GOVERNING CAPITAL

GOVERNING CAPITAL

International Finance and Mexican Politics

SYLVIA MAXFIELD

Cornell University Press

Ithaca and London

Copyright © 1990 by Cornell University

First published 1990 by Cornell University Press.

International Standard Book Number 0-8014-2458-5
Library of Congress Catalog Card Number 90-55137
Printed in the United States of America
*Librarians: Library of Congress cataloging information
appears on the last page of the book.*

♾ The paper used in the text of this publication meets the minimum requirements of American National Standard for Information Sciences—Permanence of Paper for Printed Library Materials, ANSI Z39.48-1984.

Contents

Preface

As capital moves ever more easily across territorial boundaries, it draws national financial systems into an international web. In the 1980s capital flows also seemed to spread monetarist economic ideology—from Volcker's Federal Reserve to Thatcher's England to Pinochet's Chile and beyond. The Nobel committee honored a few scattered Keynesians, but few observers would deny that the theory and praxis of nonmilitary demand management died with the Age of Aquarius.

This book details political struggles between Keynesians and monetarists and takes an unpopular stand in the debate. It suggests that in an increasingly internationalized world, capital should be governed. Finance should be regulated, foreign exchange circumscribed, and profits from short-term financial operations heavily taxed. Under these conditions, demand stimulus could take its rightful place among the tools used to overcome the massive health and welfare crisis confronting the poorest third of the world's population. Capital-controlling economic policies can have benefits that, especially for the newly industrializing countries addressed here, outweigh the efficiency costs of government intervention.

Few of those who helped with this project, least of all the more than one hundred Mexican businessmen and public servants I queried, had any idea this book would address such controversial issues. Still, most requested anonymity. I owe thanks to countless others who should also be absolved of any responsibility for the arguments herein. I am indebted to Leslie Armijo, Ernest Bartell,

Preface

Roderic Camp, Wayne Cornelius, Jonathan Fox, Celso Garrido, Stephan Haggard, Roger Haydon, Terry Lynn Karl, Robert Kaufman, Robert Keohane, Vivianne Márquez, Alejandra Mizala, Guillermo O'Donnell, Enrique Quintana, Carlos Rico, Luis Rubio, Barbara Stallings, Francisco Valdés, Laurence Whitehead, and two anonymous reviewers. Financial and institutional support came from the Committee on Latin American and Iberian Studies and Center for International Affairs at Harvard University, from the Institute for the Study of World Politics in New York, the Centro de Estudios de Estado y Sociedad in Buenos Aires, the Centro de Investigación y Docencia Económica and Instituto de Banca y Finanzas in Mexico City, the Center for U.S.-Mexican Studies at the University of California–San Diego, and the Kellogg Institute at the University of Notre Dame. Danny Lederman was the best research assistant one could hope for. Unless otherwise noted, the translations from Spanish are my own.

On a personal note, I cannot adequately thank Jonathan, Sally, and Maurice Fox and Francis Fox Piven for their support and encouragement during early stages of the project. This book is dedicated to Chris, Maria, Solveig, and Tip.

Sylvia Maxfield

New Haven, Connecticut

GOVERNING CAPITAL

1

International Financial Integration and the Politics of Economic Policy Making

"In the last two or three years . . . a group of Mexicans . . . supported and advised by the private banks has stolen more money from our country than the empires which have exploited us since the beginning of history. . . . They've robbed us . . . but they will not rob us again." With these words, Mexican president José López Portillo nationalized his country's private banks and imposed foreign exchange controls for the first time in Mexican history. Many present at this State of the Union address stood to applaud, the president himself wept, and one banker fainted. "The revolution will speed up," continued Mexico's chief of state; "the state will no longer be intimidated by pressure groups."

The bank nationalization was the most dramatic move against the Mexican private sector since Mexico's 1938 oil nationalization.[1] The architects of the bank nationalization were being "handed the heart of the private sector on a plate," recalls a journalist, using the imagery of Aztec sacrifice.[2] How could such a dramatic violation of private property rights occur in a capitalist country with a long tradition of encouraging development of private enterprise, partic-

[1] The 1938 oil nationalization was a move against foreign capitalists in Mexico, whereas the bank nationalization was primarily a move against domestic capitalists. The one major foreign bank operating in Mexico, Citibank, was exempted from the 1982 decree. Other differences between the two nationalizations are discussed in Maria Emilia Paz Salinas, "Crisis y expropriación, una análisis comparativa," *Revista Mexicana de Sociología* 45 (1983), pp. 441–452.

[2] Alan Robinson, "Portillo Pockets the Banks," *Euromoney*, October 1982, p. 3.

ularly banking? How could it occur in a country where, most scholars tell us, state autonomy is limited and the state is unable or unwilling to undertake radical reform?[3] The answer lies partly in the impact of external events, specifically the international integration of national financial markets and the loss of national sovereignty it implies.

In the 1980s there were dramatic bank nationalizations in countries as varied as Mexico, France, and Peru; this cross-national similarity in otherwise different national contexts suggests international forces must be at work. The international integration of financial markets has altered the context of national industrialization all over the world. Capital is more mobile than ever before. For national capitalists, short-term investments in domestic financial markets or foreign investments often provide higher, lower-risk returns than investments in long-term industrial expansion. Yet inducing nationals to invest in long-term industrial projects at home is among the most urgent tasks facing national governments. The rise of international markets, which curtails state capacity for this task, may feed nationalism.[4]

Indeed frustration over declining state capacity to induce and guide industrial investment lay behind the decision of a group within Mexico's political elite to nationalize the country's banks. Government advisers linked this declining state control over allocation of economic resources to the internationally facilitated accumulation of wealth and power by financial-industrial conglomerates. Popular perception also held that national bankers were becoming rich and powerful thanks to opportunities provided by international financial markets. The nationalization was an effort to implement policies, including exchange controls, state guidance of bank credit allocation, and breakup of financial-industrial conglomerates, that would help the government manage international financial integration.

---

[3]See Nora Hamilton, *The Limits of State Autonomy* (Princeton: Princeton University Press, 1982); Steven E. Sanderson, *Agrarian Populism and the Mexican State* (Berkeley: University of California Press, 1981), pp. 201–203; Juan M. Martínez Nava, *Conflicto estado-empresario* (Mexico, D.F.: Editorial Nueva Imagen, 1984), pp. 56–57; and Julio La Bastida Martin del Campo, "Los grupos dominantes frente las alternativas de cambio," in Jorge Martínez Rios et al., eds., *El perfil de Mexico en 1980*, 7th ed., vol. 3 (Mexico, D.F.: Siglo XXI, 1980), p. 126.

[4]See Howard M. Wachtel, *The Money Mandarins: The Making of a Supranational Economic Order* (New York: Pantheon, 1986), p. 15.

Ironically, the interaction of a changing international financial landscape with the balance of power between domestic political coalitions both catalyzed and limited the bank nationalization. Architects of the Mexican bank nationalization intended to break the power of financial-industrial conglomerates, increase state control over investment patterns, and help improve the state's financial position. But the influence of the Mexican bankers' alliance, including large-scale capitalists, their allies in the state, and their increasingly influential international partners, hindered effective implementation of the nationalization decree. The influence of the bankers' alliance shaped crucial decisions made during the implementation stage of the bank nationalization. These decisions limited the extent to which the original goals of the nationalization could be met. The Mexican bank nationalization amounted to an unsuccessful effort to restore the Mexican state's command of the economic heights, perceived as eroding in the face of growing international capital mobility.

In short, the Mexican bank nationalization is an episode we cannot fully explain without examining how international economic change, in this case international financial integration, interacts with domestic structures. This book examines the bank nationalization in the context of economic policy making in Mexico historically and in light of the interaction between historical structures of economic policy making and international financial integration. In this way the following chapters contribute to, and I hope will stimulate, investigation of how international financial integration affects the politics of economic policy making in industrializing countries.

International Financial Integration

A variety of terms are commonly used to capture the interconnectedness of national financial markets and their gradual transformation into a single globe-encompassing financial exchange: international capital mobility, international financial integration, internationalization of finance, emergence of transnational finance, and even the supranational financial market. *International capital mobility* is typically used loosely to refer to large flows of funds across national borders, without distinction between capital

3

(relatively long-term financial products) and money (shorter-term financial products). *International financial integration* is more precise and reflects the extent to which an actor can purchase and sell the same financial products in a variety of countries for a roughly similar price. If all national financial markets were fully integrated, any given product would be available anywhere at the same price.[5] *Internationalization of finance* refers to financial actors and institutions, based originally in one nation, operating increasingly in a variety of nations. Their operations may be denominated in local or foreign currency, and they most likely operate under local legal requirements, although they are backed in the case of insolvency by their home country monetary authority. International financial operations overlap with operations referred to as *transnational*. The latter are financial activities with, rather than in, foreign countries; they are typically carried out in the home headquarters of the lead institution, are denominated in Eurocurrencies, and are likely to be subject to the legal regulations of the home country.[6] *Supranational* refers to financial activities that are above and beyond the nation.[7]

Supranational accurately evokes the *problématique* I address here, but the word is cumbersome. In this book the defining aspect of growing international capital mobility, internationalization of financial markets, and rising international financial integration— used interchangeably in the following chapters—is the more frequent ability of investors in one nation to choose financial products for their portfolio that are denominated in foreign currencies or issued in foreign markets. To the extent that financial markets are integrated and transactions costs are low, private investors will circumvent national boundaries to maximize the utility gained from investment. Investors' decisions about what financial products to include in their portfolios depend on relative returns adjusted for inflation, expected exchange rate changes, taxes, and risk. Naturally, in countries with limited capital markets, inflation, or exchange rate instability, investors will prefer financial products de-

---

[5]Ralph C. Bryant, *International Financial Intermediation* (Washington, D.C.: Brookings Institution, 1987), pp. 76–77.

[6]Dimitri Germidis and Charles Albert Michalet, *International Banks and Financial Markets in Developing Countries* (Paris: OECD, 1984), pp. 22–28.

[7]Wachtel, *The Money Mandarins*.

nominated in foreign currencies or originating in more developed markets.[8]

The definition of *international financial integration* used here— the ability of individual and institutional investors to purchase and sell (borrow or lend) financial products in foreign markets—includes but is broader than the sovereign lending boom of the 1970s and the spectacular capital flight of the 1970s and 1980s. Technological advances, specifically in telecommunications, the shift to flexible exchange rates, and widespread decline in exchange controls and domestic financial regulation have all contributed to an unparalleled level of international financial integration. Yet we have no reliable quantitative measure of the extent of international financial integration. Empirical research on substitutability of financial assets denominated in different currencies indicates that integration, measured this way, has risen greatly, but the research does not yield reliable numerical results.[9] Research on integration that compares returns on similar financial products in different national markets yields similarly vague quantitative conclusions.[10] Controversy also rages over how to interpret results of studies that try to measure international financial integration by investigating the correlation between domestic investment and savings rates.[11]

[8]Miguel A. Rodriguez F., "Consequences of Capital Flight for Latin American Debtors," in Donald R. Lessard and John Williamson, eds., *Capital Flight and Third World Debt* (Washington, D.C.: Institute for International Economics, 1987).

[9]Substitutability of financial assets in different currency denominations has been studied to evaluate the efficacy of exchange market intervention. See Dale W. Henderson and Stephanie Sampson, "Intervention in Foreign Exchange Markets: A Summary of Ten Staff Studies," *Federal Reserve Bulletin* 69 (1983), pp. 830–836; Paul Boothe et al., "International Asset Substitutability: Theory and Evidence for Canada," *Bank of Canada Review*, February 1985, pp. 9–10; and Kenneth Rogoff, "On the Effects of Sterilized Intervention," *Journal of Monetary Economics* 14 (1984), pp. 133–150.

[10]For an introduction see Maurice Obstfeld, "Capital Mobility in the World Economy," in Karl Brunner and Allan H. Meltzer, eds., *The National Bureau Method, International Capital Mobility and Other Essays*, Carnegie-Rochester Conference Series on Public Policy 24 (Amsterdam: North-Holland, 1986), pp. 55–103; Richard M. Levich, "Empirical Studies of Exchange Rates: Price Behavior, Rate Determination and Market Efficiency," in Ronald W. Jones and Peter B. Kenen, eds., *Handbook of International Economics*, vol. 2 (New York: North Holland, Elsevier Science Publishers, 1985).

[11]See Martin Feldstein and Charles Horioka, "Domestic Savings and International Capital Mobility Flows," *Economic Journal* 90 (1980), pp. 314–329; James Tobin, "Comments on 'Domestic Savings and International Capital Flows,'" *European Research Review* 21 (1983), pp. 153–156; and Bryant, *International Financial Intermediation*, pp. 82–86.

The best quantitative measures of the extent of international financial integration available include indirect indicators such as the growth of Eurocurrency transactions, the rise in the number of foreign bank branches, and the increase in total bank profits derived from international transactions. For example, Eurocurrency transactions, which are only a portion of total international banking activity, which in turn is only a portion of all international financial activity, grew approximately twice as fast as world trade and two-and-one-half times as fast as world gross domestic product between 1964 and 1985.[12] Regarding bank branches, although banks have engaged in foreign activity since the Middle Ages and British and French banks built a network of foreign branches in European countries and the colonies during the nineteenth century, not until the 1970s was there rapid, large-scale expansion of international networks led by U.S. banks. U.S. banks, which had only 8 foreign branches in 1960, had 125 by 1975.[13] Even these numbers underestimate the banks' international spread because they do not include growth in the number of representative offices, subsidiaries, and associated banks.

In short, we have a qualitative indication and several indirect quantitative measures that international financial integration has grown. We also have a qualitative indication that integration is globally uneven. The extent to which individual and institutional investors in different countries have access to foreign financial assets varies greatly. It is much higher in the United States than in Zambia, for example. Also, within countries, there is unequal access. The latter inequality is at the crux of animosity felt for Mexican bankers during the 1970s; they facilitated access to profitable financial assets that were beyond the reach of the majority of Mexicans. The fact that this access had increased rapidly and become more visible during the course of the 1970s also added to popular animosity.

Theoretical literature related to the international integration of financial markets analyzes its potentially negative consequences in several ways.[14] The loss of autonomy in national economic policy

[12]Bryant, *International Financial Intermediation*, pp. 20–21.
[13]Germidis and Michalet, *International Banks and Financial Markets in Developing Countries*, p. 16.
[14]Bryant, *International Financial Intermediation*, pp. 87–119.

making is one. To the extent that financial markets are internationally integrated, money and capital flow to the markets, instruments, and currency denominations that offer the highest return. National economic policy makers must act within the constraint of a policy's impact on capital inflows and outflows or suffer the balance of payments consequences. Sudden inflows or outflows can arbitrarily, from a national government's viewpoint, raise or lower domestic investment, the money supply, or the tax base.[15]

Another way to analyze the potentially negative consequences of international financial integration is to explore how, to the extent one assumes financial markets are less than perfect, international financial integration leads to divergence between private and social welfare.[16] Financial transactions motivated by short-term considerations can drive prices of financial products above their "social value"—determined by long-term profit and risk calculations. Keynes explains that financial markets take investments that are "fixed" for the community and turn them into "liquid" investments for individuals. Unfortunately, this transformation of long-term community costs and yields into short-term, private ones introduces "precariousness" into investment decisions.[17] Professional investors and speculators are concerned primarily with how the market—under the influence of mass psychology—values alternative investments, rather than what these investments are worth to the professional entrepreneur or person investing "for keeps." Keynes concludes that because financial markets may value investments differently than society values them, "there is no clear evidence that the investment policy which is socially advantageous coincides with that which is most profitable."[18]

In more concrete terms, the rational utility-maximizing behavior of individual or institutional investors in one country can lead to

---

[15]Ibid.; Rodriguez, "Consequences of Capital Flight."

[16]Debate rages among eminent economists over the extent to which financial markets price perfectly efficiently or allow for 'overvaluation' and speculative bubbles. In the Yale Economics Department, for example, internationally renowned finance professor Stephen Ross holds the efficiency of financial markets sacrosanct and opposes government intervention, whereas his Nobel prize–winning colleague James Tobin strongly urges financial market regulation.

[17]This theme is evocatively echoed in Joan Robinson's work. She argued that investment is driven by the "animal spirits" of capitalists.

[18]John Maynard Keynes, *The General Theory of Employment, Interest Rates and Money* (New York: Harcourt Brace Jovanovich, 1964), pp. 149–157.

purchases or sales of financial products (lending or borrowing) that help them but hurt society by destabilizing domestic financial markets, raising or lowering the marginal cost of government borrowing, or raising or lowering investment, the money supply, or the tax base. When local investors are able to operate on a global basis, the returns to investment and economic growth in their own country cease to be crucial to their interests and are increasingly beyond government control.[19]

The Mexican case study and the brief comparison of Mexico with other Latin American countries in the following chapters suggest that international financial integration tends to divert national financial resources away from long-term industrial investment at home. Nevertheless, it also indicates that a history of "capital-controlling," or "heterodox," macroeconomic policy can mitigate the negative impact of international financial integration on long-term industrial investment. An economic policy pattern of flexible exchange rates with controlled convertibility and state intervention in domestic financial markets to help create and guide credit allocation can increase a nation's success in managing international financial integration. Such policies allow governments to influence the allocative decisions of national capitalists in favor of long-term industrial investment. This government capacity is crucial for managing capital accumulation in the context of increasingly internationalized capital markets. One of the two central arguments of this book is that differences in macroeconomic policy patterns help explain cross-national variations among newly industrializing countries in the extent of capital flight and short-term financial activity (relative to long-term private sector investment) that tend to occur when national capitalists gain easier access to international financial investment opportunities. To put it another way,

---

[19]Other negative consequences surveyed by Bryant are that national financial instability can spread more easily and that the financial innovation that appears to accompany international financial integration has high opportunity costs. Tobin makes the latter point, arguing that financial innovation uses up scarce human and capital resources and requires government attention that could more profitably be spent on other social issues. See James Tobin, "On the Efficiency of the Financial System," *Lloyds Bank Review*, July 1984, pp. 1–15. A final point departs from Hirschman's contention that capitalists relate to their national governments through either exit, voice, or loyalty. To the extent that the international integration of financial markets makes exit easier, it may undermine the exercise of voice or loyalty. See Albert O. Hirschman, *Exit, Voice and Loyalty* (Cambridge: Harvard University Press, 1970).

macroeconomic policy patterns and the policy alliances that shape them are crucial intervening variables between international financial markets and the state's capacity for economic management. The second contention developed in the following chapters is that historical continuities in national economic policies reflect the relative institutional and organizational power of competing policy alliances.

The Mexican Case: Alliances, Economic Policy, and International Financial Integration

When the groundwork was being laid for Mexican industrialization, during the regime of dictator Porfirio Díaz (1876–1911), economic policy was made by Díaz himself and a small circle of technocratic advisers. Foreign domination of the economy, low wages, and rigidity of the political system led to rising discontent among peasants and the bourgeoisie, culminating in revolutionary struggle lasting from 1910 to 1917. Mexican economic policy, from 1917 at least until the 1982 bank nationalization, has been shaped by the struggle between two competing policy alliances: the Cárdenas coalition—named after Mexican president Lázaro Cárdenas (1934–1940)—and the bankers' alliance. The bankers' alliance was made up of private bankers, many dating to the Porfirian era, large-scale traders and industrialists, and public sector monetary authorities. The Cárdenas coalition included state-organized labor and peasant groups, and government officials favoring their interests and often occupying ministerial positions concerned with agriculture or labor. The bankers' alliance dominated the government in the 1920s and early 1930s, from the mid-1950s to 1970, and after 1982. Its periods of dominance coincided with years of heavy Mexican reliance on foreign credits.

Chapter 2 describes the origins of these two coalitions. In the 1920s government officials working in alliance with private bankers shaped state economic policy-making institutions in a way that helped give the bankers a strong voice in policy making. The Cárdenas coalition, its institutional base laid in the 1930s with the mobilization of state-organized peasant and labor groups in the ruling Partido de la Revolución Mexicana (Party of the Mexican

9

Revolution, or PRM), had different interests and less influence over economic policy after its short-lived heyday in the late 1930s.[20]

This "coalitional" view of the forces shaping Mexican economic policy formation differs from existing views by focusing on policy alliances that cut across state and society. Most existing approaches focus on the relative power of the state versus society in policy formation. They tend to treat the state and private sector as aggregate units with relatively unified interests and policy preferences. The "power elite" view suggests that the economic and political elite are closely linked and that their interests and policy preferences coincide. The state has virtually no identifiable interests of its own. Foreign and large-scale national business dominates the economic policy-making process.[21] At the other extreme is the view that the state usually takes independent initiative in Mexican economic policy making. In this view the state has identifiable interests that differ from, and are often imposed over, the preferences of the private sector.[22]

The relative autonomy approach suggests that Mexican business interests and their foreign allies are the most powerful social group influencing policy. Yet they are not in charge of the state, as posited by the power elite model. In other words, although autonomously derived state interests can be discerned, authors taking this position argue that business interests prevail in most instances.[23]

The view suggested here departs from debates over the extent of state autonomy from society that undergird the three approaches outlined. According to the model of Mexican economic policy making presented in this book, economic policy is shaped by the

[20]The original party created by Mexican President Calles was the Partido Nacional Revolucionário (National Revolutionary Party, or PNR); the PRM replaced it and was in turn replaced by the Partido Revolucionário Institucional (Party of the Institutionalized Revolution, or PRI), which dominates contemporary Mexican political life.

[21]Examples of those who take this position include James D. Cockcroft, *Mexico: Class Formation, Capital Accumulation and the State* (New York: Monthly Review Press, 1983); and Ramiro Reyes Esparza et al., eds., *La burguesía mexicana* (Mexico, D.F.: Editorial Nuestro Tiempo, 1978).

[22]See, for example, Susan Kaufman Purcell, *The Mexican Profit Sharing Decision* (Berkeley: University of California Press, 1975); Merilee S. Grindle, *Bureaucrats, Politicians, and Peasants in Mexico* (Berkeley: University of California Press, 1977); and Miguel Basañez, *La lucha por la hegemonía en Mexico* (Mexico, D.F.: Siglo XXI, 1982).

[23]Recent examples of this viewpoint include Roderic A. Camp, *Enterpreneurs and Politics in Twentieth Century Mexico* (New York: Oxford University Press, 1989); and Judith A. Teichman, *Policymaking in Mexico* (Boston: Allen and Unwin, 1988).

preferences of interest coalitions that include both state and non-state actors and may be opposed by other coalitions of state and social actors.

This view is similar to interpretations of Mexican economic policy making by Cordera and Tello and Hamilton.[24] Tello, one of the architects of the Mexican bank nationalization, analyzes the nationalization in terms of competition between a "neoliberal" policy current that opposed it and a "national populist" current that supported it. The neoliberals are businessmen and government officials who espouse a contemporary version of nineteenth-century Manchester liberalism emphasizing economic laissez-faire. The national populists support state intervention in the economy to protect the interests of the poor. Tello places the nationalization in the historical context of a *disputa por la nación* (fight for the nation) between these two policy currents.

Hamilton focuses on the 1920s and 1930s, which she characterizes as involving competition between a "conservative" alliance of Porfirian-era businessmen and -women, entrepreneurs who made their fortunes during and shortly after the revolution, and government officials loyal to President Plutarco Elías Calles (1924–1930), on the one hand, and a "progressive" alliance of government officals supporting agrarian reform (including Cárdenas), workers, and peasants, on the other. Hamilton's historiography shows that the "conservative" alliance, comparable to the bankers' alliance, dominated government policy making from 1924 to 1933.[25]

---

[24]Carlos Tello, *La nacionalización de la banca* (Mexico, D.F.: Siglo XXI, 1984); Rolando Cordera and Carlos Tello, *Disputa por la nación* (Mexico, D.F.: Siglo XXI, 1979); Hamilton, *The Limits of State Autonomy*. Brandenberg posits that there are three factions in the ruling elite with "allies" from different social sectors. These factions are the revolutionary left, center, and right. He identifies Cárdenas and his supporters as the revolutionary left. See Frank Brandenberg, *The Making of Modern Mexico* (Englewood Cliffs, N.J.: Prentice-Hall, 1964).

[25]The primary concern of the Calles government, where policy making was shaped by the "conservative" alliance, was to consolidate central power in the face of opposition from the military, the Church, and regional *caudillos*. In 1929 Calles formed the PNR to centralize political power nationally. To help provide a fiscal base for central government, Calles also expanded the role of the Finance Ministry both within and outside the government. Hamilton writes, "Centralization of political power in the federal executive was accompanied by a centralization of financial control within the executive in the Ministry of Finance." See Hamilton, *The Limits of State Autonomy*, p. 80. Agrarian reform and labor rights were very low priority for the "conservative" alliance, and little progress was made on these issues between 1924 and 1933. See Hamilton, *The Limits of State Autonomy*, pp. 90–100; Barry Carr, *El movimiento obrero y la política en*

In the early 1930s several events converged, leading to a shift in power and policy emphasis in favor of the "progressive" alliance led by Cárdenas.[26] The difference in policy preferences of the "progressive" and "conservative," or bankers' and national populist, alliances is evident in debate over the Six-Year Plan for the Cárdenas administration approved by the nominating convention of the PNR in 1933. The extent and nature of agrarian reform was the primary issue disputed. The Cardenistas won; and even before Cárdenas assumed office in 1934, several aspects of the plan were put into effect.[27]

Nevertheless, the Cárdenas administration was not a monolith of officials supporting agrarian reform and workers' rights. There were several important continuities between the eras of "conservative" and "progressive" dominance (1924–1933 and 1934–1940 respectively). Cárdenas could not completely exclude such representatives of the previously dominant "conservative" alliance as Central Bank director Luis Montes de Oca, who had business allies outside the state and opposed Cárdenas's support of striking unions and land reform. The Cárdenas administration continued the "conservative" alliance's effort to promote private capital accumulation. At the same time, however, it intended to control private capital. This goal of promoting yet controlling private capital led to

---

Mexico, vol. 1 (Mexico, D.F.: Sep-Setentas, 1976); Enrique Krauze, *La reconstrucción económica: Historia de la revolución mexicana*, vol. 10 (Mexico, D.F.: Colegio de Mexico, 1977); and Lorenzo Meyer, *El conflicto social y los gobiernos del maximato: Historia de la revolución mexicana*, vol. 12 (Mexico, D.F.: Colegio de Mexico, 1978).

[26]Labor leaders independent of the PNR emerged and the depression hit, hurting agricultural exports and squeezing the peasantry. This development led to a rise in popular mobilization. Concomitantly, within the government a group that strongly supported agrarian reform coalesced. Formation of this pro-reform group led to serious policy conflict with Calles loyalists; nevertheless, by 1933 one of the *agraristas*, Cárdenas, managed to win support for his presidential bid from the proponents of agrarian reform and from Calles loyalists. Although a staunch supporter of peasant and worker interests, Cárdenas had been careful to avoid alienating Calles. This approach was essential because in Mexico the outgoing president has ultimate say over whom his successor will be. On the rise of the *agraristas* and Cárdenas's candidacy see Ramona Falcón, "El surgimiento del agrarismo cardenista—una revisión de las tesis populistas," *Historia Mexicana*, January–March 1978, pp. 333–386; and Wayne Cornelius, "Nation-Building, Participation, and Distribution: The Politics of Social Reform under Cárdenas," in Gabriel A. Almond and Scott C. Flanagan, eds., *Crisis, Choice and Change: Historical Studies of Political Development* (Boston: Little, Brown, 1973).

[27]Hamilton, *The Limits of State Autonomy*, p. 120; Tzvi Medi, *Ideología y praxis de Lázaro Cárdenas* (Mexico, D.F.: Siglo XXI, 1972); Arnaldo Córdova, *La política de masas del cardenismo* (Mexico, D.F.: Ediciones Era, 1974).

sometimes bitter debates, between "conservatives" in the bankers' alliance and "progressive" Cárdenas loyalists, over monetary policy and public spending policy, exchange controls, and taxation.

The bankers' alliance had a strong interest in tight monetary policy and a firm commitment to free exchange convertibility and fixed exchange rates, low taxation, and limited state regulation of financial markets. Although the most salient issues for the Cardenistas were agrarian reform and labor rights, their economic advisers also favored loose monetary policy, exchange controls, stiffer wealth and profit taxes, and state control of at least those industries deemed nationally strategic. In the 1930s, thanks to organizational features of the state (dating to the previous decade) and of capital (dating to the Porfirian era), the bankers' alliance won on the issues of exchange controls and taxation. But despite the best efforts of public sector monetary authorities, the bankers' alliance did not succeed in swinging monetary policy in line with its interests until their hand was strengthened by the weight of international creditors in the 1950s.

Members of both policy alliances shared a general goal of helping promote private capital accumulation. Disputes over monetary policy and public spending policy, exchange policy, and tax policy reflected differences in opinion over how this general goal should be furthered and at what cost. There was sufficient agreement to produce policies that between 1920 and 1950 increased the state's control of the economy's "commanding heights."[28] Although the Mexican government did not take a direct ownership stake in large manufacturing industry or completely control foreign trade, between 1920 and 1950 it reconstructed the financial system and created state banks, vastly improved the national transport system, took an increasingly large role in the provision of electricity and communication services, and nationalized the oil industry. In the 1940s the administrations of presidents Manuel Avila Camacho and Miguel Alemán (1940–1946 and 1946–1952, respectively) introduced a system of trade controls and credit and subsidy schemes to provide state support for import substitution industrialization

---

[28]The commanding heights are economic sectors the Soviets declared would be under state control in their 1921 "New Economic Policy" of building a mixed, rather than purely socialist, economy. These sectors included large industry, credit and banking, transportation, and trade.

(ISI), a development strategy followed until the 1980s in Mexico and most other Latin American countries.

Although politico-economic studies of developing countries have placed considerable emphasis on development strategies, and on trade policy as their defining aspect, Mexico's pursuit of an ISI model is not central to the argument detailed in the following chapters. The conventional wisdom is that ISI, associated with high state intervention, was followed in Latin America because urban business and labor are politically strong. Asian countries, where urban social forces are weaker, followed export-led industrialization (ELI) strategies, which accounted, according to common argument, for their development success relative to that of Latin American countries.

This focus on development strategies is problematic for two important reasons. First, most countries in both Asia and Latin America have followed a mixture of ISI and ELI policies. Second, focusing on development strategies does not help explain cross-national variation in nontrade policies or development outcomes in countries that share the same broad development strategy. For instance, both Mexico and Brazil protected import substituting industry heavily; yet Brazil has greater and more sophisticated industrial capacity than Mexico.

This book focuses on policies that shape the movement of investment capital nationally and internationally, rather than on development strategies or trade policy, for three reasons. First, these are the types of policies that are theoretically most likely, under a variety of economic assumptions, to explain cross-national variation in the impact of international financial integration on long-term industrial investment.[29] Second, in the comparison between Mexico

[29]Economists following the monetary approach to the balance of payments tend to emphasize monetary policy and the exchange rate regime. In light of the perceived failure of this approach to account for Southern Cone experiences in the late 1970s these economists also stress the timing of trade and capital account liberalization. See Nicolas Ardito Barletta, Mario I. Blejer, and Luis Landau, *Economic Liberalization and Stabilization Policies in Argentina, Chile and Uruguay: Applications of the Monetary Approach to the Balance of Payments* (Washington, D.C.: World Bank, 1984). Under the classic Mundell-Fleming model of international economics, domestic economic performance is shaped by the interaction between the exchange rate regime and monetary and fiscal policy. Under floating rates, monetary policy is effective and fiscal policy is not; under fixed rates, fiscal policy is effective and monetary policy is not. So-called structural monetarists, such as Ronald McKinnon, highlight the interaction between capital account liberalization and the extent of competitiveness in financial markets. See Ronald T. McKinnon, "Financial Policies," in John Cody, Helen Hughes, and David Wall, eds.,

and Brazil explored in chapter 7, there are striking differences between the two countries in these policy areas. Third, although there has been some work on the politics of monetary, exchange rate, tax, and financial policy in advanced industrial countries, there has been very little focusing on newly industrializing countries.[30]

Chapter 2 outlines the origins of the bankers' alliance and the Cárdenas coalition, and chapter 3 shows that the overall pattern in policies shaping the movement of investment capital nationally and internationally in Mexico from 1917 to 1970 conformed closely to the interests of the bankers' alliance. The government promoted the relatively unregulated development of private financial markets, maintained free exchange convertibility, rarely taxed profits or luxury consumption, and pursued tight monetary policy, albeit with some exceptions. In this policy context the incentive structure created by international financial integration in the 1970s drew resources away from industrial finance. Chapter 4 contends that small and medium-sized industrialists, without preferential access to credit markets, were financially squeezed. Industrial and financial conglomerates profited heavily from short-term financial activity. The boom in nonoperational profits of large corporations fueled mergers. Wealth and financial resources became increasingly centralized and concentrated in the hands of a relatively small

---

Policies in Industrial Progress in Developing Countries (Oxford: Oxford University Press, 1980). "Radical" economists also tend to focus on exchange rate policies, specifically exchange freedom, as determining the impact of international financial integration. See Manuel Pastor, Jr., "Capital Flight and the Latin American Debt Crisis," paper prepared for the Latin American Studies Association meetings, New Orleans, March 1988.

[30]See John Goodman, "The Politics of Central Banking," paper presented at the American Political Science Association annual meeting, Washington, D.C., September 1–4, 1988; John Goodman, "Monetary Politics in France, Italy, and Germany: 1973–1985," paper prepared for the Centro Europa Ricerche project, "The Political Economy of International Cooperation and the Domestic Base of Foreign Economic Policies of European Countries," September 1987; Gerald Epstein and Thomas Ferguson, "Monetary Policy, Loan Liquidation, and Industrial Conflict: The Federal Reserve and the Open Market Operations of 1932," *Journal of Economic History* 44 (1984), pp. 957–984; Leslie Armijo, "The Political Economy of Brazilian Central Banking, 1965 to 1987," paper presented at the American Political Science Association annual meeting, Washington, D.C., September 1–4, 1988; Gerald Epstein and Juliet Schor, "Corporate Profitability as a Determinant of Restrictive Monetary Policy: Estimates for the Postwar," in Thomas Mayer, ed., *The Political Economy of American Monetary Policy* (Cambridge: Cambridge University Press, 1990); and Donald Kettl, *Leadership at the Fed* (New Haven: Yale University Press, 1986).

number of conglomerates. Foreign exchange flowed disproportionately into oligopolistic manufacturing sectors, in some cases displacing existing or potential domestic suppliers. In the Mexican economic policy context, international financial integration benefited the wealthy by fueling luxury consumption and capital flight.

By strengthening large-scale Mexican industrialists and financiers economically, financial liberalization and international integration heightened the potential political influence of Mexican capitalists forming part of the bankers' alliance. But economic concentration also generated heightened resentment against the bankers' alliance and created a greater incentive for the Cárdenas coalition to organize in opposition to government policies. Ironically, in the period when the most salient feature of the international financial markets was great enthusiasm for Third World lending, the bankers' alliance found its influence over policy formulation slightly weakened. For example, tight monetary policy was needed but hard to justify politically when foreign exchange was pouring into the economy. Chapter 5 shows how, in the boom period of the 1970s and 1980s borrowing cycle, international financial integration contributed to policy stalemate in Mexico. It worked against the policy adjustments that would have been necessary to optimize the benefits of financial integration for long-term national industrial investment. This stalemate, combined with the political impact of the economic inequalities heightened by foreign borrowing, culminated in the dramatic 1982 bank nationalization, followed by the successful mobilization of the bankers' alliance against it. Chapter 6 covers the politics of the bank nationalization and its aftermath.

The relative influence of the bankers' alliance over Mexican economic policy has been shaped in part by the country's international financial situation. In the 1920s the bankers' alliance derived power in domestic debates indirectly from its monopoly of relations with Mexico's international creditors. In the 1930s and 1940s, when Mexico was in default on its debts and largely isolated from international financial markets, the bankers' alliance was less successful in imposing its policy preferences. Access to foreign loans became important to the Mexican economy again in the 1950s, and this change in Mexico's international financial situation marked a turning point for the bankers' alliance. It was finally able to impose its preference for tight monetary policy, with the assistance of foreign allies: international creditors. The gradual international integration of Mexican financial markets in the 1970s provided the bankers with profitable business, but easy access to foreign exchange during the debt boom temporarily weakened their policy influence. International financial integration in the 1970s and 1980s provided profits for bankers but, even before the boom went bust, aggravated inequalities and bottlenecks in Mexico's industrial structure and income distribution. The bankers briefly suffered as scapegoats for problems caused by the government's incapacity to steer the economy in the face of massive inflows and outflows of capital facilitated by international financial integration. As the leverage of international creditors over Mexico has once again become strong, the fortunes of the bankers' alliance have improved. As international financial integration fitfully proceeds, other nationalistic backlashes are possible. But in the twenty-first century the disciplinary force of international financial flows will increasingly narrow the scope for "national populist" policies. If the possibilities for popular reform in Mexico have been slim, international financial integration makes them even slimmer.

Cross-National Comparison and Theoretical Implications

The last chapter of this book puts the Mexican case just outlined in comparative perspective, contrasting it with the situations in Brazil, Argentina, and Chile. The chapters on the Mexican case emphasize the origins of a relatively strong bankers' alliance in Mexico, its influence on economic policy, and how these domestic alliances and policies interact with international financial changes. Changes in the extent of Mexico's vulnerability to sudden capital outflows and reciprocal need for capital inflows explain variations over time in the ability of the bankers' alliance to shape economic policy. The comparative emphasis shifts in the final chapter to explaining cross-national variations in the Latin American experience with international financial integration. The explanation lies in the comparative strength of each country's bankers' alliance and the different economic policy patterns associated with stronger and weaker bankers' alliances.

As stated earlier, this book makes two key theoretical contentions. The first is that characteristics of policy alliances, particularly the strength of bankers' alliances, explain economic policy

17

patterns. The second is that alliances and the policies they shape explain the impact of international financial integration. The theoretical context of the first contention, central to both the longitudinal and cross-national aspects of this study, is addressed here. Evaluation of the theoretical implications of the second contention is left for the final chapter.

The argument about the politics of economic policy making outlined here stresses policy "currents," or "networks" in which state and social actors with similar interests form implicit or explicit alliances to press for desired policies. This approach differs significantly from state- or society-centered explanations of economic policy in Latin America and from explanations based purely on ideology or international factors. Frieden, for example, argues that class structure explains cross-national variations in Latin American economic policy.[31] Where class conflict is low, elite cohesion is limited and economic policy is heterodox. High class conflict leads to elite unity and orthodox economic policy. Such an explanation has two major shortcomings. First, class conflict is difficult to define and measure. It varies considerably over time within any given country. In Mexico, a high class-conflict country according to Frieden, class conflict was low during the most orthodox policy period (1954–1970) and high as heterodoxy appeared (1970–1976). Second, arguments based on class conflict are unlikely to yield proximate explanations of specific economic policies. Understanding the institutional context is vital in linking social structure to policy.

Sikkink, Geddes, and Schneider provide examples, in the Latin American context, of state-centered approaches.[32] Sikkink draws heavily on Geddes's characterization of the Brazilian bureaucracy in her effort to explain differences in Brazilian and Argentine eco-

[31]Jeff Frieden, "Classes, Sectors, and Foreign Debt in Latin America," *Comparative Politics* 21 (1988), pp. 1–20.

[32]Kathryn Sikkink, "State Autonomy and Developmentalist Policy Making in Argentina and Brazil," paper presented at the Latin American Studies Association meetings, New Orleans, March 1988; Kathryn Sikkink, "Institutional Approaches to Latin American Political Economy," paper presented at the American Political Science Association annual meeting, Washington, D.C., September 1–4, 1988; Barbara Geddes, "Building 'State' Autonomy in Brazil, 1930–1964," paper presented at the Latin American Studies Association meeting, Boston, October 1986; Ben Ross Schneider, "Partly for Sale: Privatization and State Strength in Brazil and Mexico," *Journal of Interamerican Studies and World Affairs* 30 (1988–1989), pp. 89–116.

nomic performance in the 1950s. Both authors focus on Kubit-schek's bureaucratic reforms, which inculcated merit-based hiring and efficiency criteria in parts of the economic policy-making aparatus. However, Sikkink suggests that internal state characteristics are insufficient for explaining the substance of policy. International circumstances and ideas determine policy substance. Yet, although the ideas of the United Nations' Economic Commission on Latin America (ECLA) were in the air all over Latin America in the 1950s and 1960s and the international circumstances faced were similar, economic policy patterns varied considerably across nations. Among the variables Sikkink identifies, bureaucratic characteristics are the only ones that vary sufficiently to explain differences in policy patterns. Yet some analysts suggest there is less variation among Latin American bureaucracies than Sikkink implies.[33]

In short, one cannot move directly from class conflict to policy without observing intervening variables, including state behavior. Nor can one explain policy purely on the basis of bureaucratic characteristics. Ideological explanations beg the question of how ideas translate into policy.[34] One must view the impact of international economic circumstances in interaction with domestic structures in order to explain cross-national variation in response to otherwise similar international forces. The approach developed here stresses interaction among the state, social actors, and the international economy and therefore bears some resemblance to theories that stress these factors separately. For example, we rely on international factors to explain variation over time in the relative strength of different policy currents in any given country. Furthermore, the first of three defining elements of the policy currents approach, that interest shapes political behavior, is common also to the class conflict approach.

The validity of using self-interest models of political behavior is hotly debated. Criticisms include that human beings define their interests as the pursuit of moral principles such as justice or the

[33]Ben Ross Schneider, "Bureaucratic Careers and State Strength in Comparative Perspective," mimeo, Political Science Department, Princeton University, 1988.

[34]As Goldstein points out, "ideas influence policy only when they are carried out by individuals or groups with political clout." See Judith Goldstein, "The Impact of Ideas on Trade Policy," *International Organization* 43 (1989), pp. 31–72.

betterment of others, that the decision to act politically is not made on the basis of calculations of cost and benefit, that interests are inconsistent over time and too complex to measure, and that interest-based explanations, although perhaps accurately capturing part of social reality, drastically oversimplify.[35]

To the extent that one values theoretical parsimony, the latter criticism loses urgency. We can also partially circumvent the problem of long-run complexity and inconsistency by using a "relative" definition of interest. The proposition is, for example, that if one person or group is more severely hurt by a policy than another, it is more likely than the other to act against the policy. As for the relative importance of altruism or moral principle versus avarice in shaping political behavior, Green suggests self-interest will be stronger the clearer and more salient the tangible stakes and the more information available with which to evaluate the stakes.[36] When the stakes are clear and information to facilitate evaluating them is abundant, self-interest is more likely than models based on morality or altruism to tell us which actors will take what political action regarding a particular policy. The self-interest assumption is more viable where the stakes are economic rather than political, as they obviously are in the financial, monetary, tax, and exchange rate policies observed here. The assumption is viable because the costs and benefits of these policies are salient and easily measured. Similarly, the self-interest model is more viable in the study of elite politics than of mass politics because elites tend to have more information with which to evaluate costs and benefits. The use of the self-interest assumption in this study, which focuses primarily on elite politics, is justified in part by this observation.[37]

[35]On these criticisms see Roberto Michels, *First Lectures in Political Sociology* (Minneapolis: University of Minnesota Press, 1949); Max Weber, *Economy and Society* (Berkeley: University of California Press, 1978); Alexis de Tocqueville, *Democracy in America* (New York: Vintage Books, 1945); Graham Wallas, *Human Nature in Politics* (New York: F. S. Crofts, 1921); David Plotke, "The Political Mobilization of Business, 1974–1980: Do Classes Have Interests?" paper presented at the American Political Science Association annual meeting, Washington, D.C., September 1988; and a summary in Donald Green, "Self-Interest, Public Opinion, and Mass Political Behavior" (Ph.D. diss., University of California–Berkeley, 1988).

[36]Green, "Self-Interest, Public Opinion, and Mass Political Behavior."

[37]The salience condition explains in part why the higher the stakes in a policy debate, the greater the number of actors participating in policy currents. See Jonathan A. Fox, "The Political Dynamics of Reform: The Case of the Mexican Food System, 1980–1982" (Ph.D. diss., MIT, 1987), chapter 1.

A second defining element of the policy currents approach is that the relationship between government officials and private individuals or groups in a policy current is not characterized by capture of one by the other. Joseph characterizes policy currents as "ideological bridges" between the state and "class fractions" that allow government officials to anticipate the opinions or reactions of different "constituencies."[38] Sociologists have been defining the concept of networks both within and between organizations to depict a form of relationship that lies between those governed by hierarchy on the one hand and the market on the other. Policy currents are a form of network as these sociologists use the term.[39] Public and private actors in a policy coalition are linked by shared support of or opposition to a particular policy. They seek one another's support, and, depending on the context, there may be asymmetries in political leverage between them; but they do not explicitly coerce one another. In other words, to speak of policy currents is definitely not to suggest that state actors function as "the executive committee of the bourgeiosie." The relationship is more nearly one of reciprocal interaction.

Although there is no reason to limit the concept of policy currents to government-business relations, it has often been used to differentiate between segments of the business community and their allies in government. In a study of U.S. financial policy Michael Moran finds that deregulation has been "pursued by a coalition of public and private interests between the biggest banks and some Federal regulatory agencies. It has been opposed," he argues, "by a coalition likewise spanning private and public institutions, encompassing state regulatory agencies, small deposit-takers and powerful Congressmen."[40] In the design of postwar U.S. foreign economic policy toward the Third World, protectionist and internationalist

---

[38]Paul Joseph, *Cracks in the Empire* (Boston: South End Press, 1981).

[39]See, for example, Edward O. Laumann and David Knoke, *The Organizational State* (Madison: University of Wisconsin Press, 1987). Policy currents are also similar to what Heclo calls "issue networks," which have fluctuating participation and no hierarchy among their participants. The key difference is that material interest plays a slightly larger role in a policy current than in an issue network, where "material interest is often secondary to intellectual or emotional commitment." See Hugh Heclo, "Issue Networks and the Executive Establishment," in Anthony King, ed., *The New American Political System* (Washington, D.C.: American Enterprise Institute, 1980).

[40]Michael Moran, "Politics, Banks and Markets: An Anglo-American Comparison," *Political Studies* 32 (1984), p. 188.

21

businesses, together with their allies in government, formed competing policy currents.[41] The struggle between these competing policy currents shaped U.S. foreign policy toward the developing world in the 1950s. Students of Latin American political economy have noted a growing struggle between industrialization and financial stability–oriented policy currents in many Latin American countries.[42] World Bank adviser George Lamb expands on this point.

> No government is monolithic. All contain powerful alliances. . . . [T]he impact of these alliances on policy is evident in virtually every country: examples are the usually interventionist role of ministries of industry and commerce with respect to trade and protection, the expansionist role of ministries of irrigation, transport, construction or public works vis-à-vis public investment, and so forth. Particularly in periods of economic difficulty, there can be considerable tension between ministries which promote the interest of "their" sectors . . . and the core economic and financial agencies normally charged with imposing financial discipline and devising stabilization and recovery programs.[43]

These analysts see business-government policy currents coalescing on the basis of interests deriving from size, international competitiveness, and need for state economic support. This study singles out policy currents defined by their members' role as financiers. Fiscal sociology suggests there is a historical tendency for private financiers and government officials to develop close relations and

[41]Sylvia Maxfield and James H. Nolt, "Protectionism and the Internationalization of Capital: U.S. Sponsorship of Import Substitution Industrialization in the Philippines, Turkey, and Argentina," *International Studies Quarterly* 34 (1990), pp. 49–81.

[42]Carlos Fortín, "The Relative Autonomy of the State and Capital Accumulation in Latin America: Some Conceptual Issues," in Diana Tussie, ed., *Latin America in the World Economy* (London: Gower, 1983), p. 205.

[43]Geoffrey Lamb, "Managing Economic Policy Change, Institutional Dimensions," World Bank Discussion Papers 14 (1987), p. 9. Grant McConnell's classic study *Private Power and American Democracy* also uses the idea of policy currents to capture the texture of business influence on public policy in the United States. McConnell's use is more instrumentalist than mine. He argues that business groups gain control over specific parts of government; this control constitutes "the formation of separate narrow constituencies for particular parts of government" (Grant McConnell, *Private Power and American Democracy* [New York: Knopf, 1967], p. 254).

strategic interdependence.[44] Bates and Lien's analysis, for example, suggests that government-business policy currents were born historically as European monarchs gave the men and women of finance and commerce greater voice in government policy making in a mutual accommodation that had the entrepreneurs agree to taxation.[45] Following an interest-based model we would expect to find

---

[44]Rudolph Goldsheid, "A Sociological Approach to Problems of Public Finance," in Richard A. Musgrave and Alan Peacock, eds., *Classics in the Theory of Public Finance* (New York: Macmillan, 1958); Richard A. Musgrave, "Theories of Fiscal Crisis: An Essay in Fiscal Sociology," in H. Aaron Boskin and Michael Boskin, eds., *Economics of Taxation* (Washington, D.C.: Brookings Institution, 1980); Margaret Levi, *Of Rule and Revenue* (Berkeley: University of California Press, 1988).

[45]Robert H. Bates and Da-Hsiang Lien, "A Note on Taxation, Development and Representative Government," *Politics and Society* 14 (1985), pp. 53–70. Asymmetrical resource dependency theory, a sociological theory of organizational behavior, suggests that financiers have leverage over and within a wide variety of social groups, institutions, and organizations. Mintz and Schwartz, among others, argue that there is asymmetrical resource dependency between financiers, on the one hand, and industrialists and other groups in society, on the other; that is, nonfinancial organizations' dependence on banks for external finance is greater than the dependence of financial institutions on nonfinancial organizations for deposits. Asymmetrical resource dependency theory, a "soft" version of bank control theory, suggests that we look at financiers because of the leverage they have over social groups and institutions—industrial corporations, labor unions, and governments—that rely on external bank financing. Asymmetrical resource dependency theorists and fiscal sociologists tend to use differing methodologies. Fiscal sociology is frequently macrohistorical, as is this book. Authors trying to prove asymmetrical resource dependency tend to use a quantitative approach. Mintz and Schwartz, for instance, reason that the resource-providing role of financiers should put them at the center of social and political networks. Statistical network analysis of financiers in the United States reveals that they are disproportionately represented at the center of organizational networks. See Beth Mintz and Michael Schwartz, *The Power Structure of American Business* (Chicago: University of Chicago Press, 1985), on asymmetrical resource dependency; Jeffrey Pfeffer and Gerald R. Salancik, *The External Control of Organizations: A Resource Dependency Approach* (New York: Harper & Row, 1978), on resource dependency theory; and David M. Kotz, *Bank Control of Large Corporations in the U.S.* (Berkeley: University of California Press, 1978), on bank control theory.

The work of financial instability theorists such as Minsky and Kindleberger and of political economists such as Zysman and Thurow suggests that financial actors gain leverage not only through provision of finance to those who need it but from the key role they play in shaping industrial growth and adjustment and macroeconomic performance most generally. Zysman argues that a nation's financial system is the crucial aspect of domestic structure that explains cross-national variation in industrial policies and modes of adjustment among developed countries. Similarly, Thurow argues that the institutional relationship between financiers and industrialists explains West German and Japanese industrial success relative to that of the United States in the 1980s. Minsky and Kindleberger argue that structural instability is inherent in capitalist financial systems and suggest that this instability is the cause of most of the broad economic ills. See Hyman P. Minsky, "The Financial Instability Hypothesis," in Charles P. Kindleberger and Jean-Pierre Laffrage, eds., *Financial Crises* (Cambridge: Cambridge University

some general correlation between the institutional and organizational strength of bankers' alliances and the extent to which economic policy patterns conform to their interests. A rough picture of bankers' interests developed on the basis of deductive logic and reports from the limited empirical research available indicates that bankers prefer tight monetary policy, free foreign exchange of currencies, and little financial regulation beyond lender-of-last-resort protection.

Research in settings as widely varied as Brazil, the United States, and Western Europe suggests that central bankers favor tight monetary policy largely because the private financial community does.[46] Both archival research and econometric models of the U.S. Federal Reserve Bank's behavior suggest that it is guided by the profit considerations of private financiers.[47] In his research on postwar leadership at the Fed, Kettl finds that private bankers are at the center of the "sound finance constituency" the Fed primarily serves.[48] The opposing "cheap credit" constituency would tend to include farmers, people in construction and real estate, and producers of consumer durables whose sales depend partly on the cost of consumer credit. Private financiers fear cheap credit and inflation because it erodes their real interest earnings.[49]

Exchange rate policy, and particularly the issue of exchange controls, is another policy arena of central concern to financiers. Although Gowa may be correct in suggesting there is little interest

---

Press, 1982); Charles P. Kindleberger, *Manias, Panics and Crashes* (New York: Basic Books, 1978); John Zysman, *Governments, Markets, and Growth* (Ithaca: Cornell University Press, 1983); Lester Thurow, "Putting Capitalists Back into Capitalism," paper presented at the American Economics Association annual meeting, New York, December 1988.

[46]Goodman, "The Politics of Central Banking"; Goodman, "Monetary Politics in France, Italy, and Germany"; Epstein and Ferguson, "Monetary Policy, Loan Liquidation, and Industrial Conflict"; Armijo, "The Political Economy of Brazilian Central Banking."

[47]Epstein and Ferguson, "Monetary Policy, Loan Liquidation, and Industrial Conflict"; Epstein and Schor, "Corporate Profitability as a Determinant of Restrictive Monetary Policy."

[48]Kettl, *Leadership at the Fed.*

[49]They will tolerate inflation to the extent that their own real borrowing costs fall proportionately to their decline in real income and that their liabilities are short term so they can raise interest charged in accord with inflation. In other words, they can live with inflation if it is predictable and if they have flexibility to adjust their lending rates. This may explain Goodman's findings that private financiers in Europe simply want monetary stability. See Goodman, "Monetary Politics in France, Italy, and Germany."

group politics involved in exchange rate policy, its formulation and implementation do involve bureaucratic and elite politics related to the institutional and economic interests of key actors.[50] Central bankers, for instance, oppose exchange controls to the extent that such controls accord authority over rules of exchange distribution and cost to other executive branch agencies. Private financiers object to controls because the free international flow of finance increases the financiers' opportunities for arbitrage and for fees earned arranging international transactions. Exchange controls are sometimes adopted as a form of protectionism aimed at taxing export earnings and subsidizing imported inputs for domestic industry. In this case exporters may join financiers in their opposition to controls. More rarely exchange controls subsidize exporters. In this case exporters might find themselves opposing financiers.[51]

Financial regulation is a third issue area of central concern to financiers. Financial regulation refers to controls on lending and borrowing. Selective credit controls, for example, can impose sectoral loan allocation priorities on banks. Other regulations specify required ratios between different bank assets or liabilities. Central bankers are proponents of minimal regulation that is sufficient to ensure private bank solvency and the capacity to control the money supply, both of which are among the central bank's primary responsibilities. Variation in the central bank lending rate to private financiers and variation in reserve requirements are the key regulatory tools necessary to protect central bank sovereignty in controlling the money supply. Private financiers tolerate these controls in return for lender-of-last-resort protection but tend to oppose further controls on their lending and borrowing activities unless there is obvious financial gain involved. For example, market-segmenting

---

[50]Joanne Gowa, "Public Goods and Political Institutions: Trade and Monetary Policy Processes in the United States," *International Organization* 42 (1988), pp. 15–33.

[51]Preferences regarding exchange values are harder to predict. In a world of fixed or adjustably pegged rates, central bankers in newly industrializing countries tend to be realists, arguing for devaluation as soon as they detect sustained downward pressure on the nation's currency. Private financiers tend to be concerned about the inflationary impact and predictability of exchange rate movements. Correct or not, they associate sustained overvaluation with inflation. In these circumstances they favor devaluation insofar as they are forewarned and can reallocate assets and liabilities to cover losses— or even gain from exchange arbitrage. The preferences of other private actors will depend on the actors' international position, demand elasticities, and tastes. Roughly speaking, overvaluation hurts exporters and devaluation hurts producers of nontradeables with imported inputs.

regulations such as Glass-Steagall help keep competition down and profits up for specific sectors of the financial community.

In sum, the first two defining characteristics of the policy currents approach suggest that the economic position of public and private financiers gives them a shared interest in and basis for mutually beneficial political collaboration to achieve tight monetary policy and free capital mobility both domestically and internationally. The third, and final, defining characteristic of the approach regards the translation of interest into political outcomes. Interest does not always translate into action nor action into prevailing influence—institutional and organizational factors intervene. Where institutional and organizational development has provided financiers with allies both inside and outside the state who favor their policy preferences, the predominant policy pattern is likely to emphasize monetary stability over expansion of production, and development of financial markets and capital mobility over financial regulation or exchange controls. If financiers find themselves institutionally tied to actors with different interests, or if a strong opposing coalition is organized, economic policy is likely to be more heterodox.

Specifically, economic policy is more likely to reflect bankers' preferences under three conditions: (1) if the central bank is relatively autonomous from the legislature and the chief executive of the government, and was founded in close collaboration with private financiers; (2) if the finance ministry is allied with the central bank and exercises hegemony over other state economic policy-making agencies; and (3) if state industrialization or planning authorities have relatively little ability to control the flow of investment funds. One factor strongly influencing the latter is the extent of funds provided within private bank–industry conglomerates or through private financial (credit and capital) markets.[52]

Figure 1 simplifies the conditions for strong and weak bankers' alliances heuristically by characterizing possible relations among private bankers, industrialists, and state monetary authorities. In the case where bankers' ties to industry are relatively limited and

[52]There is a simultaneity problem here. The stronger the bankers' alliance, the less likely the state will be able to implement policies that facilitate its own control of investment finance. The less its control, the stronger the bankers' alliance. We break into the cycle of interaction between structure and policy by starting with the constraints on policy implied by the historical organization of state agencies and of capital.

Figure 1. Key dimensions of the private financial elite's alliances

		Linkage with industry*	
		Limited	Close
Linkage with state monetary authorities**	Limited	Weakest bankers' alliance	
	Close		Strongest bankers' alliance

*Through ownership or management.
**Evaluated on the basis of the private bank role in central bank founding and by patterns of communication and joint presence on boards of directors of private banks or public financial institutions such as the central bank or industrial development banks.

their links to the state are primarily through monetary authorities, which are relatively weak in relation to state planning authorities, or through state planning authorities themselves, the bankers' alliance is likely to be weak. Economic policy is more likely to be oriented toward industrial growth at the expense of monetary stability. The goal of industrial development will tend to legitimize certain restrictions on capital mobility. Where the bankers' alliance is weak, there is a greater likelihood that heterodox policies will be adopted. In the case where private bankers' ties to industry are close, through either management or ownership, and their links to the state are primarily through monetary authorities who are hegemonic among state economic policy-making agencies, the bankers' alliance is likely to be strong. The resulting economic policy patterns in this case are likely to favor monetary stability and free capital mobility.

In the case of a strong bankers' alliance—the case of close bankers' ties to industry and to state monetary authorities—there is an implicit assumption that state monetary authorities sit at the top of a power hierarchy among the state economic policy-making institutions. The bankers' alliance would not be as strong in a case where bankers had close ties to both industry and state monetary authorities but where state monetary authorities were subordinate in the policy-making process to other state agencies. In this case it is harder to predict what policy patterns will look like. They are

27

likely to be less coherent and consistent over time or to mix elements of capital control and tight monetary policy or vice versa.[53]

Conclusion

This chapter began by suggesting that the Mexican bank nationalization was a backlash against domestic bankers who were benefiting disproportionately from the opportunities provided by Mexico's growing international financial integration. This integration, defined by the more frequent ability of Mexican investors to choose financial products denominated in foreign currencies or issued in foreign nations, rose significantly in the 1970s. This book's comparatively framed case study of the interaction between domestic structures and international financial integration in Mexico confirms the warning of some economic theorists that international financial integration can have negative consequences for industrial growth and national economic sovereignty. Although we find evi-

[53]Japan in the prime of its industrialization drive falls into this intermediate category. The Bank of Japan was chartered in 1942 to "ensure appropriate application of the state's total economic power" (Eisuke Sakakibara and Yukio Noguchi, "Dissecting the Finance Ministry–Bank of Japan Dynasty," *Japan Echo* 4 [1977], p. 100). Private financiers had little to do with its constitution. At least through the mid-1960s the bank operated, in accord with its mandate, "exclusively with a view to accomplishing the purposes of the state" (Sakakibara and Noguchi, "Dissecting the Finance Ministry–Bank of Japan Dynasty," p. 100). State planning and industrialization authorities, chiefly MITI, had considerable control over the flow of investment funds, thanks to the limited development of private stock and bond markets and to cooperation from the Ministry of Finance and the Bank of Japan in imposing selective credit controls. For instance, the 1946 Order of Priority in Industrial Loans prevented banks from making loans to industries designated "unimportant" or "not urgent" without permission from the Ministry of Finance (Koichi Hamada and Akiyoshi Horiuchi, "The Political Economy of the Financial Market," in Kozo Yamamura and Yasuhichi Yasuba, eds., *The Political Economy of Japan, vol. 1: The Domestic Transformation* [Stanford: Stanford University Press, 1987], p. 239). Since banks depended heavily on the state to provide their financial resources, there was considerable incentive to comply with these restrictions. The postal saving system also provided the state with a sound fiscal base from which to distribute investment financing. On the other hand, private banks were closely linked to industry through *keiretsu*, former *zaibatsu* family holding companies reconstructed around banks. Furthermore, the Ministry of Finance, which shared economic policy-making power to some extent with MITI, was not consistently growth oriented. These conditions created a mixed institutional environment for the implementation of bankers' preferences. Monetary policy was conservative, but strict financial and exchange controls were imposed. (Yutaka Kosai, "The Politics of Economic Management," in Yamamura and Yasuba, *The Political Economy of Japan*, vol. 1, pp. 555–595.)

dence that international financial integration diverts resources away from long-term investment in national industry in Latin American countries, the case material also suggests that the negative impact is mitigated in countries with a history of strong capital-controlling policies. This evidence leads us to one of the two main conclusions of the book: that cross-national variation in economic policy patterns helps explain the divergent impact of international financial integration in different countries.

The second central argument of this book is that macroeconomic policy patterns are shaped by policy currents or alliances. Mexico's economic policy patterns reflect a continuing battle between two key policy alliances: the bankers' alliance and the Cárdenas coalition. In the long run, the institutional and organizational base of the bankers' alliance was stronger than that of the Cardenistas, and therefore Mexico's long-run economic policy patterns more often reflect the policy preferences of bankers than peasants, laborers, or their national populist state allies.

Policy currents or alliances are defined as loose coalitions of public and private sector actors brought together by the desire to push for or against a particular policy. Following the tradition of fiscal sociology we place particular weight on the role of bankers' alliances, coalitions of public and private sector financiers sometimes joined by other public sector actors or business elites. The three defining features of this approach to explaining economic policy are that it is an interest-based argument, the relationship between alliance members is not directly coercive, and the interest-policy nexus is mediated by institutional and organizational aspects of state and social structure. This argument contrasts to varying degrees with existing explanations of economic policy based on ideology, international factors, state structure, or class conflict.

DOMESTIC STRUCTURES
AND ECONOMIC POLICY
IN MEXICO

2

Origins of the Bankers' Alliance and the Cárdenas Coalition

The economic and political challenges facing postrevolutionary Mexico created the context for development of two different policy currents.[1] The bankers' alliance was born in the process of establishing financial order where there had been chaos—a requisite for any widespread economic recovery. The key private sector actors in this reconstruction were the Porfirian-era bankers and industrialists who, unlike agrarian landowners, survived the revolution with much of their wealth intact. In the 1920s they collaborated with government officials in the Finance Ministry to build a new financial system. Together, Porfirian-era bankers and Finance Ministry officials negotiated and legislated governing principles for financial institutions and monetary policy. They wrote the Central Bank charter and collaborated in efforts to raise funds to capitalize it. In the process they formed a nascent "liberal," or "monetarist," policy current opposing labor rights and state intervention in the economy and holding monetary stability sacred.[2]

---

[1] The period of sustained armed insurrection lasted from 1910 to 1917. Other, non-military facets of the revolution continued long after 1917, as did sporadic armed revolts and uprisings such as the 1926–1929 *cristiada*. Two excellent books on the revolution are Friedrich Katz, *The Secret War in Mexico* (Chicago: University of Chicago Press, 1981), and Alan Knight, *The Mexican Revolution* (Cambridge: Cambridge University Press, 1986).

[2] To some extent the differences in economic ideology between the bankers' alliance and the Cárdenas coalition correspond to what came to be called the monetarist versus structuralist debate over inflation in the 1950s and 1960s. The monetarists held that inflation is incompatible with development and must be stopped through tight monetary

Domestic Structures and Economic Policy

Through collaboration in financial reconstruction, bankers and their industrial associates gained channels of communication and influence in the state policy-making process via the Finance Ministry and the Central Bank. These two state institutions became the strongholds of the bankers' alliance within the government. In turn, the policy-making authority of the Finance Ministry and Central Bank within the executive branch added to the potential strength of the bankers' alliance. The Finance Ministry's role in financial reconstruction helped establish its supremacy over other state economic policy-making agencies.

The "Cárdenas coalition" refers to peasants and workers and those political leaders and government officials loosely allied with them. Its origins lie in the 1930s, when President Cárdenas organized labor, peasants, and "new" industrialists into a "national populist," or "structuralist," policy current favoring industrial protection, extensive state intervention in the economy, and subordination of monetary stability to the goal of industrial development and modernization of agriculture.

This chapter describes the institutional bases of the bankers' and Cárdenas alliances. It provides background for the argument, made in chapter 3, that the relatively strong institutional base of the bankers' alliance accounts for continuities in Mexican economic practice that prioritize monetary stability over expansion of production and limit state efforts to regulate capital allocation. One part of the institutional base of the bankers' alliance developed as Mexican history linked private financiers to state monetary authorities. A second took form as state monetary authorities grew to enjoy hegemony over other state agencies involved in the economic policy process. The final part of the institutional base of the bankers' alliance grew out of the organization of Mexican capital,

---

policy and strict state fiscal discipline. Market imperfections and bottlenecks are caused by price and exchange rate distortions. According to the structuralists, inflation is a natural part of growth and cannot be curbed through monetary and fiscal policy without causing unemployment and a slowdown of growth. External dependence, particularly the instability of export earnings, is a structural problem that makes it impossible to curb inflation through short-run monetary or fiscal contraction. See Roberto de Oliveira Campos, "Two Views on Inflation in Latin America," in Albert O. Hirschman, ed., *Latin American Issues* (New York: Twentieth Century Fund, 1961); and David Felix, "An Alternative View of the 'Monetarist'-'Structuralist' Controversy," in Hirschman, *Latin American Issues*.

34

which, since the Porfirian dictatorship, has closely linked private financiers to industrialists in conglomerates called *grupos*.

The institutional base of the Cárdenas coalition lies in the corporatist organizations representing peasants and labor within the governing party, in the state-created business organization the Camara Nacional de la Industria de Transformación (National Chamber of Manufacturing Industry, or Canacintra) which grouped together small and medium-sized manufacturers, and in the ministries and state development banks whose policies affected these groups: the ministries of Agrarian Reform, Agriculture and Hydraulic Resources, Communications and Transport, Property and Industrial Development (abolished in 1977), Health and Public Welfare, Labor, and Public Works and Dwellings (abolished in 1976). Although the institutional base of the Cárdenas coalition laid during the 1930s has indelibly shaped Mexican politics ever since, it was not strong in one important sense. It did not provide long-standing effective channels of influence over public policy formulation to its "members." Workers, peasants, and "popular" sectors were incorporated into the party structure in a way that strongly encouraged them to ratify party actions, in return for which their sectoral organizations' leaders would represent their interests before the party leadership. This form of incorporation brought workers and peasants minimal economic guarantees but little direct access to the public policy process. The careers of sectoral leaders depended largely on the party leadership rather than on the rank-and-file they represented. Although sectoral leaders had to be sufficiently popular to be able to deliver their sector's support to the party, and varied in their efforts to represent their constituencies, the rank-and-file had relatively little ability to force sectoral leaders to intervene heavily in policy decisions of importance to them. The hierarchy among executive branch ministries also limited the influence of officials pushing for proworker, peasant, or small business policies. With control over the purse strings, the Finance Ministry tended to exercise disproportionate weight in the policy process. When allied with the president and the Central Bank, the Finance Ministry always held sway. In sum, the institutional base of the Cárdenas coalition was relatively weak compared with that of the bankers' alliance. Organizational aspects of the state, of state-society relations, and of capital limited the Cárdenas coalition's channels of influence as they facilitated those of the bankers' alliance.

35

Reconstructing the Financial System:
The Bankers' Alliance in the 1920s

The foundations of the Mexican bankers' alliance were laid during the financial reorganization of the 1920s. These foundations were constructed in two ways. First, private bankers and state monetary authorities built lasting channels for collaboration. Second, the Finance Ministry and its dependencies consolidated their policy-making prerogative within the executive branch.

Public and Private Financiers Collaborate

The first step in the reform of the Mexican financial system was establishing a constitutional guarantee for the government right to monopolize the issuance of paper money through a central bank.[3] The 1917 constitutional convention established the principle that only one institution should be authorized to issue paper money but heatedly debated whether that bank should be public or private.[4] Giving such a right to the state threatened to limit the activity of Porfirian-era private bankers. These bankers were seen as centers of counterrevolutionary reaction, and their destruction was symbolic of the revolution's tasks. Yet they retained significant power within the elite and shaped the constitutional debate. As a result, the constitution established the principle of a public central bank with the right to monopolize money issuance, but it did not set out specific guidelines or call for the establishment of such an institution.

The political fragility of the new government and divisions within the banking community slowed financial reform. Financial chaos reigned in Mexico from 1917 to 1921 as the government

[3]On Mexico's prerevolutionary banking structure see Ernesto Lobato López, *El crédito en Mexico* (Mexico, D.F.: Fondo de Cultura Económica, 1945); Gilberto Moreno Castañeda, *La moneda y la banca en Mexico* (Guadalajara: Imprenta Universitaria, 1955); and Walter F. McCaleb, *Present and Past Banking in Mexico* (New York: Harper & Bros., 1920).

[4]Virgil Bett, *Central Banking in Mexico* (Ann Arbor: University of Michigan Press, 1957), pp. 27–29; Antonio Carillo Flores, "Acontecimientos sobresalientes en la gestión y evolución del Banco de Mexico," in Ernesto Fernández Hurtado, ed., *Cincuenta años de banca central* (Mexico, D.F.: Editorial Porrua, 1976), pp. 27–28; Eduardo Turrent Díaz, *Historia del Banco de Mexico* (Mexico, D.F.: Banco de Mexico, 1982), p. 70.

struggled to centralize political power and financial control within the executive.[5] All private banks were placed under investigation by a government commission charged with deciding their right to continue operating independently; most were slated to be taken over by state insolvency boards. President Venustiano Carranza (1915–1920) had been quick to attack the financial elite in part because he was angered by their support for Victoriano Huerta, a military and political leader allied with Porfirio Díaz earlier in the revolutionary struggle. But once he realized the financial and administrative burden involved in taking over dozens of insolvent banks, Carranza worked out a "grudging accommodation" with the Porfirian-era bankers. In 1917 his administration switched to a policy of indirect control of banking.[6]

Nevertheless, few banks were able to operate between 1917 and 1921, and at least twenty-one types of paper money printed by different banks and revolutionary factions circulated in the economy.[7] As a result, financial exchange was based primarily on silver and gold.

Divisions among government officials and among private bankers regarding the preferred terms for rechartering and refinancing the nation's private banks and establishing a central bank compounded the problem of financial reform. The larger, Mexico City–based banks were relatively more solvent and less in need of government funds and largesse to reopen than were many provincial banks. Conflict soon emerged between these two factions and their respective allies within the government.

In an overture to the Mexico City banks—and particularly to Agustin Legoretta of the Banco Nacional de Mexico—President Alvaro Obregón (1920–1924) sent legislation to Congress in 1921 postponing establishment of a single-issue central bank and grant-

[5]Heliodoro Duenes, *Los bancos y la revolución mexicana* (Mexico, D.F.: Editorial Cultura, 1945); Antonio Manero, *La revolución bancaria en Mexico* (Mexico, D.F.: Talleres Graficas de la Nación, 1958); Raul Ortiz Mena, "Moneda y crédito," in *Mexico: Cincuenta años de revolución* (Mexico, D.F.: Fondo de Cultura Económica, 1960), pp. 391–393; Turrent Díaz, *Historia del Banco de Mexico*, pp. 77–122.

[6]Douglas W. Richmond, *Carranza's Nationalist Struggle, 1893–1920* (Lincoln: University of Nebraska Press, 1983), pp. 88–89.

[7]Guillermo Ortiz Martínez, *Acumulación de capital y crecimiento económico* (Mexico, D.F.: CEMLA, 1979), p. 3.

ing eight private banks (Banco Nacional among them) the right to issue currency.[8] This move to grant special privileges to a small group of large banks angered the provincial bankers, led by Chihuahua banker and venture capitalist Enrique Creel.[9] Their main ally within the Obregón administration, finance minister Adolfo de la Huerta, testified against the legislation. He argued it would create special interests that would hinder future efforts to create a central bank. He proposed the immediate founding of a 100 percent government-owned central bank. A third proposal, by Senator Antonio Manero, suggested a compromise 50 percent public–50 percent privately owned central bank.[10] Obregón withdrew his proposed legislation, but the attempt to privilege large Porfirian-era banks added to pressures leading up to de la Huerta's insurrection and effort to prevent Obregón's chosen successor, Calles, from taking the presidency in 1924. All three proposals were buried in the chaos of presidential succession.

De la Huerta had been finance minister for Obregón. When he resigned in the dispute over financial reform during the last year of Obregón's presidential term, Alberto J. Pani was appointed in his

[8]Agustin Legoretta began to work for the Banco Nacional de Mexico in 1902. He became director in the 1920s; the family controlled the directorship until the 1982 nationalization. The bank was formed in 1884 from the union of two banks started with French and Spanish capital. It enjoyed a privileged position under the Porfiriato. Legoretta's international financial contacts also made him influential with the postrevolutionary government. The Banco Nacional de Mexico continued to dominate private finance in the postrevolutionary era.

[9]Creel had married into the influential Terrazas family of Chihuahua. As manager of the Terrazas family's banks, most notably the Banco Minero de Chihuahua, he became a sought-after intermediary for foreign capitalists during the Porfirian era. He was "at the center of the intricate interplay of regional, national, and foreign economic interests during the Porfiriato" (Mark Wasserman, "Enrique C. Creel: Business and Politics in Mexico, 1880–1930," *Business History Review* 59 [1985], p. 653). During the revolution the Creel-Terrazas family supported Fransisco Madero's opposition movement briefly but turned to back the Pascual Orozco uprising when Madero threatened to expropriate private property. Orozco's failure sent the family into exile in the United States, from where they continued to manage their wealth and collaborated with Adolfo de la Huerta's insurrection. In the 1920s the family returned to Mexico and Creel became an adviser to the Obregón government. "Creel's plight during the revolution," writes one historian, "accurately mirrors the outcome of the great upheaval. Substantial damage was inflicted on the Porfirian elite, especially the landowning class, but they were not destroyed. Much of their financial and industrial power remained intact, and from this base they rose again." (Wasserman, "Enrique C. Creel," p. 661.)

[10]Enrique Krauze, *La reconstrucción económica: Historia de la revolución mexicana* (Mexico, D.F.: Colegio de Mexico, 1977), pp. 35–36.

place.[11] Pani and his advisers were "products of the rudimentary capitalistic structure of Mexico City which had been developing during the long regime of Porfirio Díaz."[12] Pani called on financial experts such as Miguel S. Macedo, who had worked with Porfirio Díaz's last finance minister, José Limantour, developing plans for financial modernization.[13] They continued that project as they laid the foundations of the contemporary Mexican financial system during the Callista era (1924–1934). In that period Pani skillfully orchestrated a fruitful collaboration between public and private financiers that set the stage for a half century of close relations between the government and private banks.[14]

Within one month of Calles's inauguration in 1924 Pani convoked the first National Banking Convention, with the goal of developing guidelines for financial organization generally and central banking more specifically. The conference opened in February 1924 with forty private bankers, government officials, and their advisers in attendance. In addition, Congress gave Pani, as finance minister, extraordinary powers to decree financial legislation in order to avoid the delays involved in congressional debate. Thanks to Pani's mediation skills and legislative authority, a spate of legislation and institutional innovation followed. On the basis of discussion at the February convention, Miguel S. Macedo authored the overarching General Law of Credit Institutions, which went into

[11]Pani publicly accused de la Huerta of grossly mismanaging the national treasury if not stealing from it. See Secretaría de Hacienda y Credito Publico, *La controversia Pani–de la Huerta* (Mexico, D.F.: SCHP, 1924).

[12]Charles W. Anderson, "Bankers as Revolutionaries: Politics and Development Banking in Mexico," in Charles W. Anderson and William P. Glade, eds., *The Political Economy of Mexico* (Madison: University of Wisconsin Press, 1963), p. 113.

[13]Limantour was the unofficial leader, from 1895 on, of the so-called *científicos*. The *científicos* were a closely knit clique of intellectuals, professionals, and businessmen who advised dictator Porfirio Díaz. Their name stems from their insistence on "scientific" administration of the state. Their main policy focus was on economic development. They believed authoritarianism was necessary to guarantee the peace needed for economic advance. Most *científicos* believed that the Indian and mestizo population was inherently inferior and that Mexico would have to rely on the leadership and capital of the native white elites and foreigners to guide the country to modernity.

[14]David Shelton, "The Banking System: Money and the Goal of Growth," in Raymond Vernon, ed., *Public Policy and Private Enterprise in Mexico* (Cambridge: Harvard University Press, 1964), p. 134; José Alvarado, "El extraño caso de la Secretaría de Hacienda," *Problemas Agrícolas e Industriales de Mexico* 5 (1953), p. 167; Maria Elena Cardero, *Patrón monetario y acumulación en Mexico* (Mexico, D.F.: Siglo XXI, 1984), p. 24.

effect in January 1925. Pani charged the National Banking Commission, established by decree in December 1924, with enforcing this legislation.

In the first year of the Calles administration Pani also appointed and presided over a three-member commission, which wrote the Central Bank statute. The three formed part of Pani's circle of *científico* advisers who had financial experience in prerevolutionary Mexico and abroad. The "three musketeers," as they came to be called, were Manuel Gómez Morín, Fernando de la Fuente, and Elías de Lima. Gómez Morín had studied economics at Columbia University, specializing in central banking.[15] De Lima was a private banker in the final years of the Porfirian dictatorship. De la Fuente, the lawyer in the group, was a department chief for Pani in the Finance Ministry. Gómez Morín and de la Fuente were also close to Luis Montes de Oca, another member of the financiers' circle, who succeeded Pani as finance minister in 1927.

There was virtually no distinction between state and society in this financial policy-making circle. Public and private sector financiers followed the pattern, established in formulation of the first General Credit Law and the Central Bank statute, throughout the 1920s and early 1930s. In 1932, for example, Pani appointed Gómez Morín, Miguel S. Macedo, and Eduardo Suárez to recommend changes in bank regulation. Suárez recounts how their recommendations were "examined . . . by [private] bankers who had won Pani's confidence, principally Agustin Legoretta."[16]

---

[15]He spent two years in New York (1921–1922) as Mexico's financial agent, trying to resolve disputes between Mexico and international banks and oil companies. While there he became convinced that Mexico should establish a central bank in order to prove Mexico's financial strength and organizational capacity to New York bankers and businessmen.

The relative absence of direct foreign influence in the formation of the Mexican financial system, especially in the establishment of the Central Bank, is striking. The Mexican case stands in contrast to the cases of Chile, Ecuador, and Peru, where the U.S. Kemmerer Commission was directly instrumental in founding central banks. International events gave only indirect impetus to formation of the Mexican Central Bank. Establishment of the Federal Reserve Bank in the United States in 1914 provided a model for Mexican authors of financial reform. Impetus also came from an international financial conference held in Brussels in 1920, which urged all nations that hadn't created a central bank to do so. Gómez Morín's suggestion from New York that establishing a central bank would help negotiations with Mexico's international creditors is another example of indirect influence.

[16]Eduardo Suárez, *Comentarios y recuerdos* (Mexico, D.F.: Editorial Porrua, 1976), p. 34.

As he did at the National Banking Convention, and to write the Central Bank charter and other financial legislation, Pani turned to private financiers to help raise capital for the Central Bank. Initially, Pani hoped to settle Mexico's accounts with international creditors, regain international creditworthiness, and obtain new foreign loans for the Bank.[17] A refinancing agreement was worked out, partly through the help of Porfirian-era bankers with whom Pani was close. Throughout the 1920s Agustin Legoretta, Sr., owner of the Banco Nacional de Mexico, worked as an international representative for Mexico to settle outstanding foreign debts and seek new loans. This collaboration in debt refinancing helped establish a close relationship between the Legoretta family and the Central Bank and Finance Ministry, which lasts to this day. However, the terms of the 1924 refinancing agreement Legoretta helped achieve were politically unacceptable at home. Political opposition to the terms of the international refinancing led Pani to resort to a domestic austerity program to raise capital for the Bank. Between 1923 and 1925 tax increases and a drastic cut in government spending converted a 58 million peso government deficit into a 25 million peso surplus.[18]

Legally established and minimally capitalized, the Central Bank became the first instrument for state intervention in the economy. Yet it also bore witness to the desire of private bankers to create a central bank that would back private financiers in crisis but not impinge on their freedom of operation and decision making. They were not willing to accept regulation of their activities' nor did they want a commercial competitor.

In the 1920s the Bank functioned as a hybrid—somewhat more successful commercially than officially. It fared relatively poorly as a central bank in the half-decade after its founding. It did not have a monopoly on the issuance of paper, which other banks continued to circulate. Central Bank monetary emission grew relatively little in the first years of operation.[19] Private banks were not legally required to become members of the Central Bank, and initially few

---

[17]For an introduction to the history of Mexico's international debt see Jan Bazant, *Historia de la deuda externa de Mexico* (Mexico, D.F.: Colegio de Mexico, 1968).

[18]Bett, *Central Banking in Mexico*, p. 33.

[19]The Banco de Mexico printed 3.2 million pesos between September and December 1925, 2.6 million in the same period in 1926, 1.8 million in the final three months of 1927, and 3.6 million for that period in 1928.

did. They perceived the Banco de Mexico as a competitor, and the Bank's limited discounting facilities were little enticement to join. Although the Bank had almost no regulatory authority in this period, it performed respectably as a profit-making enterprise. It competed successfully for deposits with other commercial banks, primarily the two large Porfirian-era banks, the Banco Nacional de Mexico and the Banco de Comercio. Profits increased tenfold between 1925 and 1927. By 1927 the Central Bank was the nation's third largest bank in terms of deposits.[20]

The hybrid Central Bank/commercial Banco de Mexico was established with a nine-member board of directors comprising representatives chosen by public and private sector stockholders. Stock was issued in two series. The "A" series, worth 510 million pesos, could be purchased only by the government and was nontransferable. The "B" series, worth 490 million pesos, could be purchased by anyone. Among the private stock purchasers were several banks, which retired public sector debt in exchange for stock in the new Central Bank. These banks included the Banco de Londres y Mexico and Legoretta's Banco Nacional de Mexico. The "A" series stockholders, the government, chose five representatives to the board, and the "B" series stockholders chose four. To safeguard the influence of the private "B" series stockholders, all resolutions had to pass with a seven-member majority.

Manuel Gómez Morín became president of the first Central Bank board, which was composed entirely of influential businessmen. Like the seven-member majority provision for passing board resolutions, business domination of the first board of directors suggests the government's strong desire to secure support of the nation's leading capitalists for the new Central Bank.[21]

In 1928 the Finance Ministry suggested that private bankers organize themselves into a bankers' association to facilitate public-private financial collaboration. Thanks to the exchange of personnel between public and private financial institutions and the close informal ties between private bankers and government officials evident during the 1920s, the Asociación de Banqueros Mexicanos (Mexican Bankers Association, or ABM) developed the reputation of enjoying a more direct channel of communication to the highest

[20]Krauze, *La reconstrucción económica*, p. 48.
[21]For a list of the board members see ibid., p. 43.

levels of the Mexican government than did any other business organization. Its collaboration with the government was, and still is, carried on through appointees to financial regulatory bodies and close personal ties with government officials. Private financiers serve on several public financial regulatory commissions. Six of the nine members of the National Banking Commission, for instance, are appointed by the minister of finance; one is a representative of private deposit and savings banks; and two represent other credit institutions.

Survey data on public and private financiers' career patterns confirm the claim that bankers have closer ties to public officials than do entrepreneurs from other sectors. Of the leading Mexican entrepreneurs who had held political jobs, Camp found that bankers were much more likely than entrepreneurs from any other sector to have held political positions.[22] Leaders of the Mexican Bankers Association are also much more likely to have had careers spanning private business and public office than are leaders of other business associations. Whereas 15 percent of the presidents of the Mexican Bankers Association have had public sector jobs, none of the leaders of the Monterrey Chamber of Commerce, for example, have held such positions.[23] Camp concludes that "the only organization of the private sector that can claim a healthy representation among businessmen who followed careers in public life, or public figures who became entrepreneurs, is the Mexican Bankers Association."[24] Analysis of the boards of directors of Mexico's top fifty firms also reveals that there are more one-time public officials on bank boards than on nonbank company boards.

Although ties between public and private sector financiers usually are established when individuals who identify themselves primarily as private bankers venture into the public sector, the reverse also occurs. Public sector financiers often come from or retire to private sector finance. For example, Gómez Morín, first chairman of the board of the Banco de Mexico, became a legal adviser to the Banco de Londres y Mexico; Montes de Oca, minister of finance from 1927 to 1932 and director of the Banco de Mexico from 1935

[22]Roderic A. Camp, *Entrepreneurs and Politics in Twentieth Century Mexico* (Oxford: Oxford University Press, 1989), p. 84.
[23]Ibid.
[24]Ibid., p. 155.

43

to 1940, founded the Banco Internacional; Eduardo Villaseñor, director of the Banco de Mexico from 1940 to 1946, became president of the Banco del Atlántico; Ramon Beteta, finance minister from 1946 to 1952, became an adviser to Banco Continental; Carlos Novoa was a private banker and president of the Mexican Bankers Association before becoming director of the Banco de Mexico, a position he held from 1946 to 1952; Rodrigo Gómez, director of the Banco de Mexico from 1952 to 1970, came to government from the private sector; and Fernández Hurtado, director of the Banco de Mexico from 1970 to 1974, became an employee of Banco BCH.[25] Adding to this evidence, Centeno's analysis of the career paths of all public sector officials who were at the level of director general or above in 1983 reveals that the Central Bank and the Ministry of Finance had the highest levels of personnel with private sector experience.[26] In short, as Camp argues, banking is a key channel for the "exchange of private and public sector leadership" in Mexico.[27]

The testimony of leading public sector financiers also confirms the suggestion that private financiers play a major consultative role in the policy process. Antonio Ortiz Mena, minister of finance from 1958 to 1970, reports: "Our contact with the private sector leaders was constant when I was in government. We would call them, give them our ideas about a policy, wait for their reactions, take them into account, and incorporate them into our final policies."[28] Likewise, Hugo Margáin, finance minister from 1970 to 1973, states: "The private sector . . . has always had an influence in this country. In all of my positions during the many years I have been in public life, they have always been active and I always lis-

[25]Roderic A. Camp, *Mexican Political Biographies: 1935–1975* (Tucson: University of Arizona Press, 1976); Alonso Aguilar M., "El estado y la burgesía," *Estrategia* 27 (1979), pp. 20–61. Smith's well-known study of the Mexican elite concludes that there is little overlap between economic and political elites (Peter H. Smith, *Labyrinths of Power: Political Recruitment in Twentieth Century Mexico* [Princeton: Princeton University Press, 1979]). Reviewers have pointed out that his study is biased because it examines only the extent to which government officials come from the private sector. It does not examine the extent to which government officials move from government into business. It also does not provide evidence on possible variations in the extent of public and private sector overlap among different sectors of the entrepreneurial class or government. The findings presented here suggest that there is relatively high overlap between public and private financial sectors.
[26]Miguel Centeno, "The New Científicos: Technocratic Politics in Mexico" (Ph.D. diss., Yale University, 1989), pp. 186–187.
[27]Camp, *Entrepreneurs and Politics in Twentieth Century Mexico*, p. 14.
[28]Quoted in ibid., p. 116.

tened to their opinions."[29] Businessmen themselves also believe that bankers have more influence on state decision making than any other nonstate group. In three different surveys of Mexican businessmen, spanning the 1960s to the 1980s, entrepreneurs report that bankers have privileged access to the public policy process.[30]

In sum, this section suggests that the process of financial reconstruction in the 1920s established a pattern of close collaboration between public and private financiers, one that lasted at least until the bank nationalization in 1982 and that is part of the strong foundation of the Mexican bankers' alliance.

Establishing Hegemony of the Finance Ministry

The second important institutional legacy of the financial reorganization process was to establish the relative autonomy and policy-making power of the Finance Ministry and its dependencies within the government. The Finance Ministry's role in the genesis of the new financial regime and its institutional control over many new public sector financial institutions contributed to establishing its growing control over economic policy within the executive branch.[31] The Central Bank's original charter provided for a Finance Ministry veto over the decisions of the private shareholders sitting on the Central Bank's board of directors. Subsequent revisions of the 1925 law establishing the Banco de Mexico were administered under the Finance Ministry's supervision.[32] Pani also strengthened the Finance Ministry by giving it jurisdiction over budgetary decisions. Beginning with the debt renegotiations of the 1920s the Finance Ministry's role in mediating Mexico's relationship with the international

[29]Quoted in ibid.

[30]Dale Story, "Industrial Elites in Mexico," *Journal of Interamerican Studies and World Affairs* 25 (1983), pp. 351–376; John F. H. Purcell and Susan Kaufman Purcell, "Mexican Business and Public Policy," in James M. Malloy, ed., *Authoritarianism and Corporatism in Latin America* (Pittsburgh: University of Pittsburgh Press, 1977); Flavia Derossi, *The Mexican Entrepreneur* (Paris: OECD, 1971).

[31]William P. Glade, "Revolution and Economic Development," in Anderson and Glade, *The Political Economy of Mexico*, p. 12; John K. Thompson, *Inflation, Financial Markets and Economic Development: The Experience of Mexico* (Greenwich, Conn.: JAI Press, 1979), p. 57.

[32]Nora Hamilton, *The Limits of State Autonomy* (Princeton: Princeton University Press, 1982), p. 81; M. H. de Kock, *La banca central* (Mexico, D.F.: Fondo de Cultura Económica, 1941), pp. 436–437; Arnaldo Cordova, *La ideología de la revolución mexicana* (Mexico, D.F.: Ediciones Era, 1973), p. 361.

economy (by stabilizing the currency, renegotiating foreign debts, and guaranteeing foreign loans) was another factor that elevated its position within the government. In addition, the Finance Ministry created three financial regulatory agencies under its jurisdiction: the National Banking Commission, the National Securities Commission, and the National Insurance Commission. Another source of Finance Ministry power is the relative infrequency of ministerial turnover. Between 1935 and 1981 there were nine finance ministers but, for example, thirteen ministers of commerce and labor.

One discussion of Mexico's early economic policy suggests that the Finance Ministry and the Banco de Mexico together with the president defined the Mexican state in the 1930s.[33] A leading historian of the Cárdenas era argues that "the centralization of political power in the federal executive was accompanied by a centralization of financial control within the executive in the Ministry of Finance."[34]

Finance Minister Pani believed so strongly in the relative autonomy and power of the Finance Ministry vis-à-vis the rest of the executive and legislature that he resigned when he began to believe that President Calles questioned his authority.[35] Pani left the government in 1927 in a power struggle with the minister of industry, commerce, and work in which President Calles supported the latter. This cleavage between the Finance Ministry and Central Bank, on the one hand, and the ministries of Commerce, Industry, and Labor, on the other, is often echoed in more recent Mexican economic history. Although most frequently siding with the Central Bank, the Finance Ministry can also play the role of intermediary between the Central Bank and ministries favoring more expansionist policy. On the few occasions when the Finance Ministry opposes Central Bank policy suggestions, the latter—despite its considerable power—has relatively little hope of prevailing.[36]

The power of the finance minister is evident in the procedure

[33]Douglas Bennet and Kenneth Sharpe, "The State as Banker and Entrepreneur," *Comparative Politics* 12 (1980), p. 175.

[34]Hamilton, *The Limits of State Autonomy*, p. 80.

[35]José de la Fuente Iturriaga, *La revolución hacendaria* (Mexico, D.F.: SEP, 1976), p. 49.

[36]One important source of Central Bank power stemmed from the Bank's personnel exchange program. Under this arrangement Central Bank personnel were "loaned" to other ministries or agencies to help on specific problems or projects. They were always guaranteed a Central Bank job to return to. (Roderic A. Camp, *The Role of Economists in Policy Making* [Tucson: University of Arizona, Institute of Government Research, 1977], p. 15.)

Cárdenas followed to appoint a Central Bank director. In 1934 President Cárdenas was considering appointing Luis Montes de Oca (finance minister from 1927 to 1932) to head the Central Bank. He consulted first with finance minister Suárez, fearing that Montes de Oca might find it difficult "to subordinate himself."[37] Suárez recalls he suggested to Cárdenas that "to maintain the necessary discipline and coordination between superior and subordinate, it was indispensable that all agreements the president wished to recommend to me or directives for the Banco de Mexico be communicated directly to me to transmit to Mr. Montes de Oca; . . . that to ensure the progress of Finance Ministry business . . . I [Suárez] should be present at any meeting the president should have with Montes de Oca."[38] Suárez reports that President Cárdenas complied with this request throughout his entire term.

Centeno's study of career paths of public sector officials in the 1980s provides evidence to support the claim that the Finance Ministry is at the top of the hierarchy of cabinet ministries. He finds that the Finance Ministry, to a greater extent than any other, "seeds" the other ministries. It is the most common place of entry into public life for the political elite; 25 percent of the political elite have spent time working in Hacienda. Centeno also finds that ministries involved in finance have the tightest network, measured by exchange of personnel, than any other functional group of ministries in the government.[39]

In short, the influence of the Finance Ministry and its dependencies within the executive branch is a second important institutional legacy of the process of financial reconstruction. This hierarchy of economic policy-making agencies within the executive and the mechanisms of collaboration between public and private financiers provide an important base for the bankers' alliance. The third part of that base lies in the organization of Mexican capital.

The Organization of Mexican Capital

The organization of Mexican capital is marked by relatively heavy concentration; business activity is dominated by a small

[37]Suárez, *Comentarios y recuerdos*, p. 163.
[38]Ibid., pp. 163–164.
[39]Centeno, "The New Científicos," pp. 197, 242.

number of large financial-industrial-commercial conglomerates. Their history varies, with some conglomerates dating to the Porfirian era, others to the 1930s and 1940s, and yet others to the 1960s and 1970s. They also vary significantly in their form of integration. Some are fully integrated financially, legally, and administratively. At the other end of the spectrum are those integrated merely through stockholding.

The most famous Mexican conglomerate, the Grupo Monterrey, grew up around a brewery built by the Garza-Sada family in the nineteenth century in the northern city of Monterrey. The group established its own banks in order to facilitate industrial expansion. In the 1970s the Monterrey Group subdivided into four separate groups: Visa, Vitro, Alfa, and Cydsa. The first two were legally, financially, and administratively linked conglomerates of financial and industrial enterprises. The latter two were industrial concerns linked to banks through interlocking directorates. At the center of the Visa group was the original Monterrey Group enterprise, the brewery. The bank integral to this group was Serfín— originally the Banco de Londres y Mexico, one of the two oldest Mexican banks. The Vitro group included another of the original Monterrey group enterprises, the glass-making factory built to make bottles for the beer. This group's bank was Banpaís.

Another set of conglomerates grew up around the state-led development push of the 1930s and 1940s. The Chihuahua-Comermex Group associated with the families Vallina and Trouyet was a closely integrated conglomerate, like Visa-Serfín and Vitro-Banpaís. The Vallina Group began with a profitable lumbering operation in the 1930s in the northern border state of Chihuahua. The group's bank, Comermex, was founded in 1934 to fund expansion. Like the Monterrey Group conglomerates, this one was jointly administered and completely integrated financially and legally. Another conglomerate dating to the 1930s and 1940s united the huge ICA construction firm with the Banco del Atlántico. Carlos Abedrop, one of the ICA owner-directors, became a major shareholder in Banco del Atlántico in the 1960s. This conglomerate was slightly less closely integrated administratively than the three others.

A final set of financial-industrial conglomerates includes two that revolved around the nation's leading commercial banks. Unlike the groups just described, these two involved banks that purchased industrial and commercial concerns rather than beginning as industrial enterprises that linked themselves with banks in order to expand. Both leading Mexican banks, Banamex and Bancomer, became conglomerates in the 1960s and 1970s as they purchased shares in a large variety of industrial and commercial enterprises.

Camp's survey of major corporate boards in the 1980s confirms that there is a high degree of interlock between the boards of banks and major holding companies. Members of the Garza-Sada family, which controls the two major industrial groups Alfa and Visa, sat on the board of Banca Serfín. Representatives of a large industrial group (Desc), of one of the country's two leading retailing chains (Aurrera), and of another banking group (Cremi) sat on the board of Bancomer. Members of the Legoretta family, which controlled Banamex, sat on eight top company boards; and in many cases representatives from those companies in turn sat on Banamex's board. Camp's data provide numerous other examples of the connections through board representation of banks and leading non-bank firms.[40] Another set of data from Camp's study suggests the centrality of bankers among Mexico's leading entrepreneurial families. Camp finds that these families were better represented in the Mexican Bankers Association than in any other business organization.[41]

The linkage of financial and industrial capital is important for two reasons. It creates a situation where industrialists can finance expansion "internally," meaning they do not have to rely on state funds.[42] They become relatively immune to state efforts to guide industrial development by manipulating the price or quantity of money. Certain policy instruments often used by state planning authorities are rendered relatively impotent by this organization of capital. Furthermore, to the extent that they are closely linked to financial enterprises, industrialists are likely to share the bankers' policy preferences. Whereas industrialists not linked to financiers will tend to prefer low interest rates, expansionary fiscal policy, and state support, those linked to bankers will tend to share their interest in monetary stability and minimal state intervention in the economy. Thus the close integration of financial and industrial cap-

---

[40]Camp, *Entrepreneurs and Politics in Twentieth Century Mexico*, pp. 177–189.
[41]Ibid., p. 148.
[42]Nathaniel Leff, "Entrepreneurship in Economic Development," *Journal of Economic Literature* 17 (1979), pp. 46–64.

ital is an institutional or organizational factor leading to a strong bankers' alliance by limiting the range of effective policies available to state planning authorities and by adding large-scale industrialists to the bankers' alliance. The historical strength of the Mexican bankers' alliance is based on institutional structures that provided for close collaboration between private financiers and state monetary authorities, for the latter's predominance over state planning authorities, and for the close integration of financial and industrial capital. The influence of the bankers' alliance in economic policy outcomes is evident in the macropolicy pattern discussed in the following chapter, in policy episodes outlined in chapter 5, and in the limitations of national populist reform efforts such as the bank nationalization analyzed in chapter 6.

The Cárdenas Coalition

Cárdenas, appointed/elected to the presidency in 1934, tried to end former president Calles's personal stronghold over national government and with it the political regime's dependence on *científico*-type elites, such as Pani. He also worked to develop a new base of political legitimacy in urban workers, the peasantry, state workers, young military officers, and a new generation of Mexico City–based industrialists, which emerged thanks to the state's protection. Thus to some extent the origins of the Cárdenas coalition lie in a reaction to the successes of the slowly emerging bankers' alliance in the 1920s.

The political period prior to Cárdenas's presidency is known as the Maximato after General Calles, dubbed the *jefe maximo* ("highest boss"), who dominated national politics from 1924 until 1934. He was president from 1924 to 1928 and ruled from behind the scenes during the subsequent "puppet" presidencies of Emilio Portes Gil (1928–1930), Pascual Ortiz Rubio (1930–1932), and Abelardo Rodríguez (1932–1934). Calles established the National Revolutionary Party in 1929 to help consolidate national power. At a national level, opposition to the both conservative and personalistic Calles regime grew in the early 1930s. Monetary policy had been severely contractionary, squeezing all who were credit short; and agricultural policy favored private farmers over the semicollective *ejido* landholders.[43] Legal changes greatly limited agrarian reform.[44]

There were several brands of anti-Callismo; Cárdenas's presidential candidacy was supported by the *agrarista* camp. *Agraristas* were united by their desire to see a national pro-*ejido*, pro–land reform policy. Although there were divisions even within the *agrarista* camp, Cárdenas emerged as the presidential candidate for several reasons. He had demonstrated his commitment to agrarian reform and peasant organization through successful efforts undertaken while he was governor of his home state of Michoacán. Thanks to this record, Cárdenas's candidacy won the support of one of the largest peasant organizations, the Confederación de Campesinos Mexicanos (Confederation of Mexican Peasants, or CCM), in May 1933. Cárdenas was also close to Calles, had widespread support from within the military, and was the favored candidate of the president in power at the time, Abelardo Rodríguez.[45]

Because of the peasant and labor mobilization that had led in part to Cárdenas's candidacy and of the continued threat of both Callista and military intervention, Cárdenas's first year in office was not easy. Calles's behind-the-scenes presence continued to be a major problem. Pressure from the *jefe maximo* had led Cárdenas to fill his cabinet with Calles loyalists. In addition, popular opinion saw Calles behind bloody anticlerical riots that took place in spring 1935. The situation came to a head in June, when Calles publicly denounced Cárdenas's prolabor policies. Calles's denunciation forced a showdown. Cárdenas fired all Calles loyalists in his cabinet and forced Calles to leave the country.[46] From mid-1935 to mid-1936 he transferred leaders of regional pro-Calles military strongholds and replaced them with military men who had been

[43]The *ejido* is a form of communal landholding legally established in Mexico by the Spanish to preserve indigenous people's control of their lands.

[44]For an overview of the *maximato* see Lorenzo Meyer, *Historia de la revolución mexicana: El conflicto social y los gobiernos del maximato* (Mexico, D.F.: Colegio de Mexico, 1978).

[45]See Lorenzo Meyer, *Historia de la revolución mexicana: Los inicios de la institucionalización, la política del maximato* (Mexico, D.F.: Colegio de Mexico, 1971), pp. 273–293; Alicia Hernández Chavez, *Historia de revolución mexicana: La mecánica cardenista* (Mexico, D.F.: Colegio de Mexico, 1979), pp. 3–121.

[46]Hernández Chavez, *La mecánica cardenista*, pp. 45–54. Frank Brandenberg, *The Making of Modern Mexico* (Englewood Cliffs, N.J.: Prentice-Hall, 1964), p. 80, presents more detail on the cabinet changes Cárdenas imposed.

excluded from political life during the *maximato*.[47] He also replaced twenty-five state governors suspected of Calles loyalties.

The confrontation with Calles and Calles's criticism of Cárdenas's labor sympathies catalyzed the process of sectoral unification that became the base for the Cárdenas coalition. In 1935 the Confederación General de Obreros y Campesinos Mexicanos (General Confederation of Mexican Workers and Peasants, or CGOCM), the Confederación Sindical Unitaria de Mexico (Unitary Labor Union of Mexico, or CSUM), and the electrical, mining, and metal-working unions joined to form the Comité Nacional de Defensa Popular (National Committee for Popular Defense), forerunner to the Confederación de Trabajadores de Mexico (Mexican Workers' Federation, or CTM), a national federation of labor unions.[48] The CTM was born in 1936; chief among the principles declared in its founding statement was support for Cárdenas.[49] Cárdenas's relationship to the labor movement was typical of how he built a base for his populist policies. He encouraged mobilization and organization of labor to support his presidency and its pro-labor policies against the conservative wing of the PRI and business, but he was careful to make sure that the CTM did not be-

[47]Cárdenas, a general himself, had an intimate knowledge of the military, which somewhat eased the task of creating a loyal force by enabling him to move men from one position to another. Many of those he elevated to key positions had been allied with insurrection leaders Carranza, Francisco (Pancho) Villa, or Emiliano Zapata in the earlier years of the revolution. (Hernández Chavez, *La mecánica cardenista*, pp. 91–95.) Strengthening political control of the military was one of Cárdenas's several crucial state-building accomplishments. There had been three military uprisings in the 1920s (1923–1924, 1927–1928, and 1929); and when Cárdenas took office, 50 percent of the country's governors and cabinet ministers were military men. Military zone heads also exercised considerable political power. In addition to the leadership changes he made in 1935 and 1936, Cárdenas also worked to build a new sense of professionalism among younger military officers. He encouraged them to believe that they were better than the old generals and that they owed their positions to him. (Arnaldo Córdova, *La política de masas del cardenismo* [Mexico, D.F.: Serie Popular Era, 1974], p. 141.)

[48]The strongest labor organization during the *maximato* was the Confederación Regional Obrera Mexicana (Regional Mexican Workers' Federation, or CROM), led by Luis Morones. The CROM was closely aligned with the Laborist Party. The depression hurt the CROM, and its leadership began to lose credibility. In 1933, hoping to separate workers from the Laborist Party, Vicente Lombardo Toledano left the CROM, taking many members with him to join other independent labor leaders in founding the CGOCM. This organization actively campaigned in support of Cárdenas's presidential bid.

[49]After the founding of the CTM, the CROM shrank dramatically, but it has continued to exist. On several occasions Mexican presidents have taken measures to strengthen the CROM in order to limit the CTM's leverage.

come an independent political force. When he began to fear that labor leader Lombardo Toledano and the CTM might gain too much power, he split civil servants, bank employees, and teachers from the CTM. He also organized peasants into a national confederation partly designed to counterbalance the political power of labor. Organized labor was a political ally; but peasants, less well organized, could be molded into a political force that would unconditionally support the government—that would be "an organic part of the state."[50]

Cárdenas's career as labor and peasant organizer began when he was governor of Michoacán. He traveled around the state encouraging organization; in early 1929 he convoked a meeting of all worker and peasant leaders, during which the Confederación Revolucionaria Michoacana (Revolutionary Federation of Michoacán) was created. Cárdenas encouraged this organization to help force agrarian reform in the state, combat religious fanaticism, and promote state-led education.[51] During the presidential campaign Cárdenas traveled throughout Mexico explaining to groups of peasants and workers how the Plan Sexenal, essentially a campaign platform adopted after considerable argument within the PNR, would benefit them, and encouraging them to organize. In July 1935, as part of his effort to consolidate power in the face of Callista opposition, he ordered the PNR immediately to set about organizing *campesinos*. He instructed the party leadership to work state by state setting up meetings attended by two representatives elected by majority from each *ejido* or town of *ejidos* in the state. These leaders should join together to form a single statewide agrarian league. After agrarian leagues had been formed in all states, Cárdenas's instructions continued, the PNR should call a national convention to form a peasant confederation. To help organize peasants, Cárdenas enlisted, in addition to party cadres, rural teachers and the Banco Nacional de Crédito Ejidal. The latter institution was founded in 1935, a splitoff from the Banco Nacional de Crédito Agricola established by Calles. It was meant not only to provide credit to *ejidos* but also to help organize *campesinos* collectively for pro-

---

[50]Córdova, *La politica de masas*, p. 112.
[51]Ibid., pp. 28–34.

duction and distribution and, by implication, politics.[52] In June 1936 the president of the Consejo Nacional Ejecutivo (National Executive Board, or CEN) of the PNR reported fourteen leagues organized; by 1937 fourteen more had been organized, including several in states where divisions among existing peasant groups were severe, such as Veracruz. In August 1938 representatives from thirty-seven state agrarian leagues attended a national meeting in Mexico City, and the Confederación Nacional Campesina (National Peasant Confederation, or CNC) was born. As part of Cárdenas's effort to build a counterweight to the CTM, rural unions in the sugar, cotton, and henequen industries, which had been organized by the CTM, were strongly encouraged to leave that organization and join the CNC.[53]

In addition to organizing peasants and government workers, professionalizing the military, and bringing the labor movement under party control, Cárdenas also set about trying to change the image of the national party from that of an elite party whose primary function was to resolve intraelite disputes to that of a popular one. In 1936, at Cárdenas's suggestion, the party's choices of state-level nominees for party positions were ratified by assemblies of worker and peasant representatives. Later that year Cárdenas decided mass ratification should be the norm at the national level as well. To facilitate such ratification, the PNR was reorganized to reflect the role of four key sectors incorporated in Cárdenas's political base: peasants, workers, the so-called popular sector (which came to include government workers, bank employees, and teachers), and the military. Membership in the PNR was individual and based on geographic representation. Membership in the renovated party, renamed the Partido de la Revolución Mexicana (Party of the Mexican Revolution, or PRM), was based on membership in one of the four sectors. Theoretically, representation in the PNR had been direct, but in practice it functioned personalistically. Representation in the PRM was indirect, operating through sector

[52]Ibid., p. 107.

[53]Cárdenas also supported the organizing of government workers but opposed their incorporation into the CTM. They were organized as an independent sector of the PNR. Cárdenas distributed arms to sixty thousand *campesinos* partly to help them protect themselves against landlords and caciques and partly to create a peasant militia to counterbalance militant industrial workers.

leaders. The rank-and-file's political power came from its voice in choosing individuals to fill specific public sector jobs.[54]

The military was soon removed from this national representational structure, but the peasant and labor organizations became part of the long-run institutional base of the Cárdenas coalition. Another institutional base of the coalition came from a sector of the business community. Cárdenas had an acrimonious relationship with much of the business community, which objected to his support of labor strikes and land distribution. In a famous confrontation with Monterrey businessmen he suggested that if they did not like operating in Mexico they should turn their enterprises over to the state.[55] Another segment of the business community, an emerging group of manufacturers supported and protected by the state, began to enjoy close and harmonious relations with the Cárdenas government and "populist" leaders of the PNR.

Beginning in the 1930s businessmen were required by law to join the business organization pertaining to their sector. They were divided into several different organizations so their political power would be limited. Canacintra was made up of small and medium-sized manufacturers, the Confederación de Cámaras Industriales (Confederation of Chambers of Industry, or Concamin) of larger industrialists, and the Confederación de Cámaras Nacionales de Comercio (Confederation of National Chambers of Commerce, or Concanaco) of retailers and other merchants. The Confederación Patronal de la Republica Mexicana (Employers Confederation of the Mexican Republic, or Coparmex) was the one independent, or voluntary, organization; it was founded by the Monterrey Group in 1929 to form a united employers' front to combat prolabor government policies. Canacintra was the organization that became allied with the Cárdenas coalition.[56]

---

[54]Collectively the four sectors divided public offices into four groups, each group to be filled by one sector. Once a sector had named a candidate for a position, all four came out to support that choice officially. One notable exception to this procedure was in the choice of president, which was, and still is, decided by the outgoing president after consultation with other high-level party members.

[55]Juan M. Martínez Nava, *Conflicto estado-empresarios* (Mexico, D.F.: Editorial Nueva Imagen, 1984), pp. 91–92.

[56]Legislation, in 1936, mandated that Mexican businesses belong to sectoral business chambers. Each chamber was integrated into a government-controlled business confederation. The minister of the economy decided when a new chamber could be created,

Domestic Structures and Economic Policy

The split within the business community between those sympathetic to Cardenista policies and those allied loosely with the more conservative bankers' alliance became starker during the administration of Cárdenas's successor, Manuel Ávila Camacho (1940–1946). In 1945 Canacintra, the business organization incorporating small and medium-sized manufacturers, signed an accord with the CTM in support of economic nationalism—meaning trade protection and restriction of foreign investment. This alliance with labor led to a deep split between Canacintra and other major business organizations, Concamin, Concanaco, and Coparmex, that had an antagonistic relationship with labor. During the Alemán administration, state intervention in the economy joined trade as a salient point of disagreement between these two groups of businessmen.[57]

The CTM, the CNC, and Canacintra—all corporatist organizations whose access to executive branch decision makers was indirect—and the state ministries usually sympathetic to them, including the ministries of Agriculture and Labor, among others, formed the institutional base of the Cárdenas coalition. This base was relatively weak in comparison with the institutional base of the bankers' alliance, which consisted of large-scale economic groups and banks enjoying direct—if behind-the-scenes—access to executive branch decision makers and the Finance Ministry and Central Bank. The weakness of the Cárdenas coalition was in part a function of Cárdenas's efforts simultaneously to mobilize and to control. In the case of the Ministry of Agriculture, for example, Cárdenas limited the ministry's functions to keep agriculture minister Saturnino Cedillo from expanding his personal political base.[58] The

---

specified which industrial categories would be grouped within which chamber, had the right to dissolve chambers and confederations, and had representatives on the chamber and confederation boards. These organizations were designated the official *interlocutores* (intermediaries) between business and government. For more on the history of Mexican business organizations see Robert Jones Shafer, *Mexican Business Organizations: History and Analysis* (Syracuse, N.Y.: Syracuse University Press, 1973); Carlos Arriola, *Las organizaciones empresariales y el estado* (Mexico, D.F.: Fondo de Cultura Económica, 1981); and Luis Bravo Mena, "Coparmex and Mexican Politics," in Sylvia Maxfield and Ricardo Anzaldua, eds., *Government and Private Sector in Contemporary Mexico* (La Jolla: Center for U.S.- Mexican Studies, University of California–San Diego, 1987).

[57]Olga Pellicer de Brody and José Luis Reyna, *Historia de la revolución mexicana: El afianzamiento de la estabilidad política* (Mexico, D.F.: Colegio de Mexico, 1978), p. 95.

[58]Brandenberg, *The Making of Modern Mexico*, p. 82.

national development banks such as Nafinsa, the Banco Nacional de Crédito Agricola, and the Banco Ejidal, part of the institutional base of the Cárdenas coalition, could not rival the Finance Ministry's authority within the state. Formally dependencies of cabinet ministries, their directors were not routinely included in the inner circle of the cabinet. More importantly, relative to the Finance Ministry their budgets were small and their beneficiaries impotent in affecting internal government policy debates. Whereas the Finance Ministry and the Central Bank could "buy" support from other ministries, which depended on them to finance their operations, the development banks had limited funds, which they distributed to nonstate actors, such as *ejidos* or utility companies, with only indirect access to government decision makers.

The transition from the Cárdenas administration to that of his successor provides telling evidence of the weakness of the Cárdenas coalition's institutional base. The "official left" of the PRM, associated with the Cárdenas coalition, found itself with little maneuverability in 1939 as it contemplated whom to select as Cárdenas's successor. With inflation eating into wages and work stoppages and strikes on the rise, labor was divided. So was the military. Internationally, fascism was powerful and could ignite anti-Cárdenas mobilization; Cárdenas allies saw potential parallels between antileft movements in Europe and the antileft movement in Mexico. To avoid sparking right-wing opposition or further labor agitation, Cárdenas and the party leadership decided on a moderate course, choosing Ávila Camacho as the party candidate. The national labor and peasant organizations were not pleased with this choice. They feared Ávila Camacho would not support their interests; but Cárdenas had cut a deal with CTM leader Lombardo Toledano, who tried to keep labor in line. Cárdenas also promised publicly to personally fight to protect labor interests after he left office.[59]

There were two opposition candidates who tried to organize support once Ávila Camacho's selection was announced. They embodied the pressures from both left and right that had led the party to choose a moderate. Joaquín Amaro took the lead in terms of

---

[59]Hernández Chavez, *La mecánica cardenista*, pp. 187–211; Luis Medina, *Historia de la revolución mexicana: Del cardenismo al avilacamachismo* (Mexico, D.F.: Colegio de Mexico, 1970), pp. 13–98.

public oppostion to Ávila Camacho with a conservative campaign statement that included advocating severe restraints on Banco de Mexico lending—something the bankers' alliance was pushing for at the time. Juan Andréu Almazán, a more left-wing candidate, campaigned more subtly.[60]

After considerable effort, the PRM managed to organize sufficient support to hold a nominating convention and ratify Ávila Camacho's candidacy. Still there was tremendous debate over the party platform—over supporting a continuation of Cardenismo or a break with it. The CTM was the leading force pressing for policies that would continue Cárdenas's social commitment; the Callistas pressed for policies that would reflect the leading role they believed private entrepreneurship should play in national development.[61] In the end, the official Plan Sexenal expressed a commitment to continuity, but little by little during the course of the campaign and later in his administration Ávila Camacho broke with the Cárdenas policies. Agricultural credit was increasingly directed to the private sector rather than the *ejido*, and land distribution slowed down.

Although a large part of the institutional base of the Cárdenas coalition came from organized sectors of the national party, their ability to influence presidential selection and public policy was limited. The Cárdenas coalition's institutional base in the party was partly a liability. The party plays an equilibrating role in Mexican political life, preventing large-scale conflict from erupting between competing policy currents. Cárdenas himself believed in the disciplining role of the party. As president of the PNR in 1930 he expelled several senators from the party for criticizing finance minister Luis Montes de Oca even though he sympathized with them. The liabilities for the Cárdenas coalition stemmed from the equilibrating role and corporatist organization of the party. Relative to the bankers' alliance its institutional base provided little direct access to and influence over the public policy process. The relative weakness of the Cárdenas coalition and strength of the bankers' alliance shaped the economic policy patterns outlined in the following chapter.

[60]See Medina, *Historia de la revolución mexicana*, pp. 98–133.
[61]Ibid., p. 134.

3

Competing Alliances and Mexican Economic Policy, 1930–1976

Since its foundation in the 1920s the Mexican bankers' alliance has pushed for an orthodox macroeconomic policy guided by laissez-faire ideology. It has promoted the relatively unregulated development of private financial markets, free exchange convertibility, tight monetary policy, and virtually no taxation of profits or luxuries. These policy preferences are evident in certain continuities in the history of Mexican macroeconomic policy from 1930 to 1976. The policy areas discussed here are not the only, or necessarily most salient, issues in Mexican economic policy debates. Nor are they the only areas of continuity. They are singled out for two reasons. First, they are issue areas of particular concern to financial elites because they potentially constrain the mobility of financial capital. Second, they are issue areas neglected by most economic histories of Mexico. Existing histories tend to focus on trade policy and state intervention in the economy generally as key areas of policy dispute.

Financial Regulation

In the history of Mexican financial policy beginning with Cárdenas and Avila Camacho in the 1930s and 1940s the government has tried to promote private financial markets—which strengthen the economic base of the bankers' alliance—and aimed to subject

59

private bank credit allocation to state control. These somewhat contradictory strands of financial policy reflect the struggle between the bankers' alliance, desirous of growing unregulated private financial markets, and the national populists, pushing for policies to control capital allocation. The brief history of Mexican financial policy presented here also shows how during the heyday of the Cárdenas coalition, when there were two consecutive finance ministers sympathetic to the concerns of labor, peasants, and small and medium-sized industry, the Finance Ministry played a pivotal intermediary role between the bankers' alliance and the Cárdenas coalition. The first of these finance ministers, Marte R. Gómez, is the only Mexican finance minister with a background in agricultural policy. This background gave him a decidedly *agrarista* outlook. The second was Eduardo Suárez, an early fan of Keynes, and a structuralist economist with great sympathy for Cárdenas's policies. He continued as finance minister for Avila Camacho.

Legislation in the Cárdenas and Avila Camacho eras aimed to promote private sector financial institutions while subjecting them to increasing Central Bank regulation. The Cárdenas administration succeeded in extending Central Bank regulatory capacity, but it did not succeed in incorporating private financial institutions into the public sector industrialization and agricultural development effort.

In the 1930s, with several revisions of the banking and credit laws, the Banco de Mexico gained regulatory capacity. The 1931 and 1932 legal revisions eliminated gold from circulation as money and prohibited further coinage of silver money.[1] This legislation forced the public to increase its acceptance of Central Bank notes. It also forced the Banco de Mexico to cease its commercial operations and charged it with the functions of centralizing national banking reserves and aiding private banks through rediscounting

[1]The legislative changes in 1931 and 1932 reflected a balance of payments crisis. The monetary system was based on a gold standard, with silver coins valued at a fixed gold rate. The balance of payments deficit induced a gold outflow and forced down the value of silver relative to gold. A Central Bank–managed system based on paper money was designed in part to relieve this problem. It also created other problems; managing the money and credit system was still intimately linked to managing the foreign exchange position of the country. The gold-silver dilemma was merely replaced by a dollar-peso dilemma.

and clearing operations.[2] An increasing number of private banks affiliated themselves with the Central Bank. Between 1931 and 1932 the number grew from thirteen to thirty-eight.[3]

Legislation in 1936 gave the Central Bank legal authority to collect mandatory reserve requirements from commercial banks.[4] Furthermore, this legislation finally made Banco de Mexico notes the only legal tender in the country. It also increased the amount of credit the Central Bank could make available and authorized it to buy and sell federal government bonds. These measures vastly expanded the Central Bank's regulatory capacity.

The regulation of private bank lending practices was intended in part to increase credit available for productive investment in industry and agriculture and to discourage "speculative" activity. In the 1930s older manufacturing companies borrowing in the short term—often for speculation—took the place of large landowners as preferred bank customers. In the 1940s, the earliest years for which data are available, the net balance between the banks and the agricultural sector favored the banks. This allocation of private bank credit led to a squeeze on peasants and on the newer industrialists soon to be organized in Canacintra. It fueled the frustration of Cárdenas allies with private bankers.[5] During the 1934 bankers' convention the minister of finance, Marte R. Gómez, lectured the private banking community on its responsibility in Mexico's development effort: "The Mexican government has done more than one could expect; bankers! . . . do the part which corresponds to you: work solidly . . . staying away from anything that is or seems to be of a merely speculative nature."[6] A legal followup to

[2]When the Banco de Mexico had to cease commercial operations, the Banco Nacional de Mexico took them over.

[3]Virgil Bett, *Central Banking in Modern Mexico* (Ann Arbor: University of Michigan, 1957), p. 59.

[4]The legislation making affiliation with the Banco de Mexico mandatory induced most foreign banks in Mexico to close their offices. Since then, further legislation has prohibited foreign banks from operating in Mexico, although they may maintain representative offices. One of the prime functions of these offices until 1985 was to encourage Mexicans to open dollar accounts in U.S. banks. A major mechanism of capital flight, this activity was prohibited in late 1985.

[5]Sanford A. Mosk, *Industrial Revolution in Mexico* (Berkeley: University of California Press, 1954); Robert Jones Shafer, *Mexican Business Organizations: History and Analysis* (Syracuse, N.Y.: Syracuse University Press, 1973), pp. 109–111.

[6]Miguel Angel Calderón, *El impacto de la crisis de 1929 en Mexico* (Mexico, D.F.: SEP/80, 1982), p. 64.

this admonition amended banking laws to include a distinction between productive and unproductive use of funds and set a minimum for productive loans.[7]

Legislation aiming to encourage private financing of development was relatively unsuccessful. Members of the Cárdenas administration accused private bankers of fomenting speculation, especially during the foreign exchange crisis following the oil nationalization in 1938. Data showing that short-term financing accounted for three-quarters of total financial resources in the 1930s lend credence to this charge.[8] Private bank credit relative to GNP expanded only sluggishly, much to the frustration of Cárdenas's finance minister, Eduardo Suárez.[9] Between 1925 and 1940, although the number of private bank offices grew, their resources fell from 12 percent of GNP to 10 percent.[10] Capital flight amounted to 900 million pesos between 1935 and 1939, more than double the value of total investment in that period.[11]

Given the perceived weakness of the private banks' contribution to the industrial and agricultural sectors, the Cárdenas regime created seven national credit institutions to help finance investment in roads, irrigation, and energy production to improve agricultural output and spur industrialization. These institutions include Banobras for public works (1933), Banjidal for rural finance (1935), Bancomext for foreign trade (1937), Nafinsa for industry (1933), and Banco Obrero for unionized laborers' personal credit needs (1939).[12] The national credit institutions did not accept public de-

---

[7]David Shelton, "The Banking System: Money and the Goal of Growth," in Raymond Vernon, ed., *Public Policy and Private Enterprise in Mexico* (Cambridge: Harvard University Press, 1964), p. 148; Charles W. Anderson, "Bankers as Revolutionaries: Politics and Development in Mexico," in Charles W. Anderson and William P. Glade, eds., *The Political Economy of Mexico* (Madison: University of Wisconsin Press, 1963), p. 118.

[8]Raymond Goldsmith, *The Financial Development of Mexico* (Paris: OECD, 1966), p. 29.

[9]Shelton, "The Banking System," p. 145.

[10]Goldsmith, *The Financial Development of Mexico*, p. 29.

[11]Enrique Fernández Hurtado, *Cincuenta años de banca central* (Mexico, D.F.: Fondo de Cultura Económica, 1976), p. 55; Juan M. Martínez Nava, *Conflicto estado-empresarios* (Mexico, D.F.: Editorial Nueva Imagen, 1984), p. 104.

[12]Calvin P. Blair, "Nacional Financiera: Entrepreneurship in a Mixed Economy," in Raymond Vernon, ed., *Public Policy and Private Enterprise in Mexico* (Cambridge: Harvard University Press, 1964); Shelton, "The Banking System," pp. 116–120; Octavio Campos Salas, "Las instituciones nacionales de crédito," in Fernández Hurtado, *Cincuenta años de banca central*; Robert L. Bennet, *The Financial Sector and Economic Development* (Baltimore: Johns Hopkins University Press, 1965), pp. 54–60.

posits and were capitalized during the 1930s by the Banco de Mexico. They were essentially administrative arms of the Finance Ministry and Central Bank and were also subject to the authority of the ministry specifically concerned with their area of lending. Banjidal, for instance, answered to both the Finance Ministry and the Ministry of Agriculture.[13] Nafinsa was the largest and most important of the national credit institutions.[14] These institutions primarily served the financing needs of Cárdenas's main constituents. Private bankers did not consider them a threat because they did not accept deposits from the public.

Under President Avila Camacho, finance minister Suárez worked with the Central Bank to strengthen financial regulation. The Central Bank switched from rediscounting to mandatory reserve requirements as its primary means for regulating private bank activity, strengthened selective credit allocation requirements, and instituted the practice of negotiating voluntary "gentlemen's agreements" guiding private bank behavior.[15]

This policy reflected the same beliefs and goals that lay behind financial regulations during the Cárdenas administration. Agricultural, industrial, and social credit needs would not be met under an unregulated market allocation system. The goals of selective credit controls were to increase long-term financing available to industry and agriculture and to prevent short-term financing for speculation. The power to enforce selective credit controls stemmed from the Banco de Mexico's authority to impose reserve requirements on private banks. By imposing differential requirements, based on the private banks' liability and asset structures, the Central Bank could encourage or discourage specific types of bank ac-

[13]Dwight S. Brothers and Leopoldo Solís, *Mexican Financial Development* (Austin: University of Texas Press, 1966), p. 55; Mosk, *Industrial Revolution in Mexico*, p. 243.

[14]Blair, "Nacional Financiera," pp. 206–230; Robert T. Aubey, *Nacional Financiera and Mexican Industry* (Los Angeles: Latin American Center, University of California–Los Angeles, 1966); Jose Hernández Delgado, *Nacional financiera como coadyudante de la industrialización* (Mexico, D.F.: Nafinsa, 1961); Joseph S. La Cascia, *Capital Formation and Economic Development in Mexico* (New York: Praeger, 1969), pp. 39–42; Mosk, *Industrial Revolution in Mexico*, pp. 242–249.

[15]In the case of rediscounting, the Bank of Mexico influenced the allocation of credit by deciding which types of borrowers and collateral were eligible for rediscounted funds. In addition to selectively varying the cost of financing through rediscounting, the Mexican government also directly set variable interest rates for specific types of lending. (Luis Sanchez Lugo, "Instrumentos de política crediticia," in Fernández Hurtado, *Cincuenta años de banca central*, p. 385.)

tivity.[16] The Banco de Mexico employed three types of reserve requirements between 1936 and 1960 to regulate private bank activity and channel lending to productive uses: cash reserve requirements, securities reserve requirements, and a directed credit requirement, referred to as a *cajon. Cajones* (boxes) refers to quotas for loans to specific types of borrowers that banks had to fill.[17] The Banco de Mexico also had several other mechanisms of selective credit control. It continued to rediscount selectively and to grant exemptions from credit ceiling and capital liability ratio requirements.[18]

During the Avila Camacho administration (1940–1946), inducing private banks to help public development banks in providing agricultural credit was one of the primary goals of financial regulation. This government policy was also a major source of controversy between the bankers' alliance and the Cárdenas coalition. The controversy is reflected in public differences between finance minister Suárez and then–Central Bank head Eduardo Villaseñor. At the annual national banking convention in 1945 Suárez chastised private banks for not authorizing sufficient credit to the na-

[16]Ruiz Equiha, *El encaje legal: Instrumento fundamental de la política monetaria mexicana contemporanea* (Mexico, D.F.: Editorial Cultura, 1963); Mario Ramon Beteta, "El banco central como instrumento del desarollo económico en Mexico," *Comercio Exterior* 11 (1961), pp. 350–354.; Clark Reynolds, *The Mexican Economy* (New Haven: Yale University Press, 1970), p. 190; Sanchez Lugo, "Instrumentos de política crediticia," pp. 381–384; Antonio Carillo Flores, "Acontecimientos sobresalientes en la gestión y evolución del Banco de Mexico," in Fernández Hurtado, *Cincuenta años de banca central*, p. 50; Brothers and Solís, *Mexican Financial Development*, p. 68; Shelton, "The Banking System," p. 173.

[17]Cash reserve requirements on both total deposits and increments (the latter called the marginal reserve requirement) were instituted in 1936. Private deposit and savings banks had to maintain a cash reserve deposit with the Central Bank equal to 7 percent of liabilities. This grew to 10 percent in the mid-1940s as Central Bank director Eduardo Villaseñor continued to criticize private banks for making loans that encouraged speculation. In 1948 the Banco de Mexico extended reserve requirements to investment banks and began to require a specific portfolio of banks assets, as well as cash reserves, to cover liabilities. This second type of reserve requirement is known as the securities reserve. The securities reserve requirement was a means of inducing private banks to purchase securities that would otherwise not be attractive. Normally the banks satisfied the requirement by purchasing government bonds or state enterprise stock issues whose prices were fixed by the Banco de Mexico and did not offer competitive yields. The private banks were offered a variety of options for meeting the cash reserve, security reserve, and directed credit requirements. For instance, higher security reserves and more directed credit allowed the banks to maintain lower cash reserves.

[18]Credit ceiling exemptions were used primarily to control the credit allocation of the national credit institutions. They were also used to a more limited extent to regulate private banks.

tion's agricultural *ejidos*. Villaseñor, in contrast, suggested that problems in Mexican agriculture were due to a lack of investment, not a lack of credit. The lack of investment, he went on, followed from the uncertainty created by social reforms such as land redistribution and state support for workers. Pointing to the Soviet Union's move away from a program of total economic nationalization with its New Economic Policy, he called for an end to social reform to "save Mexicans from hunger."[19]

Although selective credit controls continued in the period of stabilizing development (1954–1970), they did not achieve the goals initially set for them. This was due partly to the contradictions created by the renewed efforts of the bankers' alliance in the 1950s and 1960s to promote development of private financial markets. Promoting such development was the cornerstone of the stabilizing development policies championed by the bankers' alliance in the 1950s and 1960s. As part of the effort two laws were passed in 1953 and 1954 to support stock market growth, increase savings, and stimulate industrial investment. They were the Investment Banking Law (Ley de Sociedades de Inversión) and the Stock Commission Law (Ley de la Comisión de Valores). Changes in financial regulation also spurred the growth of investment banks (*financieras*). The *financieras* were exempted from reserve requirements and restrictions on liability growth. The Finance Ministry authorized them to pay higher interest rates than were otherwise available on financial instruments that, although appearing long term, were redeemable on demand. They also offered popular dollar-denominated instruments. As a result of lenient government regulation, the *financieras* took over a rising share of total private sector resources, expanding considerably faster than any other private sector financial institutions. The *financieras* operating in 1940 had 470 million pesos worth of assets, one-tenth the assets of regular commercial banks. By 1960 they had 9 billion pesos worth of assets, equal to two-thirds the assets of regular commercial banks.[20]

From 1930 until 1954 public financial institutions accounted for a continually growing majority of resources flowing through the national financial system. Markets for privately held financial assets

[19]Luis Medina, *Historia de la revolución mexicana: Del cardenismo al avilacamachismo* (Mexico, D.F.: Colegio de Mexico, 1978), p. 266.
[20]Goldsmith, *The Financial Development of Mexico*, p. 24.

were weak.[21] But in the 1960s, nurtured by government policy, private financial institutions slowly began to catch up with public bank growth. After 1960 public banks began to suffer a relative loss of control over total financial resources. In 1963 the resources of private investment banks surpassed those of Nafinsa for the first time. In that year Nafinsa controlled 163 billion pesos worth of resources compared with the 170 billion of one hundred *financieras*.[22] Public bank resources, including those of the Banco de Mexico, fell as a proportion of the system's total resources, from 57 percent a year on average from 1949 to 1958, to 52 percent from 1959 to 1965, to 43 percent from 1965 to 1970. Private bank resources rose concomitantly.[23]

To the extent that the Mexican financial system was dominated by public sector institutions, as it was in the 1930s, the government had direct control of credit allocation and influence over investment patterns. But it had to rely more and more on indirect methods of influence, such as selective credit controls, as private banks captured a larger share of national financial resources. Yet these control policies were relatively ineffective. The financing needed for long-term industrial investment projects or improving agricultural productivity was not forthcoming from the private financial system. Ironically, the growth of long-term financial instruments was limited in part because of initial government policies used to foment the growth of private intermediaries. To spur financial development, the government had authorized relatively liquid assets that bore government guarantees. Apparent nonmonetary assets were more like money than it seemed. Time deposits, for instance, were redeemable on demand, and the liquidity of other private financial sector liabilities was tacitly underwritten by the

---

[21]In 1953, for example, Nafinsa, the public industrial development bank, had to intervene in the stock market to prevent a collapse in stock prices.

[22]Goldsmith, *The Financial Development of Mexico*, p. 30.

[23]The increase in private sector resources came largely from bond issues and deposits. In the 1955–1965 period, public banks issued bonds valued at 44 billion pesos and private banks issued 29 billion pesos worth of bonds. In the 1966–1970 period, the value of private bond issues grew six times, reaching 174 billion pesos, whereas that of public bank issues only doubled, to 66 billion pesos. Nafinsa's share of overall industry financing fell. Whereas Nafinsa accounted for roughly 50 percent of total banking system resources going to industry in the mid-1950s, its share fell to 38 percent in 1965 and 30 percent in 1970. (Maria Elena Cardero, *Patrón monetario y acumulación en Mexico* [Mexico, D.F.: Siglo XXI, 1984], pp. 101, 103.)

Banco de Mexico.[24] Government measures authorized *financieras* to accept thirty-day deposits while requiring them to match asset and liability maturities. This matching requirement legally forced the *financieras* to lend short term to the extent their deposits were short term.[25]

Data from the Banco de Mexico show that between 1940 and 1970 the proportion of long-term to total credits extended by the investment banks remained constant at one-third. Commercial banks lent 8 percent of total credits at more than one year maturity in 1940, compared to 10 percent in 1970. The liquidity of the financial system was related to a bias in private credit allocation away from industry and agriculture and toward services and financial speculation. Within industry, credit was concentrated by sector, size, and, to some extent, regional location. As Table 1 indicates, private financing of industry and agriculture as a percentage of total system resources grew only modestly from 1942 to 1958. After that, financing to industry rose slightly while financing to agriculture fell. Within industry, lending was biased toward production and sale of consumer durables, commerce, and construction. Commerce and services accounted for 33 percent of private sector lending in 1957 and a barely unchanged 31 percent in 1970. Manufacturing received a declining share of private sector financing between 1957 and 1970; 34 percent of total private sector loans went to manufacturing in 1957 and only 19 percent in 1970. Within industry, private sector financing supported the most dynamic sectors and those with fast and high yields; these sectors were usually coincident with sectors characterized by high foreign ownership. Small and medium-sized producers were at a double disadvantage compared with big business. They had little access to foreign exchange or domestic credit. A Canacintra economist writing in the 1960s about the financing problems of small and medium-sized industry argued that the central problem was not an overall shortage of savings, as the banks claimed, but merely poor allocation and channeling of credit.[26]

---

[24]Shelton, "The Banking System," p. 154.

[25]Blanca Torres, *Hacia la utopia industrial: Historia de la revolución mexicana* (Mexico, D.F.: Colegio de Mexico, 1984), pp. 141–142.

[26]See Raúl A. Ollervides, "La nacionalización y la inversión de capitales extranjeros," *Comercio Exterior* 16 (1966), p. 491.

Domestic Structures and Economic Policy

Table 1. Shares of private bank lending by sector (percentages of total financial system resources)

Years	Total	Industry	Agriculture	Commerce	Federal government
1942–1948	43	14	5	17	2
1949–1958	43	15	5	15	3
1959–1965	47	16	4	14	9
1966–1970	56	18	3	17	14

Source: Banco de Mexico, *Manual de estadísticas financieras* (Mexico, D.F.: Banco de Mexico, various years).

The Mexican government did not attain significant control over credit allocation through reserve requirements, rediscounting, and credit ceiling exemptions because these mechanisms work only in systems where the price of money is fixed, where growth in the money supply is restricted, and where enterprises rely heavily on domestic credit external to the firm. A system of government-set interest rates and control of the money supply is a requisite for effective selective credit controls because it allows the government to create a situation where demand for money exceeds supply at the administratively controlled prices. Some nonmarket rationing criteria have to be adopted. As Zysman points out, the resulting set of privileges and administrative decisions implies that the government must make explicit choices about credit allocation and financing. "Intervention is a necessity, which gives government leverage on the allocation decisions of all actors in the system."[27] A credit-based, price-administered system with selective credit controls is the type of financial structure that Zysman argues will facilitate state-led industrial development. In Mexico selective credit controls did not achieve the desired goal of stimulating investment in strategic areas because the growth of financial-industrial conglomerates made credit financing low.

The policy of selective credit allocation assumed a relatively high degree of external financing of investment. Yet estimates of external financing in the 1950s and 1960s place it between 10 percent and 34 percent.[28] The only time-series data available show that ex-

[27]John Zysman, *Governments, Markets, and Growth: Financial Systems and the Politics of Industrial Change* (Ithaca: Cornell University Press, 1983), p. 130.
[28]Flavia Derossi, *The Mexican Entrepreneur* (Paris: OECD, 1971), p. 113; Alfredo Navarette R., "El financiamiento del desarollo económico," in *Mexico: Cincuenta años de*

ternal financing shrank from 29 percent in 1950 to 14 percent in 1965, reaching the low of 10 percent in 1960.[29] It appears therefore that the reality of Mexican industrial financing—high levels of internal financing, partly related to the close ties between financial and industrial firms—contrasted sharply with the conditions assumed by those touting the theoretical effectiveness of selective credit controls.[30]

The growth of *grupos* that survived the revolution and the formation of new ones—often stemming from the managerial unification of different financial institutions—became "an important barrier to achievement of greater rationality in the application of available investable resources."[31] The *grupos* hindered the effectiveness of the government's selective credit controls because a financial institution belonging to a *grupo* could comply by lending within its circle of associated companies. One study of Mexican banking in the 1960s concludes that grouping made evasion simpler

---

revolución (Mexico, D.F.: Fondo de Cultura Económica, 1960), p. 527; Goldsmith, *The Financial Development of Mexico*, p. 46; Brothers and Solís, *Mexican Financial Development*, p. 101; John K. Thompson, *Inflation, Financial Markets and Economic Development: The Experience of Mexico* (Greenwich, Conn.: JAI Press, 1979), p. 150.

[29] Their close ties with financial institutions led many industrial companies in Latin America to operate with relatively high debt-equity (gearing) ratios and relatively low liquidity. Comparative analysis of the liquidity positions of industrial firms in the United States, United Kingdom, Japan, Argentina, and Brazil in the mid-1960s shows that ratios of liabilities to assets were considerably higher in the latter three countries than in the former two. (Eprime Eshag, "The Relative Efficacy of Monetary Policy in Selected Industrial and Less-Developed Countries," *Economic Journal* 81 [1971], pp. 294–305.) An owner-manager within an economic group linking bank and industrial capital will have a personal incentive to assume the risks and potential profit of high leverage. Although individual enterprises may be highly leveraged, group assets typically include a variety of liquid or potentially liquid assets such as urban real estate and dollar-based foreign-held time deposits or securities. The firm may be relatively illiquid, whereas the *grupo* is not.

[30] Despite the fact that some data indicate individual Mexican industrial enterprises operated with high gearing ratios and low liquidity, the system of financing within industrial-financial conglomerates reduced their sensitivity to the cost and supply of credit. Under perfect competition these firm characteristics would promote sensitivity to monetary policy and selective credit controls. But research conducted in the 1960s showed no correlation between interest rate changes and private borrowing by individuals and enterprises (John Koehler, *Economic Policy Making with Limited Information: The Process of Macro-Control in Mexico* [Santa Monica, Calif.: Rand Corporation, 1968].) A definitive study of the Mexican financial system concludes that credit demand is "governed more by shifts in consumer preferences and expectations than by changes in the cost of borrowed funds" (Brothers and Solís, *Mexican Financial Development*, p. 53).

[31] Brothers and Solís, *Mexican Financial Development*, p. 198.

and facilitated the concentration of resources "in those institutions least subject to detailed regulation" (the *financieras*).[32]

> Beyond the commercial-bank-and-*financiera* nexus, groups came also to include insurance companies, capitalization banks, mortgage banks, or other institutions needed to round out the range of financial services offered, the variety of liabilities held out to the investing public, and the geographic area covered. With the nucleus of financial institutions, extension of control to include industrial and commercial undertakings was easy. For those undertakings, adherence was advantageous because it assured funds for working capital and expansion. For financial institutions, a circle of favored business borrowers meant profitable outlets for investable funds, and more importantly, a measure of supervision over the use of their money.[33]

Groups also undermined the effectiveness of selective controls by making evasion of credit regulation easier. Compliance with many of the instruments of credit policy functioned through "gentlemen's agreements" to avoid credits that fomented speculation, keep loan interest rates within a reasonable margin over Central Bank–set deposit rates, and give priority to financing long-term assets or particular economic activities. The most comprehensive history of the Banco de Mexico notes that "the method most frequently used by the Banco de Mexico has been to join the bankers in examining the diverse financial and economic problems of the country and thereby persuade them of the importance of central bank recommendations."[34] Yet Hugo Margáin notes that while he was in government in the 1960s and 1970s, "we had a difficult time with the large banking firms and groups. Generally they tended to act like clams, and were very difficult to penetrate and develop a sense of social responsibility."[35]

Even the staunchest structuralist economists, such as José Andres de Oteyza, former president López Portillo's minister of industry and trade, recognize in retrospect the futility of trying to use a limited policy of selective credit controls to regulate national capitalists' resource allocation decisions. De Oteyza's comments high-

---

[32]Shelton, "The Banking System," p. 161.
[33]Ibid., p. 159.
[34]Sanchez Lugo, "Instrumentos de política crediticia," p. 384.
[35]Quoted in Roderic A. Camp, *Entrepreneurs and Politics in Twentieth Century Mexico* (Oxford: Oxford University Press, 1989), p. 131.

light the weakness of the credit control system. It was really based on informal agreements between government officials and private bankers, he admits, and the bankers had myriad ways to escape controls. The effectiveness of Mexican credit controls, he writes, "is limited because one must depend on the ethics of commercial bankers."[36]

The history of Mexican financial policy reflects both the interests and the power of the bankers' alliance. The alliance consistently pressured policy makers to preserve both the unregulated development of domestic financial markets and unrestricted international capital mobility (which is discussed in the following section). The policy of stabilizing development successfully promoted development of private financial enterprises. But given the structure of Mexican capital, the promotion of private financiers without regulation of financial-industrial conglomeration contributed to the growth of the conglomerates. Efforts to regulate capital mobility by controlling private sector credit allocation failed because of the opportunities for evasion provided by the *grupo* structure.

Exchange Rate Policy

Capital flight and dollarization, the use of dollars rather than pesos for the major purposes usually served by money, have posed a constant problem for Mexico. The struggle to maintain confidence in the national currency as a store of value and medium of exchange is a recurring theme in Mexican financial history and that of most other developing countries. But the threat of flight to the dollar is more acute in Mexico than in other developing countries thanks to the two thousand mile U.S.-Mexican border. This fact of geography adds to the strength of the Mexican bankers' alliance. It heightens the threat of capital flight in response to unfavored policies.

Beginning with Cárdenas, the bankers' alliance has made full use of this threat to try to change objectionable government policies. In opposition to the Cárdenas-Suárez policy of inflationary development finance, the alliance used both "voice" to express this threat

[36]José Andres de Oteyza, "La política monetaria de desarollo: El caso de Mexico" (tesis de licenciatura, National Autonomous University, 1966), p. 99.

71

and "exit" to carry it out. Between 1934 and 1937 dollar deposits as a ratio of demand deposits were as high as they were in the crisis leading up to devaluation and imposition of exchange controls in 1982.[37] Central Bank reserves were drained; in 1937 alone they fell 38 percent. They were hardly sufficient to continue the policy of Central Bank currency purchases to shore up the peso's value.

Nevertheless Cárdenas resisted devaluation, equating a strong currency with national sovereignty. He considered but, at the urging of Central Bank director Luis Montes de Oca, reluctantly rejected the idea of exchange controls. Montes de Oca preferred three arguments against exchange controls: (1) they would hurt international trade, (2) they would not be efficient, and (3) they would be incompatible with democracy. "The establishment of exchange controls," the Banco de Mexico's annual report for 1938 states, "would require a series of coercive and restrictive international trade measures, that, in addition to hurting our relations with other countries, presuppose close vigilance of all operations including the private life of the individual, which is incompatible with the general ideology of a democratic country."[38] Cárdenas was finally convinced by a different argument: that Mexico's two thousand mile border with the United States would make exchange controls impossible to implement. "Exchange controls," Cárdenas stated, "can only work in highly disciplined countries where customs rules are well organized and borders can be effectively watched; exchange control in Mexico would surely be undermined by the black market."[39]

As Mexico's conflict with the oil companies over ownership escalated throughout 1937, so did public expectations of devaluation. In the absence of exchange controls, capital flight spiraled upward. Foreign exchange reserves were drained completely, forcing Cárdenas to let the peso float down.[40] The Central Bank continued to manage the float until 1940, when the peso exchange rate was fixed once again at 5:1, as Table 2 shows.

[37]Guillermo Ortiz Martínez, "La dolarización en Mexico: Causas y consecuencias," Banco de Mexico, Serie de Documentos, vol. 40 (1981).
[38]Banco de Mexico, Informe anual, 1938 (Mexico, D.F.: Banco de Mexico, 1939).
[39]Ortiz Martínez, "La dolarización en Mexico," p. 11.
[40]Ricardo Torres Gaytán, Un siglo de devaluaciones del peso mexicano (Mexico, D.F.: Siglo XXI, 1980), p. 253.

Table 2. Exchange rates and money supply, 1931–1982

	Pesos to dollar (yearly average)	Money supply (current thousand million pesos)		Pesos to dollar (yearly average)	Money supply (current thousand million pesos)
1931	2.65	.2	1957	12.50	12.5
1932	3.16	.3	1958	12.50	13.4
1933	3.50	.4	1959	12.50	15.4
1934	3.50	.5	1960	12.50	16.9
1935	3.50	.5	1961	12.50	18.0
1936	3.50	.6	1962	12.50	20.3
1937	3.50	.7	1963	12.50	23.7
1938	5.00	.7	1964	12.50	27.6
1939	5.00	.9	1965	12.50	29.5
1940	5.00	1.1	1966	12.50	32.8
1941	5.00	1.3	1967	12.50	35.3
1942	5.00	1.7	1968	12.50	40.0
1943	5.00	2.7	1969	12.50	44.3
1944	5.00	3.3	1970	12.50	49.0
1945	5.00	3.5	1971	12.50	53.0
1946	5.00	3.5	1972	12.50	64.3
1947	5.00	3.4	1973	12.50	79.9
1948	5.00	3.9	1974	12.50	97.5
1949	8.65	4.3	1975	12.50	118.2
1950	8.65	6.0	1976	15.60	154.8
1951	8.65	6.8	1977	22.60	195.7
1952	8.65	7.1	1978	22.80	260.3
1953	8.65	7.7	1979	22.80	346.5
1954	12.50	8.7	1980	23.00	461.2
1955	12.50	10.5	1981	24.50	612.4
1956	12.50	11.7	1982	57.20	991.5

Note: Money supply is total bills, coins, and checking accounts.

Sources: Banco de Mexico, *Informe anual*, 1931–1938 (Mexico, D.F.: Banco de Mexico, 1932–1939); Banco de Mexico, *Economía mexicana en cifras* (Mexico, D.F.: Banco de Mexico, 1981); Secretaría de Hacienda y Crédito Público, Dirección General de Estudios Hacendários, *Cuenta de la Hacienda Pública Federal*, 1959–1982 (Mexico, D.F.: Secretaría de Hacienda y Crédito Público, 1960–1983).

Through the 1940s the peso again became overvalued. Avila Camacho had sufficient foreign exchange to avoid having to devalue, but he left his successor a highly untenable situation. The high cost of imports during World War II drained foreign exchange reserves. Weeks before President Alemán was inaugurated, his finance minister, Ramon Beteta, suggested he devalue the peso. Alemán rejected the idea, citing the inflationary impact it could have.

Like Cárdenas before him, Alemán also rejected the idea of exchange controls as a way to safeguard foreign exchange reserves and to try to maintain the peso's exchange value. Instead, he sought foreign loans as a way to build up reserves to support the peso. Within five days of Alemán's inauguration, finance minister Beteta was negotiating loans with officials from the International Bank for Reconstruction and Development (IBRD) and the Export-Import Bank. In 1947 he obtained two $10 million loans from the IMF. However, this amount hardly compensated for that year's $100 million loss.[41] Expectations of devaluation fueled rampant capital flight. Alemán stepped up efforts to obtain foreign funds from the IBRD, the Export-Import Bank, and the IMF. In May 1948, with Central Bank reserves virtually depleted, Alemán obtained two last-minute, short-term loans from private U.S. banks and an emergency IMF peso purchase. Of course, this was only a stopgap measure. In July 1948 Alemán finally had to devalue. Private bankers blamed the need for devaluation on excess government spending to support agricultural cooperatives and to nationalize and run the railroads and oil company. Economists sympathetic to the Cárdenas coalition, including Lobato López and Ricardo Gaitan, argued that the cause lay in external shocks.[42]

Commitment to free convertibility and exchange rate stability was part of the 1950s financial reform package, which ushered in the period of stabilizing development (1954–1970).[43] Success in controlling inflation, kept to an annual average of 6 percent between 1950 and 1960, allowed for a remarkable twenty-two-year period of exchange rate stability with free convertibility.[44] The long period of peso stability, however, heightened the tendency to delay devaluation. Economist David Shelton observed in the 1960s, "Attachment to the exchange rate has reached proportions which bear little relation to its purely economic significance."[45] When the U.S. dollar began to float in August 1971, at least one adviser close to the president argued strongly for using the change in U.S. policy as an opportunity to let the then-overvalued peso float downward with the dollar. But "devaluation," said finance minister Hugo Margáin, "is a word that is not in my dictionary."[46] When Presi-

[41]Torres, *Hacia la utopia industrial*, p. 119.

[42]Leopoldo Solís, "Mexican Economic Policy in the Post-War Period: The Views of Mexican Economists," *American Economics Review* 61 (1971), p. 31.

[43]Thompson, *Inflation, Financial Markets and Economic Development*, p. 147.

[44]See ibid. and Brothers and Solís, *Mexican Financial Development*.

[45]Shelton, "The Banking System," p. 169.

[46]Leopoldo Solís, *Economic Policy Reform in Mexico: A Case Study for Developing Countries* (New York: Pergamon, 1981), p. 61.

dent Luis Echeverría was finally forced to devalue the long-over-valued peso in 1976, the devaluation drastically undercut his popular image and power within the ruling elite. "Se le cayo la tunica de Dios [His God's tunic fell off]," comments one Mexican observer.[47]

Big business has made unrestricted foreign exchange a widely recognized symbol of individual right and freedom. Alfredo Sandoval, president of Coparmex in 1984, declared that exporting capital generated in Mexico is "a form of protection and defense of savings." A PRI candidate for mayor of the northern border city of Ciudad Juárez, asked in an interview if he considered capital flight legitimate, said, "Yes, it is legitimate, if someone made money by their own effort and knows they are going to lose it here."[48] MIT economist Lance Taylor asserts that Mexico is "virtually the only developing country in which the economically powerful classes have the privilege of such an open capital market."[49]

The way the Mexican government has handled foreign exchange policy highlights three aspects of bankers' alliance power. The first concerns the institutional power of the Central Bank. Exchange policy is the one policy area in which the Central Bank, direct representative of private bank interests within the government, weighs in more heavily than the Finance Ministry. Ultimately, it is Central Bank reserves that determine the ability to sustain the peso's value. Exchange controls were rejected by Cárdenas in the 1930s and have been repeatedly rejected since then in part because of the strong case made against them by the Central Bank. The second aspect of bankers' alliance power is that free convertibility guaranteed the bankers' alliance an important weapon—the threat of capital flight—in policy disputes. The third aspect of the power of the bankers' alliance, highlighted in the way the Mexican government has handled exchange policy, concerns the tendency to delay devaluation as long as possible using foreign loans. Ultimately, foreign borrowing heightens the importance of international creditors in the domestic policy-making process and gives domestic bankers a potential international ally. Indeed, the weight of international

[47]Interview, Mexico City, March 1984.
[48]"Es una protección a lo ahorrado con trabajo," El Universal, September 24, 1984, pp. 1, 12.
[49]Lance Taylor, "La crisis y su porvenir: Problemas de política macroeconómica en Mexico," Investigación Económica 170 (1984), pp. 283–311.

creditors helped the bankers' alliance achieve a long-desired shift to tight monetary policy in the 1950s.

Monetary Policy

In the 1930s and 1940s Mexico followed a policy of loose money and high deficit spending. Whether as cause or consequence of the limited private sector contribution to national development, the Cárdenas administration launched a massive state investment campaign funded by deficit spending. The financial elite opposed this policy. Bitter debates erupted; they highlight the monetary policy preferences and rationales of the two competing coalitions. The dispute took the form of a serious rift in relations between different branches of the executive and between government agencies and private bankers. The bankers and their ally within the state, Central Bank head Montes de Oca, objected to state intervention in the economy and to deficit spending. They supported tight monetary policy and adhered to an orthodox liberal economic philosophy. On the other hand, Eduardo Suárez, finance minister under presidents Cárdenas and Avila Camacho, favored state intervention and deficit spending if necessary to promote agricultural and industrial development. His firsthand experience of the effect of tight monetary policy and strict adherence to orthodox monetary policy on the U.S. economy in the years leading up to the Great Depression made him a dedicated advocate of Keynesian economic theory.

In the mid-1950s the impact of devaluations in 1948 and 1954, combined with pressure from domestic and international bankers, brought about a shift away from the inflationary system of deficit financing characteristic of the Suárez regime. The bankers' alliance gained new international allies and became more firmly entrenched in the executive branch. Monetary policy in the 1954–1970 period more clearly reflected the alliance's ideological preferences than it had in the previous era.

Although debates between the bankers' alliance and the Cárdenas coalition were most heated in the late 1930s and early 1940s, conflict among several of the key actors during these years dates to the 1920s and early 1930s. For instance, there was considerable controversy over monetary policy related to Mexico's international debt negotiations in the late 1920s. Mexico's U.S. creditors, led by banker Thomas Lamont, were willing to refinance if Mexico agreed to try to balance the public sector budget and stop agricultural land expropriations.[50] The Montes de Oca–Lamont refinancing agreement was soundly opposed by national populists in Congress, who objected to these conditions. Bankers such as Enrique Creel and Agustin Legoretta argued for it.[51]

There was also intense controversy in 1932 over Montes de Oca's 1931 monetary stabilization package, known as the Ley Calles—after former president Calles, who was then head of the board of directors of the Central Bank. Montes de Oca's tight monetary policy drew such great criticism from labor and peasants and from other government officials that he was fired. When Cárdenas later brought him back into government as head of the Central Bank, he was again the center of controversy over monetary policy.

Although Montes de Oca, Miguel S. Macedo, Alberto Pani, and Manuel Gómez Morín occasionally had differences of opinion over policy specifies and strategy, they were among the leading ideologues of the bankers' alliance in the first several decades after the fall of Porfirio Díaz. They turned to conservative Austrian economists such as Hayek and von Mises for theoretical justification of their policy prescriptions.[52] Their views are reflected in financial legislation, public speeches, and newspaper and journal articles of the 1930s and 1940s. Macedo, for example, authored the 1936 version of the Banco de Mexico statute. In it he presents a long rationale for why "circulatory credit" (new Central Bank monetary emission) should never substitute for real economic resources. The

---

[50]Lorenzo Meyer, *Los inicios de la institucionalización: La política del maximato* (Mexico, D.F.: Colegio de Mexico, 1978), p. 217.

[51]Whereas national populists opposed the agreement because of the domestic austerity it implied, Pani opposed it because he believed Mexico should not take on any further external debt.

[52]Hayek is one of the most important representatives of the so-called Austrian school of economics. Originally a government employee in von Mises's service, he enjoyed a life-long intellectual relationship with von Mises; the two men founded a major pre–World War II European economics research institute. Hayek spent eighteen years, beginning in the 1930s, as a professor at the London School of Economics. He became a vocal critic of Keynes after publishing a two-part review of Keynes's *Treatise on Money*. Contrary to Keynes, Hayek argued that under conditions of unemployment, an increase in spending leads to inflation and ultimately to distortions in the productive structure. Unemployment, Hayek suggested, was due partly to rigidities in the labor market. Government intervention would only make it worse. In the post–World War II era Hayek continued to be a strong opponent of Keynesian demand management.

overarching reason is to "free the Mexican monetary system from all inflationary tendency."[53] Macedo's monetary legislation prohibited the Central Bank from directly financing the government. It did authorize the issue of short-term treasury certificates of a total value up to 10 percent of the average annual government revenue in the previous three years. However, the market for these securities was woefully thin. The first government bond was issued through the Banco de Mexico in 1934 for a road construction project. In that case and later ones, private bankers were unwilling to purchase government bonds and reportedly advised their clients against doing so.[54]

Suárez criticized Macedo's legislation for being too restrictive to meet the needs of a credit-short economy trying to increase agricultural productivity and industrialize. Beginning in 1936 he instructed the Banco de Mexico to resort to the printing press despite the legal restrictions imposed by Macedo's legislation. By the end of 1937 the Bank's outstanding credits to the government exceeded the legal limit by 89 million pesos.[55] A persistent shortage of bank credit, Suárez believed, justifed monetary regulation loose enough to fund productive development activity in agricultural and industrial sectors.[56] Macedo resigned from the Central Bank's board of directors out of frustration with Suárez's actions. His legislation was superseded in 1941 by new legislation that Suárez believed gave the credit system a greater ability to serve both state and private sector financial needs.

Suárez's actions were shaped by Keynesian ideas about the role of money, credit, and the state in the economy. Where the ideologues of the bankers' alliance turned to Hayek and von Mises, Suárez turned to Keynes and Wicksell. The dispute between the bankers' alliance and Suárez over the role of money and credit is highlighted in accounts of a 1938 meeting with private bankers called by President Cárdenas. The occasion for the meeting was a surge in capital flight and financial speculation and a concomitant squeeze on business credit. The position of the bankers was that they were merely passive intermediaries in this situation. Credit

[53]Antonio Carillo Flores, "Presentación," in Eduardo Suárez, *Comentarios y recuerdos* (Mexico, D.F.: Editorial Porrua, 1976), p. xxxiv.
[54]Mosk, *Industrial Revolution in Mexico*, p. 233.
[55]Bett, *Central Banking in Modern Mexico*, p. 113.
[56]Carillo Flores, "Presentación," p. xliii.

was tight because deposits were down. Deposits were down because individuals and enterprises feared that Cárdenas's aggressive social policy would destabilize the financial system. The bankers' alliance had tried to warn the government in a memo by Macedo, sent a year earlier with the approval of the Central Bank board and Central Bank head Montes de Oca, suggesting that wages and public works projects would have to be cut if Cárdenas wanted to save the health of the financial/monetary system. The bankers claimed they had no choice but to drastically restrict credit. The situation would correct itself once the government's social policy changed.

Suárez argued differently, suggesting that credit is made not by depositors but by the banking system as a whole. He argued, following Keynes, that the money supply is endogenous. If bankers, backed by the Central Bank, increased their credit lines, deposits would rise. The only other way to avoid a serious depression in times of tight credit, Suárez suggested, would be for the government to increase its spending on public works. In a more public dispute in 1938 Suárez justified a technically illegal Central Bank overdraft facility for two state-owned agricultural banks, and the general rise in deficit spending, on these grounds.

Another confrontation took place between Suárez and the bankers' alliance after the 1938 oil expropriation. Montes de Oca pushed for an austerity program, while Suárez advocated continued monetary expansion.[57] Suárez later summed up the Keynes-inspired theory of "productive inflation" that rationalized his position: "If because of a lack of savings, unemployment should appear and resources are underutilized, it is legitimate and even necessary to create money—by means of the printing press if need be—even if this implies a rise in the price level. For it would be a far greater wrong for society to accept a waste of human resources and impoverishment."[58]

The discord between Suárez and the banking community was so great in the late 1930s that the custom of holding an annual banking convention attended by private financiers and government officials—often including the president—was suspended for the only

[57]Antonio Carillo Flores, "Acontecimientos sobresalientes en la gestión y evolución del Banco de Mexico," in Fernández Hurtado, *Cincuenta años de banca central*, p. 36.
[58]Antonio Manero, *La revolución bancaria en Mexico* (Mexico, D.F.: Talleres Graficas de la Nación, 1957), p. 275.

time in contemporary Mexican history. No meetings were held between 1937 and 1941. When the national conventions did resume, they were full of debate and rancor between Suárez and the bankers' alliance. Suárez gave one of his most vicious critiques of monetarist orthodoxy in his speech to the 1943 annual bankers' meeting:

> The orthodox economists, inspired by so-called theoretical principles backed by very little experimental proof, predict that what is essential in any situation is that budgets are balanced, that metallic reserves are large, that credit is supplied following rigid lines, and that the public debt be reduced. Fortunately many countries have deviated from these theories; if the U.S. is a great country, it is because Alexander Hamilton based its development on heterodox principles, among others, that of having a large public debt. If that country has now been able to overcome the problems of the Great Depression it is because it has followed the revolutionary economic policy of the New Deal.[59]

Although Cárdenas's successor, Ávila Camacho (1940–1946), began a rapprochement with the bankers' alliance designed to heal the wounds of Cárdenas's prolabor and propeasant policy, he inherited an inflationary legacy that continued to disquiet private bankers. Suárez stayed on in the government as Ávila Camacho's finance minister. The state continued to play a major role in the economy, with 50 percent of all investment coming from the public sector, as Table 3 indicates. As financial pressure on the government grew during the 1940s thanks to government spending and the inflationary impact of World War II, the bankers' alliance and the Cárdenas coalition again articulated two very different positions.[60]

The 1944 annual convention of the Mexican Bankers Association attacked government intervention in the economy and called for the Banco de Mexico to restrain monetary expansion.[61] Pani, then retired from government, represented the view of the bankers' alliance articulated at this convention in a book attacking Suárez and

---

[59]Francisco Suárez Davila, "Bosquejo biografico," in Suárez, *Comentarios y recuerdos*, p. lxxxix.
[60]Reynolds, *The Mexican Economy*, p. 262.
[61]Robert Jones Shafer, *Mexican Business Organizations: History and Analysis* (Syracuse, N.Y.: Syracuse University Press, 1973), pp. 58, 129.

Competing Alliances and Economic Policy

Table 3. Public and private sector investment shares (gross fixed capital formation–percentages)

	Public	Private
1940	49	51
1945	50	50
1950	50	50
1955	32	68
1960	33	67
1965	32	68
1970	33	67
1975	42	58
1976	38	62
1977	38	62
1978	43	57
1979	42	58
1980	43	57
1981	43	57
1982	44	56

Source: Secretaría de Programación y Presupuesto Instituto Nacional de Estadística, Geografía e Informática, *Estadísticas Históricas de Mexico* (Mexico, D.F.: SPP, 1985).

his loose monetary policy. Pani argued in the book that inflation and devaluation were the scourges of Mexican development.[62] Suárez replied that Mexico's supreme problem was not monetary instability but rather the need to raise national output and per capita income. Furthermore, Suárez had attended the Bretton Woods, New Hampshire, monetary conference at the end of World War II; and although he was angered at the way the United States diluted Keynes's original plans, he argued that the Keynesian underpinnings of the Bretton Woods accord vindicated his fight for Keynesian policies in Mexico. In a speech on his return from New Hampshire, Suárez suggested that all financial institutions should subject themselves to the principles upheld at Bretton Woods: demand stimulation, increasing real income, better income distribution, and full use of human and material resources.[63]

The bankers' alliance contended that growth is best achieved in the context of price stability and that an unencumbered private financial system should be able to transfer savings to investors effi-

[62]Alberto Pani, *El problema supremo de Mexico* (Mexico, D.F.: Manuel Porrua, 1955).
[63]Carillo Flores, "Presentación," p. xl.

81

ciently. The low savings record of the previous two decades, the bankers' alliance argued, was due to inflationary government spending, not some inevitable shortfall of savings. Domestic policy should be guided by the need to maintain fixed exchange rates and free convertibility. The government should facilitate growth of private financial intermediation, pursue tight monetary policy, and eliminate the public deficit.

The Cárdenas coalition took a different position. It argued that there is an inevitable gap between savings and resources necessary to finance development. Therefore the state must intervene, providing and mobilizing investment capital. There is little possibility of directing savings into productive investment through policies aimed at developing private financial markets. Inflationary finance had worked well for the previous twenty years and could continue to do so. It would work better, the Cárdenas coalition noted, in a context of exchange controls. Inflation generates excess demand for foreign exchange which should be government rationed to prevent external imbalance. On the basis of this essentially structuralist economic analysis the national populists prescribed high public spending despite inflation, heavy state involvement in mobilizing investment capital, and exchange controls.

In 1948 the bankers' alliance used the occasion of Mexico's first devaluation in a decade to severely criticize the government policies it argued had induced it. Although President Alemán tried to put blame for the 1948 devaluation on international circumstances beyond Mexico's control, the head of the Central Bank and the head of the Mexican Bankers Association were quick to place the blame on prior government policy. The head of the Mexican Bankers Association contended that public spending, salary increases, agricultural reform, and oil and railroad nationalizations had been misguided policies that all contributed to the need for devaluation. The head of the Central Bank blamed government policy that permitted excessive imports, which drained international reserves.[64] Spokesmen for the national populist policy current blamed both bankers and large-scale businesses and government. They criticized both for engaging in or permitting speculation and income concentration and the government for relying heavily on foreign loans instead of conducting a tax reform. When a second devaluation became un-

---

[64]Torres, *Hacio la utopia industrial*, pp. 122–123.

avoidable in 1954, the administration bought labor support with the promise of wage increases.

Key members of Adolf Ruiz Cortines's cabinet (1952–1958) were sympathetic to arguments for monetary stabilization. Rodrigo Gómez, head of the Central Bank, favored it because, he argued, stabilization would instill confidence in the domestic financial system in Mexican savers and make Mexico more creditworthy in the eyes of international bankers. Antonio Ortiz Mena, the minister of finance appointed in 1958, shared Rodrigo Gómez's classic monetarist outlook. Ortiz Mena had close relations to international bankers who had begun pressuring for a policy change in 1953. The World Bank sent a mission to Mexico in 1953 that held out the promise of large-scale international support for Mexican development if Mexico would adopt sounder financial policies. The Bank's conditionality policy stated:

> It happens not infrequently that the Bank's examination of general economic conditions in the borrowing country reveals the existence of economic or financial practices or policies which so adversely affect the financial and monetary stability of the country that, if continued, they would endanger both the productive purposes and the repayment prospects of the Bank loan. In such cases, it is the policy of the Bank to require, as a condition of Bank financing, that the borrowing country institute mechanisms designed to restore stability to its economy. [The Bank] requires concrete evidence that the government is actually taking appropriate steps to establish stability, . . . once given such evidence, it is usually willing to make a loan concurrently with the execution of the measures adopted.[65]

Additionally, Mexican government officials in the Central Bank and Nafinsa believed that international loans from private banks would also be forthcoming if the country adopted monetary stabilization policies.[66]

The Central Bank began to restrict the money supply in 1955. In 1956 domestic money and capital markets were noticeably tight and interest rates were high.[67] Small and medium-sized manufacturers in Canacintra objected to this policy but had no strong advo-

[65]IBRD, *The Economic Development of Mexico* (Baltimore: Johns Hopkins University Press, 1953), pp. 53–54.

[66]Thompson, *Inflation, Financial Markets and Economic Development*, p. 125.

[67]Brothers and Solís, *Mexican Financial Development*, p. 83.

cate within the government.[68] Finance minister Antonio Carillo Flores played a key role in selling the tight money policy to those opposed to it. He argued that it would protect the purchasing power of workers and the middle class.[69] He also argued in the face of expansion-oriented ministries, such as Industry, that it was a grave mistake for developing countries such as Mexico to try to grow too fast. Although there was slight monetary expansion in 1957, after 1958 Rodrigo Gómez and new finance minister Ortiz Mena formed a fiscally conservative team that dominated Mexican economic policy until 1970. Central Bank subordination to the Finance Ministry, which had contributed to inflationary deficit financing in the 1930s and 1940s, facilitated the close synchronization of monetary policy and public financing, helping keep inflation low.

The political ability to tighten monetary policy rested in part on the success of the financial policy followed simultaneously. The growth of private banking allowed the Central Bank to use reserves to fund the public sector without resorting to inflation or taxation. Using reserve requirements on private banks, the Banco de Mexico reduced its credits to the federal government while pressuring private banks to increase their holdings of government securities.[70] As Table 1 shows, the major change in private bank financing patterns between the 1940s and the 1960s was an increase in private bank financing of the federal government as a proportion of total system financing. The yearly average from 1942 to 1948 was 2.3 percent; it rose to 14.4 percent in the 1966–1970 period. At the same time, public bank financing fell from 26.9 percent in the 1942–1948 period to 10.8 percent between 1966 and 1970. According to Banco de Mexico data, of total financing to the government, excluding state enterprises, the public institutions' share dropped from 93.3 percent in the 1940–1948 period to 43.2 percent between 1966 and 1970, while the private institutions' share rose from 7.9 percent to 56.2 percent.

[68]Olga Pellicer de Brody, *Historia de la revolución mexicana: El entendimiento con los Estados Unidos y la gestión del desarollo estabilizador* (Mexico, D.F.: Colegio de Mexico, 1978), p. 203.

[69]Roger Hansen, *The Politics of Mexican Development* (Baltimore: Johns Hopkins University Press, 1971) pp. 50–51.

[70]Brothers and Solís, *Mexican Financial Development*, p. 99; Shelton, "The Banking System," pp. 166–168.

Although there is debate about whether changes in monetary policy explain lower inflation rates during this period, what is important here is the role of the bankers' alliance in bringing about the shift in monetary policy. Members of the bankers' alliance finally came to control both the pivotal state economic policy-making institution—the Finance Ministry—and the Central Bank. Furthermore, the alliance found new and powerful allies in Mexico's international creditors. The growth of private financial markets created resources that the Central Bank skimmed to finance government spending without raising taxes or inflating the economy. Profits were high enough that this skimming represented relatively little burden to the private banks. In their eyes it was certainly preferable to the previous era of inflationary finance or to changes in a tax structure highly favorable to them. The cooperation of private financiers and close collaboration between the Finance Ministry and the Central Bank made the coordination of monetary policy and government spending possible.

Tax Policy

A final characteristic of Mexico's macroeconomic policy pattern is the country's extremely limited tax policy. Tax policy was limited politically by the strength of the bankers' alliance and the importance of the working class in maintaining PRI legitimacy. This latter factor put limits on the government's ability to tax workers and maintain political legitimacy while the bankers' alliance repeatedly defeated efforts to tax profits and luxuries.

During the Cárdenas administration the bankers' alliance managed to limit efforts to tax capital exports, bank profits, and "excess" profits generally. The banking community managed to achieve a substantial modification in the special bank profits tax proposed in late 1938. In 1939 Montes de Oca was successful in convincing Cárdenas and Suárez to repeal a tax on capital exports. The argument he used highlights the way the bankers' alliance used voice and exit to defeat objectionable policies. Montes de Oca argued that the tax encouraged capital exports by creating fears that it would be raised. The bankers' alliance also mobilized in 1939 to water down Cárdenas's proposed excess profits tax. Deviating from its usual strategy of negotiating behind the scenes, the Mexican Bankers Association launched an all-out public campaign, calling the proposed change in fiscal policy an attempt to create a "fascist" tax regime as part of the government's "Hitlerist totalitarianism."[71]

The growth of private financial markets in the 1950s allowed the government to fund itself through reserve requirements rather than fiscal policy. So long as this system worked it was hard to garner support for tax reform. In 1956 the suggestions of Victor Urquidi (then adviser to the finance minister and also a leading Mexican economist and longtime director of Mexico's premier graduate school) to raise taxes and mitigate the tax structure's regressiveness fell on deaf ears. At that time, personal income was taxed on a schedular rather than a global basis. Using a schedular basis meant income was divided into different categories, each taxed differently. The wealthy reported their income in many small fractions in order to avoid paying taxes.[72] Most tax income came from indirect taxation and wage earners.[73]

The next administration faced pressure from international development agencies to increase the portion of government revenue raised through taxation. President Adolfo López Mateos (1958–1964) reported to the Alliance for Progress that Mexico would do this. Through tax reform, the administration wrote, the government would increase tax revenue from 10.9 percent of GDP in 1960 to 19.8 percent in 1970.[74] In 1962 plans suggesting a switch from schedular to global income taxation were drafted and circulated. In 1963 Nicholas Kaldor, a prominent Keynesian economist, was invited to Mexico by the reformists to report on the Mexican fiscal system. His recommendations included adding a wealth and inheritance tax and eliminating anonymous bearer bonds to help enforce tax collection.[75] In response to Kaldor's report, reform

[71]Nora Hamilton, *The Limits of State Autonomy* (Princeton: Princeton University Press, 1982), pp. 112–113.
[72]Solís, *Economic Policy Reform in Mexico*, p. 22.
[73]Centro de Estudios Contables, "Es justo nuestro sistema de impuesto sobre la renta?" in Leopoldo Solís, ed., *La economía mexicana* (Mexico, D.F.: Fondo de Cultura Económica, 1960); Clark Reynolds, "Why Mexico's 'Stabilizing Development' Was Actually Destabilizing," *World Development* 16 (1978), p. 1007.
[74]Solís, *Economic Policy Reform in Mexico*, p. 22.
[75]Nicholas Kaldor, "Las reformas al sistema fiscal en Mexico," in Solís, *La economía mexicana*; Nicholas Kaldor, "Las reformas al sistema fiscal," *Comercio Exterior* 14 (1964), pp. 265–276; Reynolds, "Why Mexico's 'Stabilizing Development' Was Actually Destabilizing," pp. 275–276.

plans were taken up again by incoming president Gustavo Díaz Ordaz in 1964. The bill that finally passed into legislation during his administration was weaker than that originally proposed and fell far short of Kaldor's recommendations. It shifted income tax to a global basis but allowed for anonymous bearer bonds, continued the exemption of interest and dividends, and scrapped the excess profits tax. In practice, the reform increased the relative share of wage taxes and decreased the share of property tax in overall tax revenue.[76] Despite López Mateos's promise to raise the ratio of tax revenue to GDP to 19.8 percent by 1970, the 1965 reform brought the ratio only to 8.2 percent, as Table 4 indicates.

These tax reform efforts failed to meet stated goals largely because of a lack of support within the executive branch. The boom in private financial intermediation, and the success of government authorities in channeling private resources into government coffers in the 1950s and 1960s, bolstered the arguments of tax reform opponents. Ortiz Mena, finance minister from 1958 to 1970, believed the primary goal of the tax structure should be to aid capital formation and inspire business confidence.[77] Although there were targeted exemptions for "new and necessary" industries, the overall tax structure was designed to stimulate investment and savings indiscriminately.[78] Accordingly, the tax burden on middle and upper income individuals and on corporations was very light. The system was extraordinarily regressive, at least until the 1970s. In 1971 Mexico's ratio of tax revenue to GNP was one of the lowest in the world, as Table 4 indicates.

The irony of the substitution of monetary policy for tax policy was that it created a vicious circle in which taxes could not be raised for fear of undermining long-run confidence in the financial system. As a well-known Mexican economist and former government official writes, "The very success of monetary policy hindered

[76]Solís, *Economic Policy Reform in Mexico*, p. 22.
[77]Raul Ortiz Mena, "Moneda y crédito," in *Mexico: Cincuenta años de revolución* (Mexico, D.F.: Fonda de Cultura Económica, 1960).
[78]"Necessary" industries were defined by the Finance Ministry as those in which domestic production did not satisfy at least 80 percent of domestic demand. The Ministry of Finance also had another completely discretionary program for granting tax relief to individual firms in return for their agreement to specific quality, price, or employment requirements. See Timothy King, *Mexico: Industrialization and Trade Policy since 1930* (Oxford: Oxford University Press, 1970), pp. 98–106; and Mosk, *Industrial Revolution in Mexico*, pp. 189–197.

Table 4. Government tax revenue in historical and cross-national perspective (percentages)

Ratio of Mexican government tax revenue to GDP	
1925	1.4
1935	1.4
1940	2.2
1950	7.1
1955	7.7
1960	6.5
1965	6.6
1970	8.2
1975	11.2
1980	15.3
Ratio of government tax revenue to GNP in 1971	
West Germany	37.9
United Kingdom	34.4
Denmark	28.2
Finland	26.3
United States	22.5
Venezuela	21.3
France	17.3
Italy	16.9
Canada	15.4
Kenya	14.7
South Africa	14.4
Peru	14.4
Turkey	13.7
Spain	12.7
Colombia	12.3
Uganda	11.4
Japan	10.9
Ecuador	9.5
Brazil	9.0
Mexico	7.2

Sources: Data provided by the Secretaría de Programación y Presupuesto, Instituto Nacional de Estadística, Geografía e Informática; United Nations, *Statistical Yearbook,* 1972.

tax flexibility and tax reform."[79] Repeatedly, in the 1960s and 1970s, tax reform proposals were watered down, if not defeated, by government officials and private businessmen who argued that they would seriously damage the investment climate.

Luis Echeverría, more sympathetic to national populist ideology than many previous presidents, made several unsuccessful efforts to increase taxes on the wealthy.[80] Fifteen days after taking office Eche-

[79]Solís, *Economic Policy Reform in Mexico,* p. 28.
[80]The political system had been severely shaken by student uprisings in 1968. This political instability encouraged Echeverría to incorporate relatively left-wing political

verría announced his plans to place a 10 percent tax on luxury goods. The announced plan provoked a storm of protest from virtually the entire business sector. Businessmen in the bankers' alliance objected at least as much to the procedure followed as to the plan's substance. The tax proposal had been sent to Congress before the customary consultation with private sector leaders. Coparmex, the business organization closely associated with the Monterrey Group, complained that whereas "in recent years the highest government authorities have followed the healthy custom of advising national business organizations of legislative initiatives which . . . could affect the economic life of Mexico," this time "we've been called together to be informed of actions practically consummated."[81]

Four of the nation's largest business organizations signed a joint declaration saying that increased state revenues should come from greater efficiency in tax collection, not higher rates or new taxes. They also demanded that private sector representatives be consulted before economic decisions were taken and threatened that the fiscal reform, if implemented, would cause a decline in private investment.[82] Even Canacintra, with a large constituency of small and medium-sized entrepreneurs usually supportive of the government, denounced the proposed luxury tax, arguing that it would lead to inflation and growth of a black market in luxury goods.[83]

Until Echeverría fired him in 1973, finance minister Hugo Margáin tried to play an intermediary role between the national populist and bankers' alliances. In response to protest about the proposed tax reform, Margáin rushed to consult with and reassure private sector members of the bankers' alliance. Noting that Mexico's corporate tax burden was among the lowest in the world, Margáin emphasized that he understood it had been beneficial for

---

leaders into his cabinet in an effort to regain lost legitimacy. He promised to adopt a new economic strategy of "shared development." Echeverría's reformist goals included placing greater control on foreign investors, alleviating income inequality, and developing new exports. He aimed to achieve the highest rate of growth compatible with these other goals.

[81]Carlos Tello, *La política económica en Mexico, 1970–1976* (Mexico, D.F.: Siglo XXI, 1979), p. 45.

[82]Américo Saldívar, *Ideología y política del estado mexicano, 1970–1976* (Mexico, D.F.: Siglo XXI, 1980), p. 98.

[83]Rosario Green, *Estado y banca transnacional en Mexico* (Mexico, D.F.: Editorial Nueva Imagen, 1981), p. 83.

the nation's industrial development. However, to correct incipient imbalances in the Mexican economy, Margáin explained, it would be necessary to modify the tax structure slightly to increase domestic savings. "It is not a broad reform" he stressed, "but we do need to capture a larger portion of the nation's internal savings."[84] He went on to invite the private sector to participate in deciding which items would be taxed as luxuries. A series of meetings with Finance Ministry officials gave private sector leaders a chance to limit the impact of the tax change by lobbying for exclusion of a large number of goods from the list of luxury items.

A meeting at the National Palace between private sector leaders and the president on the proposed tax change foreshadowed the conflictive relationship that would develop between Echeverría and other national populists in his administration, on the one hand, and the bankers' alliance, on the other. It is also a measure of the weight of anti-reform forces. At this meeting Echeverría agreed to limit the list of taxable items. But he did not hesitate to admonish the leaders of industry and commerce for seeking wealth and luxury at the cost of national well-being, and he reminded them that the government must act in the interest of the entire nation, not just that of one sector.[85]

Several other tax reform proposals were under consideration in 1972. Finance minister Margáin was considering an increase in fuel and energy prices, which had been unchanged for ten years. A different group, working under the direction of the Assistant Secretary for Revenue, was formed to investigate alternative ways to increase government revenue. This group began to formulate a proposal for wide-spread fiscal reform. At the first cabinet meeting about the 1973 budget, in October 1972, finance minister Margáin presented the plan to increase energy and fuel prices. In true national populist form, Echeverría expressed his dismay, considering this a very limited way to increase government resources. Minister of patrimony and industry Horacio Flores de la Peña, the strongest voice of the national populist alliance in the Echeverría cabinet, supported Echeverría's criticism of Margáin's proposal and suggested that the Finance Ministry was evincing a "lack of zeal for tax reform." At

---

[84]Hugo Margáin, "Lineamientos de finanzas públicas," *Mercado de Valores* 32 (1971), pp. 13, 23–25.
[85]Green, *Estado y banca transnacional en Mexico*, p. 84.

this point in the meeting, the director of the working group on fiscal reform came forward to report on his team's study of the viability of changing wealth and income taxes. His working group, he volunteered, could write a reform proposal quickly enough to be sent to the Chamber of Deputies for consideration as part of the 1973 budget.[86]

The group quickly drafted a tax reform proposal based on the 1964 reform suggested by Kaldor. The proposal included changing the procedures for calculating taxable income, prohibiting anonymous ownership of bonds and stocks, creating a wealth tax, closing loopholes, increasing the marginal personal income tax rate, and changing treatment of profits and dividends.[87]

The proposed reform was discussed in a cabinet meeting in mid-November 1972. The major source of disagreement was over proposals to increase taxation on interest income and financial assets. The Secretariat of the Presidency favored the full proposal, including provisions to increase interest and dividend taxes. The government representative of the bankers' alliance, director of the Central Bank Ernesto Fernández Hurtado, opposed the reform. Finance minister Margáin took an intermediate position supporting reform, provided the proposal to increase taxation of financial assets was eliminated. Margáin's concern was that raising taxes on financial assets held in Mexico would induce Mexican capitalists to hold their wealth in financial assets outside Mexico. Margáin's position was adopted, despite continued opposition from the head of the Central Bank, who argued that the reform would discourage investment, induce capital flight, and eventually lead to political instability.[88]

In keeping with the tradition of private sector consultation in policy formulation, Margáin held a series of meetings at his home to discuss the proposed tax reform with leaders of the business community. Private sector objections echoed those first raised within the cabinet by Fernández Hurtado. "The private sector representatives were very critical and presented a common front," writes Solís. "They saw the bill as a first step leading to foreign

[86]Solís, *Economic Policy Reform in Mexico*, p. 73.
[87]Ibid.
[88]Ibid., p. 74; Laurence Whitehead, "Mexico from Boom to Bust: A Political Evaluation of the 1976–1979 Stabilisation Program," *World Development* 8 (1980), pp. 843–865.

exchange controls and argued that tax administration could be improved by measures that would not hurt investor confidence as the proposed measures would."[89]

Margáin defended the need for tax reform on the grounds that it would prevent a worse evil and the scourge of the bankers' alliance: inflation. "The private sector, while still reluctant," writes an observer at the meetings, "ran out of arguments and withdrew from discussion, warning at the same time of unforeseen dangers."[90] Its most conclusive objection, echoing those of the head of the Central Bank, was that the reform would precipitate capital flight and force a politically destabilizing peso devaluation.[91] The private sector lent grudging public support to the tax proposal, while reformulating their opposition strategy.

Before the bill could be sent to Congress, the secretive thirty-two-member Consejo Mexicano de Hombres de Negócio (Mexican Council of Businessmen, or CMHN) intervened, arguing forcefully with Echeverría in private against the bill.[92] Soon after, finance minister Margáin appeared before Congress to explain that several small changes in tax rates would substitute for the proposed change in tax structure.[93] Margáin explained that aspects of the proposed tax reform, particularly the elimination of anonymous bonds and stocks, would have provoked capital flight, which the nation could ill afford.[94]

---

[89]Solís, *Economic Policy Reform in Mexico*, p. 76.

[90]Leopoldo Solís, "A Monetary Will-o'-the-Wisp: Pursuit of Equity through Deficit Spending," unpublished manuscript, 1976, p. 102.

[91]Whitehead, "Mexico from Boom to Bust," p. 847.

[92]Saldívar, *Ideología y política del estado mexicano*, p. 104.

[93]At the same time the administration was preparing to send the tax reform bill to the legislature, another important piece of reform legislation, one regulating foreign direct investment, was also being prepared (Robert E. Looney, *Mexico's Economy: A Policy Analysis with Forecast to 1990* [Boulder, Colo.: Westview, 1978], pp. 80–81). Echeverría pushed this bill forcefully while dropping tax reform entirely. One interpretation is that the Mexican government finds it easier to regulate foreign capital than national capital.

[94]Tello, *La política económica en Mexico*, p. 61. The limited tax changes eventually introduced by Echeverría made the tax structure more regressive—leading former finance minister Ortíz Mena to call it a "counter-reform" (*Excelsior*, June 15, 1984). Corporate income tax, for example, remained at approximately 2 percent of corporate income throughout the *sexenio*. The ratio of tax revenue did increase from 8.7 percent in 1970 to 12 percent by the end of Echeverría's administration. But this was far from sufficient to cover the rise in public spending. The major tax change under López Portillo (1976–1982) was a 12 percent value-added tax introduced to replace the 4 percent sales tax. This tax also had a regressive impact. For a government view on tax changes

Through the 1970s Mexican fiscal policy remained a relatively ineffective tool for raising state revenue. The tax burden on capital was remarkably light. Although the history of Mexican fiscal policy is dotted with reform efforts, they were repeatedly defeated by the bankers' alliance.

Conclusion

The dominance over economic policy making of government officials in the Finance Ministry and Central Bank sympathetic to private bankers' interests, and the growing weight of other potential bankers' alliance allies, such as international creditors, shaped an economic policy pattern of limited fiscal policy, a commitment to free and fixed foreign exchange, tight monetary policy, relatively ineffective selective credit control, and weak government influence over private investment finance.

Over time the relative influence of the bankers' alliance over economic policy has varied with Mexico's international financial situation. The greater the need for good relations with international creditors, the more weight the creditors and those bankers with close ties to them have in the policy process. In the 1920s Mexico was in default on its international debts but needed to renegotiate and receive fresh funds, in part to help capitalize the new Central Bank. In this period the bankers' alliance was relatively successful in imposing its policy preferences. The alliance was less successful in the following two decades, when Mexico once again fell into default and was isolated from international financial markets and the world economy in general. As access to foreign loans again became important in the 1950s, the fortunes of the bankers' alliance improved. As we see in the next several chapters, the opportunities provided by rising international financial integration in the 1970s strengthened the economic base of the bankers' alliance. But from 1974 to 1981, a period of excess global liquidity, the alliance

---

see Guillermo Prieto Fortín, "Aspectos de la política tributaria, 1977–1982," *Comercio Exterior* 32 (1982), pp. 240–243. For a more critical summary see *Latin America Economics Report*, January 5, 1979, and John S. Evans, "The Evolution of the Mexican Tax System since 1970," Technical Papers Series, Institute of Latin American Studies, University of Texas–Austin, vol. 34 (1982).

saw its clout decline as Mexico's international financial situation improved dramatically—if only temporarily. When the debt boom went bust and Mexico's international creditors were once again in a powerful position vis-à-vis Mexican policy makers, the influence of the bankers' alliance rose once again.

INTERNATIONAL
FINANCIAL MARKETS
AND MEXICAN
POLITICAL ECONOMY

4

The Internationalization of Finance
and Economic Concentration

In the 1970s the Mexican economy became increasingly integrated into international financial markets. The number of representative offices of foreign banks in Mexico increased dramatically, Mexican banks were encouraged to operate internationally, and foreign borrowing ballooned. Historical continuities in Mexico's economic policies, particularly the promotion of private financial markets with relatively little success regulating credit allocation, free exchange convertibility, and little or no tax of luxury goods, shaped the way international financial integration affected Mexico's industrialization effort. In the context of these policies, the boom in international financial markets and rising international financial integration spurred a boom in domestic financial activity within Mexico. Benefits from the financial boom flowed disproportionately into the hands of multisector conglomerates, or *grupos*. Allocation of domestic and foreign credit was highly concentrated among a few privileged borrowers. The market for business finance became increasingly segmented between the relatively low-cost internationally integrated market and the relatively high-cost national market. Those large-scale enterprises with access to low-cost credit benefited in several ways. They could finance investment, enjoy the benefits of foreign exchange speculation, and profit as creditors by lending in the high-cost portion of the market. The uneven access to financing squeezed small and medium-sized entrepreneurs while *grupos* had privileged access to credit for productive activity. The boom also gave *grupos* the opportunity to put profits

97

to work in lucrative short-term financial activities or conglomerate expansion.

The distribution of bank profits and dollar- and peso-denominated bank credit highlights the way the benefits of international integration were concentrated among a few large conglomerates. Analysis of the Mexican trade and capital account in the late 1970s also reveals that foreign exchange flowed disproportionately to conglomerate enterprises and upper-class consumers. Foreign exchange generated by public sector borrowing and oil exports subsidized both luxury consumption and capital flight by wealthy Mexicans. It also subsidized a rise in import elasticity in private sector–dominated oligopolistic sectors of manufacturing.

International Financial Integration and Financial Boom in Mexico

Mexico's international financial integration grew by a variety of indicators in the 1970s. First, the number of representative offices of foreign banks grew tremendously. Legislation in 1932 prohibited foreign banks from having branch offices in Mexico. But the legislation did not rule out foreign banks establishing representative offices. These offices could not legally perform domestic banking operations but could help arranging trade financing and other international transactions as well as providing information and advice. The number of representative offices grew from 26 in 1969 to approximately 140 in the late 1970s. In the 1970s the business of these offices involved a variety of under-the-table activities that violated the spirit, if not the letter, of Mexican law. The offices played a crucial role in drumming up Mexican business for foreign banks. In practice drumming up business often meant they facilitated capital flight.[1]

Mexican government officials also promoted the international operation of Mexican banks. There was no reason, they argued, that Mexican banks could not enjoy the profits that U.S., European, and Japanese banks were earning through Euromarket opera-

---

[1] The 1969 figure on the number of representative offices is from Miguel S. Wionczek, "La banca extranjera en America Latina" (Lima: Instituto de Estudios Peruanos, 1969), p. 54. Information on the 1970s comes from an interview with former finance minister Jesus Silva Herzog, Mexico City, August 1989.

tions. "For Mexican credit institutions," stated an official government publication, internationalization "is one more opportunity to increase their profitability, since acting in the international market they have greater options for obtaining and using funds."[2] Legislation passed in 1977 permitted Mexican banks to open foreign branches; tax and Central Bank regulations encouraged borrowing and lending on the Eurocurrency market. Gustavo Romero Kolbeck, director of the Central Bank, argued that the reforms would lay the groundwork for Mexico City to become an important offshore financial center.[3] Treasury secretary David Ibarra announced in 1978 that he believed Mexican banks were on the verge of becoming internationally competitive.[4] By 1981, the nation's leading banks had thirty-four branch or representative offices in U.S. and European cities as well as in other Latin American capitals and the Caribbean.

To facilitate the international competitiveness of Mexican banks, Mexican officials thought it was necessary to promote mergers among domestic financial institutions. The government adopted an official policy of promoting centralization of financial activity and a shift from the original Anglo-Saxon model of specialized banking to the West German and Japanese version of "universal" banking. This change in official policy sped up a process toward concentration and centralization already well under way.[5]

Another indicator of the pressures of integration was the creation of a high-yield, dollar-denominated financial asset. Until 1976 only foreigners and residents of border zones could hold dollar-denominated deposits in Mexican banks. The creation of "Mexdollars" in 1976 permitted all residents to hold dollar-denominated deposits. When exchange controls were imposed in 1982 and these

---

[2]*Comercio Exterior* 27 (1981), p. 373.

[3]Carlos Ramírez, "Con cada dolar por ventas de petroleo viene mayor grado de inflación," *Proceso* 176 (1980), p. 7.

[4]"La política de David Ibarra," *Proceso* 57 (1977), pp. 6–9.

[5]José Manuel Quijano, ed., *La banca: Pasado y presente* (Mexico, D.F.: CIDE, 1983), pp. 195–210. The concept "financial group" was officially introduced in 1970, providing legal recognition of financial conglomerates already in existence. For example, the Banco de Comercio (Bancomer), the nation's largest bank, had three legally separate but managerially and financially unified institutions—commercial, investment, and mortgage—which it legally merged after the 1970 legislation was passed. In 1974 new banking legislation provided authorization for "multiple banks," so called because they would provide clients with multiple financial services, including short-term loans, mortgages, and foreign exchange facilities.

Table 5. Dollarization of the Mexican financial system, 1971–1982

	Percentage of total public bank liabilities in dollars	Percentage of total private bank liabilities in dollars	Percentage growth rate of public bank dollar liabilities	Percentage growth rate of private bank dollar liabilities	Percentage of total credits in dollars
1971	5	5			17
1972	4	4	10	0	13
1973	5	6	38	71	14
1974	5	6	47	17	18
1975	5	6	38	14	16
1976	14	28	131	263	33
1977	23	23	30	50	38
1978	21	23	6	21	31
1979	25	35	20	132	37
1980	24	38	15	52	34
1981	27	46	64	70	42
1982	na	44	257	99	na

"na" = Not available.
Sources: Banco de Mexico, Informe Anual (Mexico, D.F.: Banco de Mexico, various years); Secretaría de Programación y Presupuesto, Informe de Gobierno, José López Portillo (Mexico, D.F.: SPP, 1983).

accounts were declared only partially convertible, Mexdollars were jokingly termed "ex-dollars." The Mexdollar was created in response to a decline in domestic bank deposits and to rising capital flight. Creation of Mexdollars allowed for substantial dollarization of the Mexican financial system. As Table 5 indicates, the percentage of total private bank liabilities denominated in dollars rose from 5 percent in 1971 to 46 percent in 1981.

Mexican authorities also kept domestic interest rates high in an effort to boost domestic savings and discourage capital flight. But high nominal interest rates within Mexico and the differential between domestic and foreign interest rates created attractive opportunities for short-term financial speculation. In 1974, for example, nominal three-month interest rates were 12.44 percent in Mexico and only 5 percent in the United States. By 1981 Mexican nominal rates were 34.56 percent while U.S. rates were 13.02 percent.[6] Dollar loans converted into pesos, deposited for the short term in Mexican banks, and then reconverted into dollars earned

[6]Banco de Mexico, Indicadores de moneda y banca (Mexico, D.F.: Banco de Mexico, 1975–1982).

the arbitrager a considerable profit between 1979 and mid-1982. Thanks to market segmentation and interest rate differentials, anyone who succeeded in obtaining cheap credit was assured large profits, whether through exchange speculation or through other short-term investment. The highly liquid structure of Mexican bank deposits after 1977 reflects this boom in speculative financial activity. Between 1978 and 1982 the nonliquid time deposits of over one year at Mexican private banks fell more than 75 percent, from 48 percent of total deposits to 12 percent.[7] Long-term credits extended by public sector banks fell from 46 percent of the banks' total assets in 1970 to 31 percent in 1979. Commercial banks behaved the same way; their long-term credits fell from 36 percent of commercial bank assets in 1970 to 27 percent in 1979.

As the financial system became increasingly integrated into global capital markets, high interest rates and free exchange convertibility led to a pattern of monetary intervention that invited speculation. The Central Bank, concerned about the negative economic impact of exchange speculation, announced in June 1980 that it would allow the peso to slide slightly on a daily basis in order to maintain a constant interest rate differential between pesos and dollars and at least contain the incentive to speculate. Free convertibility made this policy self-defeating. Devaluation increased internal prices. As inflation rose, real interest rates on peso deposits fell, creating the need to adjust peso interest rates upward again in order to keep attracting peso depositors. To maintain constancy in the ratio of peso interest rates to international interest rates, the Central Bank had to increase the peso slide again. From the point of view of investors, this increase was further incentive to deposit in dollars. Completing the circle, the monetary authorities then had to increase peso interest rates again.

The rise in direct private foreign borrowing was another indicator of growing international financial integration. Given the relatively high cost of domestic credit, foreign borrowing was highly attractive to Mexican private enterprise. As long as the government guaranteed exchange stability, which it did until Central Bank reserves were almost exhausted in 1982, there was little risk and considerable profit in foreign borrowing. Banco de Mexico programs

[7]Antonio Assereto Amerlinck, "Perfil de las crisis recientes del sistema financiero mexicano," *Comercio Exterior* 34 (1984), p. 962.

Table 6. Foreign debt of the Mexican private sector, 1970–1982

	Nominal value in billions of dollars	Growth rate	Percentage of total Mexican external debt
1970	1.8		30.3
1971	2.1	14.5	32.7
1972	2.6	25.6	34.2
1973	3.2	20.9	31.0
1974	4.5	42.9	31.3
1975	5.6	24.1	28.1
1976	6.3	11.5	24.3
1977	6.4	2.1	21.9
1978	7.2	11.3	21.4
1979	9.3	30.4	23.9
1980	15.0	60.5	30.7
1981	20.1	35.6	27.7
1982	21.5	6.6	26.8

Sources: Secretaría de Programación y Presupuesto, Informe de Gobierno, José López Portillo (Mexico, D.F.: SPP, 1983); Banco de Mexico, Informe Anual, 1982 (Mexico, D.F.: Banco de Mexico, 1983).

encouraged foreign borrowing by private banks as a way to increase the supply of credit available domestically. Through a variety of mechanisms the Banco de Mexico would accept dollars the banks had borrowed on the international market and convert them into pesos with the exchange rate guaranteed. The banks relent these pesos, charging a premium to cover the exchange risk already effectively guaranteed by the Central Bank.[8] Direct private sector debt grew from $1.8 billion in 1970 to $20.1 billion in 1981, as Table 6 shows. Private Mexican banks contracted close to half of this debt. Through their international branch offices and by means of certificates of deposit, time deposits, and bankers' acceptances issued by foreign offices, they raised money from the U.S. interbank market, from European central banks, and from foreign companies and investors.[9] The private financial institutions' share of total external credits rose relative to those of the whole banking system in the 1970s. The public bank share of total systemwide foreign obligations fell from 90 percent in the 1971–1978 period to 70 percent in the 1979–1982 period, reflecting a rise in private

[8] Jorge Eduardo Uriarte Seldner, "La banca mexicana en los financiamientos internacionales," Ejecutivo de Finanzas 11 (1982), p. 32.
[9] Manuel Medina Mora, "Fuentes de financiamiento internacionales atraves de bancos mexicanos," Ejecutivo de Finanzas 10 (1981), p. 56.

bank borrowing in the Euromarket. At the end of 1982 private banks held $13 billion in dollar-denominated deposits, two-thirds contracted abroad and one-third reflecting deposits by Mexicans. In 1982 private banks accounted for 38 percent of total private sector debt.

Indicators such as the number of foreign banks with representative offices in Mexico, the international operation of Mexican banks, and direct private foreign borrowing suggest that Mexico's level of international financial integration rose in the 1970s. In the context of the economic policy patterns outlined in chapter 3, this rise in international financial integration lead to the concentration of financial resources and wealth among large financial and service sector entrepreneurs and upper-class consumers in general.

Concentration of Credit Allocation by Size and Sector

Theory suggests that the oligopoly power of *grupos* in a product market gives them profits higher than the economywide average and contributes to the concentration of financial resources in their hands. Concentration of financial resources in the hands of a few conglomerates permits them considerable control over credit allocation. This control in turn reinforces their position in the product market. Credit flows to group members, contributing to the segmentation of industry between those with easy access to finance and those without it. "In effect," writes Nathaniel Leff, "the groups have taken factor-market imperfections in the LDCs and transmuted them into product-market imperfections. In the process, rapid economic growth has occurred, but the groups have also created a special form of oligopoly capitalism."[10] Evidence on the concentration of credit allocation suggests that benefits from the Mexican financial boom of the late 1970s flowed disproportionately into *grupo* hands. In 1979, 5 percent of all borrowers consumed 68 percent of all banking system credit.[11] Dollar financing by private banks to private sector borrowers was also concentrated

[10]Nathaniel Leff, "Entrepreneurship in Economic Development," *Journal of Economic Literature* 17 (1979), p. 55.

[11]Hector González Mendez, "Comportamiento de la captación bancaria en Mexico," Banco de Mexico, Serie Documentos de Investigación, vol. 20 (1981), p. 3.

in a few large internationally linked conglomerates. Ten Mexican conglomerates contracted 34 percent of private sector external debt; three of them alone, the Monterrey-based Alfa, Vitro, and Visa, accounted for 20 percent of total private foreign borrowing.[12] Foreign borrowing was also concentrated by company size. "Gigantic" companies had 52 percent of their total liabilities in foreign debt. The smallest companies had only 3 percent of their liabilities in foreign debt.[13] A 1982 study by Banamex reveals four sectors receiving between 25 percent and 45 percent of their financing from foreign loans: autos and auto parts, construction and construction materials, chemicals and pharmaceuticals, and food, beer, and tobacco.[14] Construction and food and beverages are two traditional *grupo* strongholds; the other two sectors are characterized by MNC subsidiaries and joint ventures with national conglomerates.[15]

Conglomerates also dominated stock market activity. Often, conglomerates' financial groups included stock brokerages, and as a consequence brokeraging was concentrated among a relatively small number of actors. Between 1978 and 1981 ten brokerages accounted for 66 percent of operations.[16] "Investment societies" (*sociedades de inversión*) accounted for most of the rest of stock market operations. These societies also tended to be integrated into conglomerates and were used for the groups' own short-term financial purposes. One such society devoted 53 percent of its underwriting to bonds for one economic group, which was the principal stockholder in the bank with which the *sociedad* was affiliated.[17]

The financial sector itself also became increasingly concentrated

---

[12]Quijano, *La banca*, p. 273. There was wide variation in foreign borrowing patterns among the *grupos*. In December 1981, 72 percent of the Alfa Group's liabilities were foreign debts. The Serfín Group had close to 60 percent of its liabilities in foreign debt. The Frisco Corporation, one of the largest in the Bancomer Group, had almost no foreign debt, according to information reported to the Mexican stock exchange.

[13]Quijano, *La banca*, p. 273.

[14]*Expansion*, March 1982, p. 21.

[15]Research by Quijano indicates that there was a shift in the growth of foreign lending to *grupos* and away from MNC subsidiaries. In the first half of the 1970–1981 period, private sector foreign debt was contracted primarily by MNCs for the long term; in the second half, it was contracted mostly by national conglomerates for the short term. José Manuel Quijano, Hilda Sanchez, and Fernando Antia, *Finanzas, desarollo económico y penetración extranjera* (Puebla: Universidad Autonoma de Puebla, 1985).

[16]Maria Elena Cardero, José Manuel Quijano, and José Luis Manzo, "Cambios recientes en la organización bancaria y el caso de Mexico," in Quijano, *La banca*, p. 236.

[17]Ibid, p. 237.

because the boom in financial speculation benefited a small number of large *grupo* banks. Between 1970 and 1981 the number of banks fell from 240 to 97. The number accounting for 75 percent of the system's resources fell from 18 to 6. The largest private banks saw the return on their increasingly liquid asset portfolios rise rapidly during the boom of the late 1970s. Bank profits for Banamex, Bancomer, and Serfín, the nation's three largest banks, grew from 27 percent of paid capital reserves in 1978 to 39 percent in 1981.[18]

Commercial banks and the groups with which they were associated also used a portion of their profits to purchase existing enterprises and expand their conglomerates. Existing *grupos* grew in size, and several new *grupos* were formed. A survey of the expansion of Mexico's four largest groups reveals that they made nine acquisitions between 1975 and 1977, compared with thirty-two between 1978 and 1981.[19] The total number of *grupos* grew also. Among the *Expansion 500*, the Mexican equivalent of the *Fortune 500*, there were 39 *grupos* in 1979, 90 in 1980, and 120 in 1981. By 1980, these conglomerates included 1,100 companies; by 1981, 1,600. The concentration of assets among a sample of 23 *grupos* grew from 26 percent of total assets in 1978 to almost 31 percent in 1980.[20] Of the growing number of economic *grupos* formed in the 1970s, those that linked bank and industrial capital commanded a majority of *grupo* assets.[21]

In sum, the financial boom accentuated segmentation between the relatively low-cost internationally integrated market and the relatively high-cost national market. The uneven access to dollar financing created a dualism within the Mexican industrial sector, with small and medium-sized businesses excluded from the internationalized part of the Mexican financial market. This dualism contributed to industrial concentration, leading small and medium-sized businesses to voice a crescendo of complaints about the lack and expense of credit between 1979 and 1982. The president of the Credit Union for Small and Medium-Sized Business complained in

[18]Clemente Ruíz Durán, *90 dias de política monetaria y crediticia independiente* (Puebla: Universidad Autonoma de Puebla, 1984), p. 36.
[19]Eduardo Jacobs, "Holdings: Concentración para que?" *Economía Mexicana* 3 (1981), pp. 23–34.
[20]Quijano, *La banca*, p. 265.
[21]Rafael Santin, Victor Tirado, and Salvador Cordero H., *El poder empresarial* (Mexico, D.F.: Terra Nova, 1983), p. 108.

Table 7. Percentage of total private commercial bank credits in Mexico by destination, 1975–1983

	1975	1976	1977	1978	1979	1980	1981	1982	1983
Industry	43	na	41	40	35	35	34	35	34
Agriculture	9	na	9	10	10	10	10	7	6
Services	14	na	16	17	20	23	21	18	21
Housing	5	na	3	4	4	3	3	2	4
Commerce	25	na	25	25	26	27	27	15	14
Financial activity	na	na	na	na	4	4	2	1	6
Federal government	2	na	3	2	3	16	3	21	20

Note: Columns may not add to 100 because of rounding.
"na" = not available.
Source: Banco de Mexico, Informe Anual (Mexico, D.F.: Banco de Mexico, various years).

1982 that "credit is exceptionally expensive and our industries have little access."[22] "Most of the credit," added one of his associates, "is channeled to large companies."[23] Large conglomerates had access to plentiful and relatively low-interest foreign loans that smaller borrowers could not obtain. Not only did this access allow conglomerate borrowers to obtain working capital at rates lower than those charged on scarce domestic credit, but it also brought them profits from arbitrage between the dollar- and peso-based portions of the financial market. They used these profits to buy up other enterprises, which were often vulnerable because of the financial squeeze on small and medium-sized businesses. In short, they put profits from short-term financial activity to work in other highly lucrative financial activities and conglomerate expansions.

In the context of Mexico's relatively liberal financial policy, international financial integration and the financial boom of the late 1970s led to the concentration of credit both by the size and the sector of the borrower. Table 7 shows that during the 1975–1981 period private financing to industry fell while financing to services rose, with most other sectors receiving a roughly constant share of private credits. Between 1977 and 1981 the percentage of private financing to manufacturing fell to a decade-long low. Manufacturing and construction bore the brunt of the decline in private bank credits to industry. One high-level executive in the construction industry remarked on the short-run, nonproductive nature of bank

[22]Interview with Hector de los Santos, Fogain, Mexico City, October 1984.
[23]Interview with Manuel Díaz Rivera, Canacintra, Mexico City, October 1984.

lending patterns he observed from his vantage point in the economy, concluding that Mexican banks "tend to be lazy."[24] Relatively larger portions of credit went to the oil, energy, electronics, and nonmetallic minerals sectors. The first two are state-dominated sectors, and the latter two are among the most highly concentrated sectors in Mexican private industry.[25]

The rise in financing to the service sector reflects in part an increase in the interbank market fueled by growth in short-term speculative activity by banks.[26] Other changes in commercial banks' balance sheets and income accounts also highlight the short-term speculative nature of financial growth in the 1970s. Not only did credits become increasingly short term, as already mentioned, but the share of credits in total commercial bank assets fell from 58 percent in 1970 to 48 percent in 1982.[27] The share of stocks and bonds in total assets also fell, reflecting a shift into more liquid assets, which could be used for exchange speculation or other rapid-turnover financial maneuvers. The share of reserves in total assets rose, reflecting both the desire for liquid assets and a rise in Central Bank reserve requirements.

Mexico did experience a stock market boom in 1979, but it reflected speculative buying and selling of secondary issues rather than primary stock issues. Secondary issues were a way for corporations to sell stocks in order to secure other means of financing, mostly foreign debt. A company would sell stock, a tax-free transaction, and deposit the proceeds in a local or foreign financial institution to earn interest. At the same time the company would take out a loan from that institution, or another, enjoying a tax exemption on the interest payments.[28]

In short, bank profits and dollar- and peso-denominated bank credit not only were concentrated among a few large conglomerates but also were biased away from long-term lending for industry and toward short-term financial and commercial activity. Anal-

[24]Interview with José Sanchez, ICA, Mexico City, April 1984.
[25]Quijano, Sanchez, and Antia, *Finanzas, desarollo económico y penetración extranjera*, p. 194.
[26]Federico Rodríguez and Javier Salas, "Estructura y funcionamiento del mercado de crédito interbancario en Mexico," *El Trimestre Económico* 52 (1985), pp. 293–312.
[27]Alejandro Davila Flores, *La crisis financiera en Mexico* (Mexico, D.F.: Ediciones de Cultura Popular, 1986), p. 102.
[28]Quijano, *La banca*, pp. 221–304.

ysis of Mexico's trade and capital account in the late 1970s reveals that foreign exchange also flowed disproportionately to conglomerate enterprises and upper-class consumers.

Foreign Exchange Allocation

Mexican foreign exchange inflows increased dramatically thanks to the foreign borrowing just discussed and to oil export revenues. Analyzing foreign exchange allocation is another way of gauging the domestic politico-economic impact of international financial integration. Foreign exchange inflows in the late 1970s supported an increase in luxury consumption—including capital flight, oligopolistic industry, and a partial reversal of import substitution.[29]

Table 8 shows that between 1977 and 1981 the imports of consumption goods grew an average of twice as fast, annually, as the imports of intermediate and capital goods. The fastest-growing importing sectors were textiles, commerce, beer, and furniture—all consumer goods–producing sectors. The private sector's consumer imports bill for the 1977–1981 period amounts to $4.2 billion of the total $7 billion. The increase in private sector consumer imports clearly reflects middle-class luxury consumption. Transportation sector consumer imports, largely vehicles for personal transport, accounted for 22 percent of the total increase in private sector consumer goods imports. Textiles, including the large categories of shoes and synthetic clothing, accounted for another 15 percent of

[29]Foreigners with business in Mexico have for centuries shipped income generated in Mexico out of the country; there have been many bouts of capital flight. But there are two differences between these episodes and that of the late 1970s and early 1980s. First, to the extent that it is increasingly the national bourgeoisie that generates savings and allocates them among different investment opportunities, including international ones, capital export is a grave politico-economic problem. Although few would expect foreign businessmen who dominated Latin American economies until the early twentieth century to take a country's long-run growth into account in making their investment decisions, these considerations should weigh more heavily with national capitalists. If they will not invest in their country's future, who will? The second difference lies in the magnitude of capital flight relative to domestic saving and investment. Facilitated by international financial integration, government policy, and excess global liquidity, the magnitude was much greater in the 1970s than in any previous period. For a discussion of the difference between "normal" outflows and capital flight see Robert Cumby and Richard Levich, "On the Definition and Magnitude of Recent Capital Flight," in Donald R. Lessard and John Williamson, eds., *Capital Flight and Third World Debt* (Washington, D.C.: Institute for International Economics, 1987).

Table 8. Public and private sector imports by type of goods, 1977–1981 (percentages)

	1977	1978	1979	1980	1981	Annual growth	Percentage of total import growth accounted for
Total							
Private	64	63	66	63	65	50	65
Public	36	37	34	37	35	89	35
Consumer							
Percentage of total imports	5	6	8	13	12	88	14
Private	78	80	84	49	58	66	8
Public	22	20	16	51	42	198	6
Intermediate							
Percentage of total imports	64	64	62	60	57	38	55
Private	63	59	64	63	62	37	33
Public	37	41	36	37	38	38	21
Capital							
Percentage of total imports	38	34	34	29	28	40	31
Private	62	66	66	71	72	47	23
Public	38	34	34	29	28	32	8

Source: Banco de Mexico, *Informe Anual* (Mexico, D.F.: Banco de Mexico, various years).

the increase. Food manufactures imports, including alcoholic beverages, meat, and butter—all luxury items by average Mexican living standards—accounted for another 15 percent of the increase. A category including TV and radio receivers and transmitters, phonographs, cameras, and watches accounted for another 14 percent of growth in private sector consumer imports. Finally, paper and books accounted for 9 percent of the increase.[30]

[30]The growth in public sector consumer goods imports was also dramatic, reflecting a crisis in Mexican food production in the late 1970s. All public consumer goods imports rose an annual 1977–1981 average of 198 percent, shooting from 3 percent in 1977 to 785 percent in 1980. Private sector consumer imports, starting from a much higher absolute level, also rose, but at one-third this rate. Despite the boom in public sector consumer goods imports, private sector consumer goods imports still accounted for 55 percent of the total nominal growth in Mexican consumer goods imports between 1977 and 1981. Behind the rapid rise in public sector consumer imports was stagnation in agricultural production, reflecting both chronic and conjunctural problems. Food manufactures, mostly sugar and powdered and dried milk imported by the state food marketing agency, Conasupo, accounted for 51 percent of the total increase in public consumer imports. Conasupo accounted for one-fifth of total public sector imports between 1977 and 1981. The rise in Conasupo sugar imports reflected both the conjunctural factor of poor weather and a bad cane harvest in 1979 and growing per capita sugar consump-

Finance Ministry evaluations of consumer imports by sector of final use within the economy show that the fastest-growing sectors include wheat and corn milling, oil and vegetable fat production, beer and soft drink production and furniture manufacturing. The first two categories are of basic food items, but the other categories fall into the area of luxuries. All the consumer goods–producing sectors are relatively concentrated, which points to the concentration of imports among a small number of companies within them. In the tortilla (corn and wheat grinding) sector, of close to 8,000 producers in 1975 (the latest year for which data are where available), 24 accounted for 38 percent of total sectoral production.[31] In the beverage industry, 56 of 1,551 producers accounted for 41 percent of production.[32]

Tourism abroad and capital flight are also forms of luxury consumption. In 1981 Mexicans spent more abroad than foreign tourists did in Mexico.[33] In 1982 Mexicans had $29 billion worth of deposits in U.S. banks, according to the U.S. Federal Reserve.[34] Real estate holdings add considerably more to this figure. The boom in Mexican real estate purchases in the United States was so great that U.S. media reports referred jokingly to Mexico's "reconquest of lost territory." The main concentrations of Mexican prop-

---

tion. Sugar was among the government-subsidized food staples. A large portion of the sugar subsidy, however, benefited manufacturers using sugar as a major input—particularly soft drink manufacturers. Public sector milk imports reflect increased demand and dietary improvements for the Mexican middle class and, to some extent, the lower-middle class. Agricultural manufactures accounted for 51 percent of the increase in public sector consumer imports, and agricultural products accounted for another 34 percent. Again this reflects agricultural stagnation caused by both long-term industrially biased development and poor 1979 weather conditions. As a consequence of these two factors, public sector agricultural imports rose from $10 million in 1979 to $297 million in 1980. The short-lived Mexican Food System program, launched in 1980, was partly a response to the fear that agricultural imports would completely consume new oil earnings; 1979 projections had agricultural imports consuming 50 percent of oil export earnings by 1985 and 73 percent by 1990. (Casio Luiselli Fernández, "Agricultura y alimentación: Premisas para una nueva estrategia," in Nora Lustig, ed., *Panorama y perspectivas de la económia mexicana* [Mexico, D.F.: Colegio de Mexico, 1980], p. 911.)

[31]Saúl Trejo Reyes, "Concentración industrial y política económica en Mexico," *Comercio Exterior* 33 (1983), p. 821.

[32]Ibid.

[33]Henry C. Schmidt, "The Mexican Foreign Debt," *Mexican Studies/Estudios Mexicanos* 2 (1985), p. 227.

[34]The Mexican deposits registered with the U.S. Federal Reserve also include Mexican Central Bank deposits in the United States, but in 1982 these deposits were negligible because of Mexico's severe balance of payments crisis.

erties were in San Diego, El Paso, San Antonio, Houston, Dallas, Los Angeles, Miami, Denver, Vail, New York, and San Francisco. According to a University of Texas study, most of the value of Mexican holdings was concentrated in a small number of luxury properties. Many Mexican properties in the United States in 1982 were relatively low-cost investments near the border. The study found that 10 percent of the properties accounted for 80 percent of the value of Mexican real estate in the United States and 80 percent accounted for 15 percent of the value.[35] By 1981, with twenty-nine U.S. real estate firms operating offices in Mexico City, the pace of Mexican investment in the United States had become alarming to the Mexican government. Unable to prohibit it, the Mexican government aimed to slow this form of capital flight by banning advertisement of U.S. real estate in the Mexican media.[36]

The World Bank estimates that Mexican capital flight between 1978 and 1982 amounted to $27 billion, a figure that corresponds roughly with Banco de Mexico calculations. Nongovernment economists in Mexico have made estimates ranging from $40 billion to $55 billion.[37] The investment bank publication *World Financial Markets* reports that Mexico's $97 billion debt would be only $12 billion were it not for capital flight.[38]

Even though consumer goods imports grew rapidly, intermediate and capital goods imports accounted for 85 percent of the total growth in imports, excluding purchases of foreign assets held abroad, between 1977 and 1981. In the categories of intermediate and capital goods imports, private sector imports grew faster and were absolutely larger than public sector imports. Producer and

[35]This study is reported in José Reveles, "800 milones de dolares al año se iban," *Proceso* 310 (1982), pp. 16–17.

[36]It was not an outright ban but a declaration that permission would be based on prior approval, which government officials are quoted as saying they never intended to grant. See Reveles, "800 milones de dolares al año se iban"; and Rafael Rodríguez Castañeda, "Freno a la publicidad que induce a la fuga de capitales," *Proceso* 266 (1981), pp. 6–7.

[37]See Jaime Ros, "Mexico from Oil Boom to the Debt Crisis: An Analysis of Policy Response to External Shocks," in Rosemary Thorp and Laurence Whitehead, eds., *Latin American Debt and the Adjustment Crisis* (Pittsburgh: University of Pittsburgh Press, 1987), p. 74; Edmar Salinas, "La coyuntura inflacionaria, soló un factor mas," *Uno Más Uno*, June 2, 1985; *El Día*, July 4, 1985, p. 9. Variations among different estimates of capital flight depend on what is included in the definition and how it is measured. Transfer pricing by MNC subsidiaries and over- and underbilling by Mexican exporters and importers are often not included in official estimates.

[38]Morgan Guaranty Trust Company, *World Financial Markets*, February 1986.

Financial Markets and Political Economy

intermediate goods imports were concentrated in the oil, petrochemicals, and manufacturing sectors.[39]

Data for the 1976–1981 period show that manufacturing in-
curred a large trade deficit and that the state-owned oil and petrochemical sectors generated a strong surplus.[40] The private sector
accounted for a growing share of the total manufacturing sector
deficit: 49 percent in 1977 and 68 percent in 1981.[41] By sector
origin, excluding the consumer category of food manufactures, the
largest categories of manufactured imports were steel, chemicals,
and machines. By tariff chapters, the largest categories were machines, transport-related goods, common metals (including steel),
and chemicals. Data showing imports by sector of final consumption reveal a more complicated picture. Some of the same sectors
are present: transport-related goods, steel and non-ferrous metals,
metal products and machines, and the specific chemical subsector
producing medicinal products. Paper, commerce, and oil and electricity complete the list of sectors accounting for the greatest expense in imports.[42] The metal products and machine industries were
also among the fastest-growing importing sectors.

Many of the high-import private sector–dominated industries

[39]Analysis of producer goods imports is more difficult than that of consumer goods
imports because of data limitations and the methodological complexity of tracing these
imports through the production structure. To build an accurate input-output matrix for
the Mexican economy would be a monumental project given that existing matrices are
dated and based on extrapolations from earlier matrices, which do not completely capture structural change in the Mexican economy. In the analysis that follows two sources
of data were used. First, data from the Treasury Secretary showing imports by sector of
final consumption (which eliminates the need for an input-output matrix) were available
for the period 1977–1979—although with no breakdown for public and private sector
importing. For the 1980–1982 period a different series, with a public-private breakdown, was available. A second set of data, from the Planning and Budget Ministry,
presents imports by their tariff categories and sector of origin. With no accurate input-
output matrix, however, the data are useful only when matched with import data collected from business organizations representing the major importing sectors of the economy. At best this matching still yields only a partial analysis. The general results are
presented here.
[40]For specific data on trade balances by sector see Mario Dehesa, "Tipos de empresa y
el comercio exterior de manufacturas," Economía Mexicana 4 (1982), p. 140.
[41]Ibid., p. 141.
[42]The single catch-all commerce sector accounted for more of the increase in total
imports between 1979 and 1981 than any other single sector. Unfortunately, this category is so broadly defined that with existing data one cannot evaluate the economic
impact of this import expense. Like manufacturing, however, this sector—including
commerce, restaurants, and hotels—used up a disproportionately large share of imports
relative to investment.

have an oligopolistic structure. The auto industry, accounting for the high import of transport-related goods, is dominated by multinational subsidiaries and is highly concentrated; 33 of a total of 930 companies in the transport sector account for 85 percent of production.[43] In the high-import machine tools industry, 59 firms of a total 24,296 account for close to 50 percent of production.

Banco de Mexico data for a list of twenty-six major Mexico-based firms support the overall hypothesis of capital and intermediate imports being biased toward the largest firms in the relatively highly concentrated machinery, steel, chemical, and auto sectors. Individual firm-level data from the Central Bank also support this hypothesis. The twenty-six listed firms accounted for an annual average of 20 percent of total private sector imports between 1977 and 1981. Eleven of the firms were in the auto and transport sector, four in chemicals, three in steel, and five in metal products and machinery. Seventeen were MNC subsidiaries.

Foreign exchange allocation for producer goods imports favored highly concentrated manufacturing industries and supported unnecessarily import-intensive production. Taylor estimates that less than two-thirds of the total increase in imports reflected normal income elasticity.[44] Underlying the boom in manufactures imports was a growing elasticity of industrial import demand relative to internal demand. According to one study, the coefficient of imports to internal demand went from 2.4 percent in 1978 to 3.1 percent in 1980, reflecting some displacement of domestic industrial supply and thus "reversing the trend of import substitution."[45] Another study, by Mexican economist Nora Lustig, calculates an import substitution index of imports relative to total product supply. This index shows that the proportion of imports rose for all sectors of manufacturing between 1975 and 1980. The increase was greatest for capital and intermediate goods. The index for capital goods rose from 29.5 percent to 34.2 percent, and for intermediate goods from 9.2 percent to 13.2 percent. Lustig's measurement of the extent of backward linkages for industry, including the oil sector,

[43]Trejo Reyes, "Concentración industrial y política económica en Mexico," p. 821.

[44]Lance Taylor, "La crisis y su porvenir: Problemas de política macroeconómica en Mexico," *Investigación Económica* 170 (1984), pp. 283–311.

[45]CIDE, "La evolución reciente y las perspectivas de la economía mexicana," *Economía Mexicana* 3 (1981), p. 11; Gerardo Bueno, "Endeudamiento externo y estrategias de desarollo en Mexico: 1976–1982," *Foro Internacional* 24 (1983), p. 84.

shows a decline. This conclusion is corroborated by data showing that growth in manufacturing output began to decline in 1980 and failed to keep pace with GDP growth in 1980 and 1981.[46] Brailovsky and Barker find that participation of imported goods and services in total demand grew from 8.8 percent in 1977 to 14.7 percent in 1981. In machines, for example, the participation of imports in satisfying total domestic demand grew from 31 percent in 1978 to 43 percent in 1980. Another indicator of increasing substitution of imports for domestic production is that imports grew more rapidly than capacity utilization between 1979 and 1981.[47]

A direct comparison of investment and import levels between the oil and manufacturing sectors—the former public, the latter private sector–dominated—shows a much higher ratio of investment to imports in the oil sector. In 1979 and 1980 the manufacturing sector accounted for something under two-thirds of total imports but only one-quarter of total investments. Although there are numerous examples of profligate importing by public sector enterprises, mainly in the energy area, the contrast with private sector–dominated manufacturing areas is striking. Imports in the oil sector account for 14 percent of total imports in 1979 and 9 percent in 1980, whereas oil investment accounts for 32 percent and 37 percent of total investment. Manufacturing, in contrast, accounts for a very high portion of total imports and a relatively low level of investment.

Of the highest-importing sectors in manufacturing between 1979 and 1981, there were only four in which investment grew almost as fast as imports: electricity, transport, nonferrous metallic minerals, and basic iron and steel. These are all sectors with high state participation. In the other private sector–dominated categories imports grew much more rapidly than investment. The fifteen sectors in which imports grew the fastest between 1979 and 1981 are iron minerals, nonferrous metallic minerals, wheat milling, corn milling, vegetable fats and oils, hard liquor, beer, soft drinks, textiles—

---

[46]Lustig points out that the data she presents do not separate out consumption goods produced in economic branches that produce both consumer and producer goods. Nora Lustig, "Capital Formation during the Oil Boom," paper prepared for workshop "Government and Private Sector in Contemporary Mexico," Center for U.S.-Mexican Studies, University of California–San Diego, April 1986.

[47]Vladimir Brailovsky and Terry Barker, "Recuento de la quiebra," *Nexos* 71 (1983), p. 21.

other, furniture, structural metal products, electrical machinery and equipment, construction, commerce, and restaurants and hotels. Investment grew almost as fast as imports only in the categories of beer, soft drinks, and furniture.

Mexico's foreign exchange bonanza, partly a consequence of international financial integration, led to a large increase in nonproductive imports. Consumer imports grew exponentially. But in absolute terms, foreign exchange expenditure on producer goods was much greater. Producer goods imports accounted for 85 percent of the growth in the nominal value of imports. In many cases artificially cheap imports replaced domestic production instead of representing a net addition to domestic investment. The import substitution index measuring the relationship between imported and total producer goods supplied shows that the proportion of imports rose for all sectors of manufacturing between 1975 and 1980. The trade surplus generated by the public sector–dominated oil and petrochemical sectors subsidized a rise in import elasticity in private sector–dominated, oligopolistic sectors of manufacturing. Like bank profits and credit, foreign exchange flowed disproportionately to conglomerate enterprises and upper-class consumers.

Conclusion

The incentive structure created by international financial integration and government policy drew resources away from industrial finance. Small and medium-sized industrialists without preferential access to credit markets were financially squeezed. Industrial and financial conglomerates profited heavily from short-term financial activity. The boom in nonoperational profits of large corporations fueled mergers. Wealth and financial resources became increasingly centralized and concentrated in the hands of a relatively small number of conglomerates. Foreign exchange flowed disproportionately into oligopolistic manufacturing sectors, in some cases displacing existing or potential domestic suppliers. It disproportionately benefited the wealthy by fueling luxury consumption and capital flight.

The Mexican experience was not unique. As chapter 7 describes, to varying degrees across the continent in the late 1970s the internationalization of finance drew resources away from long-term industrial finance and into short-term financial and commercial activity and led to increased polarization of the industrial structure and to a concentration of wealth and income. These similar trends in widely varying Latin American countries reflect the weight of international forces in Third World development.

Despite the similarities, not all Latin American countries suffered to the same extent from these unanticipated consequences of international integration. In the Chilean and Argentine cases liberal financial policy and the internationalization of financial markets in the late 1970s led to deindustrialization. Other countries in Latin America, such as Brazil and Colombia, managed to harness the benefits of international financial integration to industrial development. Mexico falls somewhere in between. In contrast to the deindustrialization in Chile and Argentina, there was net new industrial investment in Mexico during the 1970s. However, the increase in new capital formation in Mexico was due primarily to the buoyancy of public sector investment in oil, not to a rise in private sector industrial investment. In Mexico the share of the private sector in national gross fixed capital formation fell from 62–65 percent in the 1971–1976 period, to 56–58 percent in the 1977–1981 period.[48] Also, private sector investment shifted from manufacturing toward services. Private sector investment in manufacturing fell from 46.4 percent of total private sector investment in 1977 to 36 percent in 1980.[49] The Mexican government was able to prevent the contraction of private sector capital formation that international financial integration encouraged in Argentina and Chile. It was not able to manage international financial integration as successfully as countries such as Brazil. Mexican private sector investment lost dynamism relative to the public sector and shifted away from manufacturing.

Why wasn't Mexico more successful at managing the international integration of its financial markets? The answer lies in Mexico's long-run economic policy patterns and the historically and institutionally shaped alliances that explain them.

---

[48]Data from the Central Bank and the Ministry of Budget and Planning vary somewhat, with the Central Bank data showing slightly lower private sector investment.
[49]Lustig, "Capital Formation during the Oil Boom."

5

International Liquidity and
the Politics of Economic Policy
in the 1970s

The incentives created by Mexico's economic policies and international financial integration channeled resources into short-term financial activity and growth of economic *grupos*. This resource allocation strengthened the economic base of the bankers' alliance. But at least in the short run a stronger economic base did not translate into an increased capacity to influence economic policy. Access to foreign loans hurt the bankers' alliance in the short run because it temporarily undermined the rationale for monetary stability and restraint. The result was a period of heightened struggle between policy currents. Partly because of the availability of unconditional foreign loans, the bankers' alliance lost struggles over public spending during both the Echeverría and the López Portillo administrations and in 1980–1981 also lost a push for devaluation that it argued would have helped restore monetary stability.

Although the bankers' alliance lost several battles over monetary restraint, its institutional base remained largely intact. The bankers' continued power is evident in policy issues that were kept off the agenda; the bankers' alliance was also able to weaken threatening proposals that did reach it. Until 1982 financial regulation and exchange controls—representing two policy arenas in which the national populists would have liked to see change—were not seriously considered. Also, the bankers' alliance was able to eliminate capital control provisions in the 1979 Industrial Plan. Without these provisions, the plan lost much of its potential effectiveness. This type of compromise solution to policy conflicts is also evident

117

in the 1980 Plan Global de Desarollo (Global Development Plan, or PGD).

These struggles and compromises over economic policy led to heightened frustration for both the bankers' alliance and the national populists. Both policy currents perceive the López Portillo administration as one in which they lost ground. As is evident in the brief survey of government income and expenditure at the end of this chapter, foreign borrowing allowed the government to avoid the political difficulties of changing development strategy in either the monetarist or the structuralist direction.

Conflict over Monetary Restraint and Industrial Policy

The bankers' alliance began to lose ground in preserving monetary stability in a fight over public spending with Echeverría. Then it lost the battle over oil development strategy and public spending during the López Portillo administration. It also failed in efforts to convince López Portillo to devalue the peso in 1980–1981, when it believed there was still time to try to restore monetary stability and avert a financial crisis. Despite these failures, in debates over industrial planning the bankers' alliance was able to eliminate provisions making private sector compliance mandatory.

The Fight over Public Spending, 1973–1976

Echeverría's cabinet included representatives of both the national populist alliance and the bankers' alliance. Industry and national patrimony minister Flores de la Peña, a blunt, outspoken economist and self-proclaimed leftist, was considered the anchor of the left wing of the cabinet. In keeping with this role, he voiced repeated criticisms of big business. He was suspicious of the conservatism traditionally associated with the Finance Ministry and Central Bank and had a particularly antagonistic relationship with finance minister Margáin.

As finance minister, Margáin tried to play an intermediating role between the national populists and the bankers' alliance; yet his primary allegiance was to the latter. His role as intermediary gave members of the bankers' alliance confidence that any potential leftward drift would be checked. Large-scale businessmen believed that, at that time, Margáin was their best interlocutor in the Eche-

118

Table 9. Public sector finances, 1973–1982

	Deficit as percentage of GDP	Internal debt as percentage of GDP	External debt as percentage of GDP
1973	5	3	13
1974	5	8	14
1975	9	11	16
1976	7	11	17
1977	5	11	28
1978	7	12	26
1979	7	14	22
1980	7	14	18
1981	14	18	22
1982	17	28	36

Sources: Calculated using data from IMF, International Financial Statistics (Washington, D.C.: International Monetary Fund, 1974–1983); Secretaría de Programación y Presupuesto, Primer Informe de Gobierno, 1983 (Mexico, D.F.: SPP, 1984).

verría administration. Margáin, one businessman said, "was a complete gentleman, he always consulted us before sending legislation to the legislature."[1] When he was fired in 1973 for opposing Echeverría's public spending on the grounds that it was inflationary, private sector confidence in the government plummeted.

Margáin was fired for refusing, in the absence of any serious effort to increase government revenue, to authorize increases in public spending that he considered inflationary. The nation's treasury, Margáin argued, was virtually empty. Referring to the possibility of foreign borrowing, Echeverría declared he would appoint a finance minister who could find the money needed for expanded government expenditures.[2] After Margáin was fired, the Central Bank director was alone in trying to staunch the national populist wave, which, ironically, was made possible in part by loans from international bankers. Following Margáin's departure the public sector deficit grew from 5 percent of GDP in 1973 to 9 percent in 1975, as Table 9 shows. Foreign debt relative to GDP rose from 13 percent in 1973 to 16 percent in 1975.

[1]Américo Saldívar, Ideología y política del estado mexicano (Mexico, D.F.: Colegio de Mexico, 1980), p. 104.

[2]Not long after Margáin's firing, rising inflation forced Echeverría to adopt a stabilization plan—Latin America's first heterodox stabilization plan. Because of its heterodox nature the plan was varyingly described as a victory for monetarists and for structuralists. González notes the conflict between these two currents both in the plan and in Echeverría's rhetoric. Eduardo González, "La política económica, 1970–1976: Itinerario de un projecto inviable," in Pedro López Díaz, ed., Capitalismo y crisis en Mexico (Mexico, D.F.: Ediciones de Cultura Popular, 1978).

Echeverría's public statement in response to concern about the consequences of Margáin's firing further upset businessmen in the bankers' alliance. Asked in an interview about widespread business opinion that Margáin's dismissal would hurt the value of the peso by causing capital flight, Echeverría responded that nothing would happen to the peso because "finances are managed from Los Pinos." (Los Pinos is the Mexican White House.) Businessmen interpreted this response as a sign that Echeverría intended to increase his personal control over economic policy. In the days immediately following Margáin's dismissal, wealthy Mexicans sent half a billion dollars out of the country.[3]

Capital flight continued, but it did not convince Echeverría to change his policies. During the rest of his administration he neither reverted to the monetary and fiscal policies of the stabilizing development era preferred by the bankers' alliance nor clamped down on capital in order to prevent capital fight as he tried to shift to a more populist development model. His response was simply to run a bigger and bigger deficit and borrow more abroad.

The initial defeat of the bankers' alliance over monetary restraint in the 1970s spurred a wave of organization among business leaders sympathetic to the alliance's ideological position. Margáin's departure from the government gave the Flores de la Peña wing of the cabinet, representative of the national populist line, more room to maneuver. Businessmen in the bankers' alliance felt increasingly helpless to stop Echeverría's inflation and foreign loan–fueled public spending boom and growth of state intervention in the economy.[4] Echeverría's policies spurred election of a new breed of more confrontational leaders of business associations. Coparmex, for example, took a significant turn toward political confrontation with the PRI after Guajardo Suárez, who had been president of Coparmex since 1960, was forced to resign.[5] He was replaced by Andres Marcelo Sada, who believed that the government was out to de-

---

[3]Adrian Lajous, "Quien la manejó," *Excelsior*, November 9, 1984, p. 7.

[4]Juan M. Martínez Nava, *Conflicto estado empresarios* (Mexico, D.F.: Editorial Nueva Imagen, 1984), p. 176.

[5]Guajardo Suárez had close ties to Echeverría and did not support the more confrontational strategy desired by many Coparmex members. See Carlos Arriola, *Las organizaciones empresariales y el estado* (Mexico, D.F.: Fondo de Cultura Económica, 1981), p. 78; Elvira Conchiero, Antonio Gutierrez, and Juan Manuel Fragoso, *El poder de la gran burguesía* (Mexico, D.F.: Ediciones de Cultura Popular, 1979), p. 123.

stroy free enterprises and that only through political action could businessmen defend the place of private property in Mexico.[6]

The Mexican Bankers Association remained relatively discreet, evincing complaints only in private and remaining publicly aloof. However, Concanaco, Concamin, and some provincial business organizations joined Coparmex's aggressive public stance. Canacintra was alternately conciliatory and defiant, reflecting the increasing heterogeneity of opinions represented among the enterprises in the organization.

Formation of an umbrella business organization, the Consejo Coordinador Empresarial (Business Coordinating Council, or CCE), was the clearest manifestation of the rise of a new adversarial group within the business community in response to the perceived leftward drift of the Echeverría administration. In a 1973 bulletin the American Chamber of Commerce of Mexico invited businessmen to join and coordinate action to confront "growing hostility toward private enterprise"[7] Several months later, in a speech in Monterrey, a former president of the Chamber of Commerce elab-

---

[6]Conchiero, Gutierrez, and Fragoso, *El poder de la gran burgesía*, p. 126; Saldívar, *Ideología y política del estado mexicano*, p. 175. Relations between Echeverría and the private sector deteriorated from 1973 on. Almost all bridges between the Monterrey Group and the Echeverría administration were burned after the death of Monterrey patriarch Garza Sada. Garza Sada was assassinated, and Monterrey capitalists placed the blame on Echeverría for failing to maintain law and order. See Arriola, *Las organizaciones empresariales y el estado*, pp. 87–89; and Martínez Nava, *Conflicto estado empresarios*, pp. 182–184.

The confrontations reached a climax in 1976 over a proposed urban housing law and land expropriations in the northern states of Sonora and Sinaloa. The urban housing law would have made federal and municipal governments responsible for zoning all urban growth nationwide. The private sector worried that this law could hurt industrial expansion and would give the government the right to regulate private property. At the height of the controversy Echeverría accused Monterrey capitalists of holding clandestine meetings to plan opposition to the zoning proposal. He accused them of wishing for a military government in Mexico and engaging in the "most decadent" forms of U.S. consumerism. The president of the PRI at the time, Porfirio Muñoz Ledo, exhorted a group of workers to take "direct action to correct the wrongs of business interests." López Portillo, then minister of finance, got into the act also, noting the "Ku Klux Klan" style of the opposition business meetings. As a result of the controversy, the proposed zoning legislation was substantially watered down. See "Government Business Flare-ups in Mexico," *Business Latin America*, April 28, 1976, p. 135.

From 1977 to 1981 more moderate business leaders regained leadership positions they had lost during the Echeverría years. However, as the oil boom began to go bust in 1981, the hard-liners once again began to move to the forefront.

[7]Carlos Arriola, "Los grupos empresariales frente al estado (1973–1976)," in *Los hombres del control del estado mexicano* (Mexico, D.F.: Colegio de Mexico, 1976), p. 471.

orated on the need for coordination among businessmen. The majority of Mexican businessmen are politically inept, he suggested, and the private sector's views are virtually absent from the media. To combat creeping socialism in Mexico, he continued, the private sector would have to organize.[8]

Oil Policy, Industrial Strategy, and Public Spending

When López Portillo accepted the presidential sash in 1976, he took responsibility for a deeply divided nation undergoing its worst financial crisis and economic recession in twenty years. Under Echeverría's administration, foreign debt ballooned from $4 billion to $20 billion, real growth came to a halt, and inflation reached 40 percent a year, very high for Mexico. Low private sector investment and approximately $4 billion in capital flight during Echeverría's tenure reflected the private sector's profound mistrust of the government and uncertainty about the economic environment. On top of Echeverría's abrupt expropriation of private land in the northern states of Sonora and Sinaloa in mid-1976, the devaluation on September 1, 1976, sparked rumors that bank accounts would be frozen or the banks nationalized, even that a military coup was imminent.

As López Portillo faced up to the tasks of his new office, his predecessor's legacy constrained him. He had to try to rebuild private sector confidence in the government while working within the guidelines of an IMF agreement Echeverría had signed. The political and economic crisis López Portillo inherited underscored the bankruptcy of the Mexican model of import substitution industrialization. But the prognosis for foreign exchange inflow from oil and loans presented an opportunity for change.

There were three positions within the government regarding how fast to develop Mexico's oil resources and how to include them in the goal of industrialization: the positions of the national populist

[8]Ibid., p. 472. Several Mexican authors have argued that the CIA was involved in the formation of the CCE and, beginning in 1973, in the rising politicization of the private sector (Miguel Basañez, *La lucha por la hegemonia en Mexico* [Mexico, D.F.: Siglo XXI, 1981], pp. 89–90; Saldívar, *Ideología y política del estado mexicano*, p. 196). Given what is known to have been large-scale CIA involvement in Chile during this same period, the argument is plausible. In any case, private sector opposition clearly existed before 1973, and U.S. intervention, if it existed, would at most have accelerated an established trend.

alliance and the bankers' alliance, and the position taken by "oil minister" Díaz Serrano to further his career within the bureaucracy. The national populist current took a "protectionist" view of oil development, the bankers' alliance favored a "contractionary" plan, and Díaz Serrano spearheaded an "expansionary" campaign intended to increase his power within the bureaucracy. He found a social constituency with the employees of the state-owned oil company, Pemex.[9] As head of Pemex, Díaz Serrano argued for the most rapid possible development of oil production capacity. He believed that oil export revenues would alleviate Mexico's chronic capital shortage—which according to him was the only thing constraining Mexican industrial growth.[10] The position Díaz Serrano took differed sharply from that taken by the previous administration. Although Echeverría had had information indicating the size of Mexican oil fields, he followed a "go-slow" policy. He chose not to publicize news of Mexico's oil wealth, believing that oil still in the ground was an important form of national insurance.

De Oteyza, López Portillo's minister of national patrimony and industry, opposed Díaz Serrano's preferred policy of rapid oil development. He and other opponents warned of "petrolization" of the economy. They thought the nation's industrial structure should be built up first, so that oil wealth could be assimilated without the ill effects of Arab-style petrolization. They argued Mexico should develop its own technology and industrial capacity to drill, pump, and refine oil. Rapid development would require contracting with foreign firms for work Mexico could hope to do itself within several years. This was the "protectionist" view held by the national populists.

In addition to wanting controlled oil development, the national populists called for using oil revenues to deepen import substitution in the short run, to expand manufactures exports in the long run, to support public spending, and to increase the size of the domestic market by increasing the share of wages in national income. Besides calling for continued protection for some sectors of industry, this current also called for tax reform, the maintenance of

[9]Vladimir Brailovsky and Terry Barker, "Recuento de la quiebra," *Nexos* 71 (1983), pp. 13–23.
[10]Antonio Yunez Naude, "Los dilemmas del desarollo compartido: La política económica de 1971 a 1976," *Trimestre Económico* 48 (1981), pp. 210–234.

123

a strong state role in the economy, and limits on foreign direct investment. These policy proposals reflected a structuralist, in some cases "post-Keynesian," economic logic: that the roots of stagflation are on the supply side and that an increase in public investment is the best way to overcome stagflation.

Inside the state the strongest proponents of this view were minister of patrimony de Oteyza and Carlos Tello, minister of the newly created Secretariat of Budget and Planning. The social constituency supporting their view included organized labor and small and medium-sized business. Concanaco and Canacintra came out in favor of the national populist line of using oil and public spending to industrialize and expand the domestic market slowly.

A third position on oil development and industrialization, that of the bankers' alliance, was "contractionary." The bankers' alliance argued that the oil boom should be restrained until inflation could be squeezed out of the economy. It called for increased international integration of the Mexican economy, including the reduction of trade barriers and the encouragement of foreign direct investment. Public spending, it argued, should be cut and the role of the state in the economy curtailed. Proponents of this view within the government were the head of the Central Bank, Romero Kolbeck, and minister of finance Moctezuma Cid. This was also the viewpoint of most large-scale businessmen in industry, commerce, and finance. Coparmex and the CCE argued for cutting public spending to control inflation and using oil revenue to expand nonoil export capacity.

The strictures of Mexico's 1976 IMF agreement bound López Portillo to adopt a "go-slow" position, at least in rhetoric. At the end of 1976, however, Pemex director Díaz Serrano announced plans to increase refining capacity 93 percent during the course of the *sexenio*. Production capacity would increase from 5.2 million metric tons to 18.6.[11] In practice, oil policy was biased in the fast-growth direction Díaz Serrano had pushed for.[12] It was common

[11]"Mexico Initiates Aggressive New Policy of Oil Exploration," *Business Latin America*, January 12, 1977, p. 11.

[12]For more on the oil debate see the special issues of *Foro Internacional* 18 (1978) and *El Economista Mexicano* 12 (1978). Also see Heberto Castillo, "Necesario plan nacional de energeticos," *El Economista Mexicano* 12 (1978); and Francisco Colmenares, *Petroleo y lucha de clases en Mexico, 1864–1982* (Mexico, D.F.: Ediciones Caballito, 1982).

for production goals to be reached early, as much as two years ahead of schedule. A 2.25-million-barrel-per-day ceiling was set in 1977 for the end of 1982. This level of production was reached in 1980. The government then raised the ceiling for year-end 1982 to 2.75 million. Production reached this ceiling by mid-1982 and surpassed it by 10 percent by the end of the year, despite oversupply in international oil markets.[13]

President López Portillo had ultimate authority over the oil policy decision, as over most economic policy, and he admits in retrospect that he chose the fast-production track in part because it would allow Mexico to increase its foreign borrowing. The link between developing oil production capacity and being able to benefit fully from cheap international loans was crucial. "We had to take the opportunity," said López Portillo in an interview. "Delaying the decision to use oil as the central force to finance development would have been cowardly and foolish. Not to do so [exploit oil reserves to their fullest] would have meant that we might never again have the opportunity to finance expansion. With oil exploitation slowed, no one would have lent us money."[14] Oil export would both bring in foreign exchange to finance Mexican growth and also call forth massive new inflows of foreign loans. In the context of excess global liquidity and the rapid growth of international lending, the foreign exchange benefit of rapid oil production was great. The enticement of being able to borrow heavily at the relatively low interest rates of the 1970s was an important argument for pursuing rapid development of Mexico's oil reserves.

Although the availability of foreign loans had encouraged López Portillo to follow Díaz Serrano and Pemex's desire to push ahead

[13]Dale Story, *Industry, the State and Public Policy in Mexico* (Austin: University of Texas Press, 1986), p. 169. Díaz Serrano's success in getting López Portillo to support unbridled expansion of Mexico's oil reserves and the advantage this gave Serrano in his closed-door campaign to succeed López Portillo led to considerable resentment within the bureaucracy. When Díaz Serrano cut oil prices in mid-1981 in response to the fall in international prices, preelection infighting led to his firing. Following a pattern of independent decision making, Díaz Serrano had discussed the decision to cut prices only with López Portillo. As one observer noted, "The Pemex chief had been caught out before on the same score, but his close ties to López Portillo helped deflect the talk generated by his independent style." In this case, however, his colleagues pushed for his resignation partly to eliminate competition for the presidential spot. ("Surprise Move at Pemex," *Business Latin America*, June 10, 1981, p. 177.)

[14]Interview reprinted in "Salvé al país del caos," *Excelsior*, July 26, 1984, pp. 1, 13–14.

full steam with oil production, the bankers' alliance still put up a fight to control the extent of public spending associated with rapid oil development. Its efforts were hindered by the partial erosion of its institutional base within the state. The Ministry of Finance's dominance over economic policy began to decline after 1970 as the two-term minister of finance, Ortiz Mena, and his two-term ally at the Central Bank, Rodrigo Gómez, left the government. Margáin's dismissal in 1973 was another blow to the position of the Finance Ministry within the bureaucratic hierarchy. The creation of the Ministry of Budget and Planning in 1976 introduced more contention over the locus of economic policy making.[15] Budget and Planning was charged with controlling public spending, and an entire section of the Finance Ministry was moved intact to the new ministry. The creation of Budget and Planning introduced tensions because Budget and Planning became responsible for formulating spending policy, which the previously hegemonic Finance Ministry would then oversee. In a defensive move in 1977 Finance created a General Directorate of Treasury Planning, with Undersecretary Miguel de la Madrid in charge. This subsecretariat competed directly with Budget and Planning.

These institutional tensions were aggravated by López Portillo's appointment of ideologically opposed ministers to head the competing ministries. The president appointed national populist Tello to head Budget and Planning and monetarist Moctezuma Cid to head Finance. Tension came to a head within the first year of the administration. In the fall of 1977 a dispute erupted over the 1978 budget. Tello, following a structuralist economic interpretation, called for an increase in public spending to eliminate inflation caused by supply side bottlenecks to help expand the domestic market, and to increase social welfare. He proposed expanding the money supply and liberally supporting all state-owned enterprises with central government funds. His proposed budget amounted to 900 billion pesos. Moctezuma Cid, on the other hand, called for an austere budget in order to meet IMF guidelines. He proposed a budget of 780 billion pesos, limiting the money supply to IMF ceilings and supporting Pemex while contracting funds transferred to all other state-owned enterprises.

[15]For more on the history of Budget and Planning see John J. Bailey, "Presidency, Bureaucracy and Administrative Reform in Mexico," *Inter-American Economic Affairs* 34 (1980), pp. 27–59.

López Portillo explained the situation in an interview: "I chose the people I thought were best fit for these posts. . . . [U]nfortunately they didn't agree in fundamental ways about the responsibilities I gave them. . . . They didn't present me with alternatives but rather methodological and informational problems which made intelligent decision-making impossible. . . . [A]s a consequence I had to ask for their resigations."[16]

Firing these two ministers did not resolve the tensions between the two policy currents.[17] Tello complained that de facto the monetarist current had won the battle and Moctezuma Cid claimed the reverse. In fact, although the planned budget was closer to Moctezuma's position, actual public expenditure in 1978 reached the level Tello had proposed.[18] Replacing Tello at Budget and Planning was García Sainz, a former business leader with considerable government experience. Unlike Tello, he had the trust of many businessmen. Yet he lasted only a year in the position, resigning in early 1979 after being publicly rebuked for failing to fund priority public sector projects.

Foreign Loans and Devaluation Delay

Chapter 3 outlines how part of the Mexican economic policy pattern is a commitment to foreign exchange stability and convertibility. It has been Mexican government policy to overcome public fear of devaluation and consequent dollarization and capital flight by intervening in the exchange market to guarantee the peso's value. However, the commitment to exchange stability introduced rigidity in exchange policy and encouraged a pattern of foreign

[16]Interview reprinted in "Salvé al país del caos," *Excelsior*, July 26, 1984, pp. 1, 12–13. Tello and Moctezuma Cid both had close ties to López Portillo. Both worked for him during the Díaz Ordaz (1964–1970) years, when he was head of the Commission of Public Administration of the Secretariat of the Presidency—essentially the precursor of the Budget and Planning Ministry. Tello was undersecretary of revenue at Finance when López Portillo was the minister (1973–1976).

[17]For more on this episode see Carlos Marín, "Seís años en busca del rumbo y del equipo," *Proceso* 314 (1982), pp. 6–12; Rodolfo Guzman, "Pero cuál es la ruta económica?" *Proceso* 55 (1977), pp. 6–8; Rodolfo Guzman and Carlos Ramírez, "La omnipotencia presidencial en el origen de la crisis," *Proceso* 56 (1977), pp. 6–10; Miguel López Azuara, "El presidente se fortalece, la presidencia se debilita," *Proceso* 133 (1979), p. 6; and "How Mexico's Opposition Defines the Debate over Economic Policy," *Business Latin America*, July 29, 1981, p. 233.

[18]"Recibe la Cámara un presupuesto 'tellista,'" *Proceso* 59 (1977), p. 23.

borrowing to delay devaluation. The negative impact of a such a policy on industrialization efforts in the context of the internationalization of finance is clear in the pattern of foreign exchange allocation in Mexico in the late 1970s. The public sector maintained a positive balance of payments through foreign borrowing, whereas the private sector maintained a negative balance. Under conditions of complete exchange freedom and limited import controls between 1978 and 1981, the Mexican government's policy of supporting the value of the peso amounted to subsidizing the price of foreign exchange.

As Table 10 indicates, the public and private sectors generated roughly equal shares of foreign exchange in 1978. By 1982 the public sector generated 65 percent of Mexican foreign exchange, whereas the private sector generated only 35 percent. The public sector's foreign exchange earnings rose absolutely and relatively. Although the public sector provided an increasing share of foreign exchange through borrowing and export earnings, it consumed a declining share of foreign exchange, transferring the surplus to the private sector. The Mexican state essentially transferred dollars to

Table 10. Sources and uses of foreign exchange, 1978–1982 (percentages)

	1978	1979	1980	1981	1982
Public Sources	48	53	49	64	65
Exports	12*	17	30	26	40
Borrowing	35	37	20	37	35
Private Sources	52	47	51	36	35
Exports	45	36	34	25	29
Borrowing	6	10	17	11	5
Public Uses	49	49	40	33	33
Imports	15	13	17	15	10
Debt payments	32	32	20	17	27
Private Uses	51	51	60	67	67
Imports	40	29	44	40	36
Debt payments	11	9	10	10	10
Errors and omissions	0	0	5	14	15

*Subcategories may not add up to main totals because lesser subcategories are not listed.
Source: Data provided by the Central Bank.

the private sector through Central Bank interventions, which supported an increasingly overvalued exchange rate.[19]

As early as 1978 the Mexican peso was considered overvalued in relation to the U.S. dollar. In the following three years the foreign exchange bonanza put more upward pressure on the peso. In that period the peso appreciated at least 34 percent.[20] A 4 percent slide in the peso's value during 1981 was clearly insufficient to correct this overvaluation. The Central Bank spent increasingly large amounts of foreign exchange to intervene in the market to support the peso's value. The need for devaluation of the Mexican peso began to be mentioned by international bankers in 1978. Fearing financial crisis the bankers' alliance began to bring pressure to bear domestically in 1980. By late 1980 finance minister Ibarra and Central Bank director Romero Kolbeck began to press President López Portillo to devalue. They were opposed in the economic cabinet by the future (but still undesignated) president, de la Madrid, then minister of budget and planning, and de Oteyza, minister of patrimony and industry. De Oteyza was a key government actor in the national populist alliance, which was pushing at the time for exchange rate controls rather than devaluation.

Throughout the first half of 1981 there was a continuous debate about the extent to which the Mexican economy was overheated and about the role of growth-induced inflation in causing overvaluation and the sluggish performance of Mexico's nonoil exports. Two Cambridge University post-Keynesian economists wrote a long, technical article de Oteyza and other structuralists in the government used as ammunition against the bankers' alliance proposal for slower growth and devaluation.[21] On the other hand, the Asociación Nacional de Importadores y Exportadores de la República Mexicana (Mexican Association of Importers and Exporters, or Anierm), Concamin, CCE's research and investigation division, and Canacintra of Nuevo Leon, for example, all called for a slowdown in economic growth as the only way to combat inflation.

---

[19]Lance Taylor, "La crisis y su porvenir: Problemas de política macroeconómica," *Investigación Económica* 170 (1984), p. 292.

[20]Taylor, "La crisis y su porvenir," p. 294.

[21]John Eatwell and Ajit Singh, "Se encuentra sobrecalentada la economía mexicana?" mimeo, 1981. This report is described in the *New York Times*, October 24, 1982. See also *Expansion*, August 5, 1981, p. 23.

Inflation, they argued, was making the peso overvalued. José Luis Coindreau, then president of Coparmex, called for a "total change in economic policy."[22]

Ibarra and Romero Kolbeck pressed the issue of devaluation with more urgency when oil prices fell in mid-1981. Instead of devaluing, however, López Portillo took de Oteyza's suggestion of correcting the international accounts imbalance by increasing the number of items covered by import licenses and further subsidizing exports.[23] To placate Ibarra and Romero Kolbeck, López Portillo agreed to increase the peso's slide to 14 percent for the second half of 1981, up from 10 percent in the first half. A 4 percent cut in the government budget and an increase in domestic interest rates were also announced.

Throughout the rest of 1981 Ibarra and Romero Kolbeck continued to push for devaluation as it became apparent that the other measures were proving ineffective in correcting the trade imbalance, controlling inflation, and halting capital flight. Divisions within the cabinet grew. As overvaluation increased, capital flight mounted, rising from $2.5 billion in the first half of 1981 to $8.5 billion in the second half.[24] Between April and December 1981 capital flight equaled two-thirds of new foreign debt contracted.

In 1981 and the first half of 1982 the transfer of resources from the public to the private sector became increasingly politicized. A declaration by two major independent unions claimed that the public sector had subsidized 46 percent of private sector foreign exchange expenditure.[25] Although the estimate may be incorrect, denunciations of this type reflected the increasingly obvious extent of capital flight and Banco de Mexico expense in dollars used to inter-

[22]In May 1981 *Expansion*, a business magazine representing the views of large-scale industry and commerce, complained about discrepancies implicit in the Ministry of Patrimony and Industry and the Central Bank's analyses of the cause of Mexico's apparent lack of international competitiveness. The Central Bank placed blame on inflation and peso overvaluation. De Oteyza, on the other hand, called this analysis simplistic. The article called de Oteyza's assertions disconcerting, noting the doubt generated about government capacity to run the economy when "a minister of state calls the Central Bank simplistic." (*Expansion*, May 27, 1981, pp. 18–19.)

[23]For more on this increase in tariff protection see Bela Balassa, "Trade Policy in Mexico," *World Development* 11 (1983), p. 805; and "Mexico Raises Some Tariffs," *Business Latin America*, May 27, 1981, p. 168.

[24]Carlos Tello, *La nacionalización de la banca* (Mexico, D.F.: Siglo XXI, 1984), p. 77.

[25]Clemente Ruíz Durán, *90 dias de política monetaria y crediticia independiente* (Puebla: Universidad Autonoma de Puebla, 1984), p. 47.

vene in the currency market. The national populists wanted exchange controls to guarantee equitable distribution of foreign exchange.[26]

While labor exerted pressure publicly, Ibarra and Romero Kolback continued to exert their pressures in private meetings with López Portillo.[27] But the fall in oil prices and the urgency it lent to the need for devaluation came at a time when López Portillo felt he could not afford to suffer a loss of prestige and presidential power. He needed power to be able to impose his choice for president (the *destapado*) from among the various possible candidates, each with a particular constituency. Ibarra and budget and planning minister de la Madrid were competing to be the president's choice of successor. Ironically, whereas Ibarra stressed bad news and the need for devaluation, de la Madrid's way of campaigning was to be optimistic, stressing that the oil price fall was only temporary and therefore a devaluation was unnecessary.[28] López Portillo found de la Madrid's position convenient. He stressed two reasons for not devaluing: his belief, supported by de la Madrid, that he could overcome the financial crisis without it, and his fear that both he personally, and the political system generally, would lose power and prestige:

> I did everything humanly possible to avoid devaluation. I delayed day after day thinking the country would recover before it was emptied of dollars. Devaluation hits Mexicans psychologically. It is a problem of national dignity, not financial adjustment. . . . I grew tired during my administration of saying that the fixed dollar parity

[26]Interview with Ajit Singh, September 1987.

[27]When one somewhat naive government official pushed the issue at a meeting attended by fifty government officials, he was soundly trounced by Ibarra and Romero Kolbeck. He had expected them to support his push for devaluation and was rudely surprised. They explained to him later that his tactics had been wrong: "You didn't understand that you can't corner the President publicly, much less on such a sensitive issue. . . . If López Portillo had even let the overvaluation of the peso be discussed, several people would have left the meeting directly to buy dollars and spread the word of imminent devaluation. It could have created a panic which would have led to uncontrollable devaluation." (Lajous, "Quien la manejó," p. 7.)

[28]For more on the 1982 succession see "Mexico Starts to Zero in on Issues and Candidates for Presidental Choice," *Business Latin America*, July 8, 1981, p. 213. Other candidates besides Ibarra and de la Madrid included labor minister Ojeda Paullada; commerce minister de la Vega Domínguez; interior minister Oliveres Santana; Moctezuma Cid, who took over Pemex when Díaz Serrano was fired; and Garcia Paniagua, head of the PRI.

had ceased to be a necessary condition of progress and stability. . . . Yet I was tremendously anxious to avoid the political weakness of devaluing before the Presidential succession. . . . I didn't want to weaken the political system with a devaluation when there only remained a few months before the choice of my successor. . . . I thought I could straighten out the nation's finances without need for devaluation.[29]

López Portillo ordered Romero Kolbeck not to raise the issue during cabinet meetings and stipulated that it be discussed only in private, secret meetings between the two of them. Not even Ibarra was to be informed. Romero Kolbeck soon found it increasingly difficult to get an appointment to see the president. At a semipublic meeting in early February 1982 López Portillo complained bitterly that it seemed as though the close of the presidential term inevitably brought with it lack of confidence in the president. Obviously referring to Romero Kolbeck and Ibarra, López Portillo complained that even his closest collaborators were questioning his judgment.

By this time Central Bank reserves were almost gone as a result of interventions to support the peso's value. Finally, in mid-February López Portillo authorized Romero Kolbeck to stop intervening in the market and let the peso float downward. Although he fired Ibarra and Romero Kolbeck to try to deflect some of the political fallout from the move, he himself accepted a considerable portion of the blame, in part to try to regain private sector confidence. "I know," he said in a speech before a meeting of Concanaco, "that a president who devalues, is devalued; without doubt this devalued president has faults and defects and has committed errors, he may not have the right—but does have reasons—to make a solemn and formal petition to the class here represented. I ask that you help us manage the current situation."[30]

Foreign loans allowed López Portillo to delay devaluing the peso. This delay contributed to financial instability and fueled capital flight. The bankers' alliance had hoped to prevent financial instability by pressuring for devaluation. The national populists focused

[29]Interview reprinted in "Salvé al país del caos," *Excelsior*, July 26, 1984, pp. 1, 13–14.
[30]Carlos Ramírez, "La salida de Ibarra, consumación de la quiebra del desarollismo," *Proceso* 281 (1982), pp. 5–10.

on the way overvaluation effectively subsidized capital flight and lobbied for exchange controls. The multiple pressures on López Portillo and within his cabinet led to policy paralysis. Neither the bankers' alliance nor the national populists were able to achieve the policy changes they desired.

Industrial Planning

Industrial planning was another area of policy conflict; in this case the bankers' alliance was somewhat more successful in attaining policy modifications than it was in the public spending fight during the Echeverría administration or in the oil development strategy and devaluation debates just outlined. Industrial planning became an issue shortly after López Portillo's inauguration, when López Portillo announced an Alliance for Production with labor and business. Heralded as a new form of planning—"negotiated" (*concertada*) rather than indicative planning—it involved developing a series of sector-specific industrialization targets.[31] The Alliance amounted to a series of general statements of intent by private sector organizations to involve 140 companies in increasing investment in ten branches of industry.[32] The private sector was not bound to these agreements; nor were government incentives spelled out in detail.[33]

Part of the problem in making the Alliance stick was the wide divergence of opinion within the government about what the appropriate public and private roles should be in national develop-

---

[31]Jose Reveles, "Podrán bailar sin codazos ni pistones, predice de Oteyza," *Proceso* 127 (1979), p. 6.

[32]Accords were signed in several sectors. In mining, private sector companies agreed to make 4 billion pesos worth of new investments under the Alliance. In petrochemicals and autos, they agreed to 1 billion pesos each. López Portillo also courted northern agro-industrialists and agro-exporters in an effort to bring them back into the PRI's fold after the traumatic 1976 land expropriation. Satisfied with the indemnization López Portillo gave them, a group of leading Sonora and Sinaloa businessmen eventually signed an Alliance for Production accord agreeing to make 600 million pesos worth of new investments.

[33]For more on the Alliance for Production see John Weiss, "Alliance for Production: Mexico's Incentives for Private Sector Industrial Development," *World Development* 12 (1984), pp. 723–742; *Business Latin America*, March 2, 1977; *Proceso* 75 (1978), p. 25; Robert E. Looney, *Economic Policymaking in Mexico* (Durham, N.C.: Duke University Press, 1985), p. 134; and Daniel Bitrán, "Rasgos sobresalientes de la economía y de la política económica de Mexico en el umbral de los ochenta," *El Trimestre Económico* 50 (1983), pp. 60–65.

ment. The national populist current, represented by Tello, believed the Alliance was a trick to get workers to accept lower wages. "This alliance," he said, "has basically been supported by workers who have limited their wage demands. The responsibility of businessmen is to invest and create employment. . . . I feel this hasn't been done. The commercial sector hasn't lived up to its side of the bargain. There is still speculation. . . . This alliance has limited possibilities for success."[34]

Tello believed public sector investment had to grow because the nation could not expect the private sector to cooperate in industrialization efforts. Moctezuma Cid, on the other hand, believed the private sector should be allowed to, and would, take the lead in industrialization. He argued that the Alliance for Production had a great chance of success.

Tension between the national populists and the monetarists over industrial planning was also evident in the formulation and implementation of the March 1979 Industrial Plan. A plan for using oil revenues, written under the direction of de Oteyza at the Ministry of Patrimony, it reflected a partial victory for the national populists. However, opposition from businessmen in the bankers' alliance to the plan's potentially obligatory nature resulted in weak implementation. The plan's major goal was to use oil revenue for industrial development. It aimed to increase production of basic consumer and capital goods, to decentralize industrial activity away from Mexico City, and to promote small and medium-sized entrepreneurs. The plan named seventy priority industries (accounting at the time for 60 percent of national value added) that would be eligible for government support.[35] Government instruments would include fiscal incentives, direct and indirect subsidies of finance and industrial inputs, and government purchase orders.

[34]Rodolfo Guzman, "Pero cuál es la ruta económica?" *Proceso* 55 (1977), p. 7.
[35]The seventy priority industrial branches were divided into two preference categories: (1) agro-industry and capital goods, including steel and cement, and (2) consumer durables/nondurables and intermediate goods, including textiles, shoes, soap, paper, appliances, furniture, parts and engines for transport vehicles, petrochemicals, metallurgical products, and construction materials. One of the major problems with the plan was that it assumed no problems in stimulating such a broad array of different industries. For more see *Comercio Exterior* 25 (1979); Secretaría de Presupuesto y Planificación, *Plan nacional de desarrollo industrial* (Mexico, D.F.: SPP, 1979); and Francisco Javier Alejo, "Las empresas publicas y el plan industrial," *El Economista Mexicano* 13 (November–December 1979).

Large-scale businessmen in the bankers' alliance had two major criticisms of the plan. They denounced it for increasing the government's role in the economy and for involving mandatory private sector performance levels. Business saw the mandatory nature of the plan as most threatening and lobbied hard, and successfully, against it.

The original implementation phase of the plan began with creation of an interministerial Industrial Development Commission to coordinate all decisions related to the plan. The commission would develop "growth programs" for each prioritized industrial branch. In these programs, firms would agree to specific goals for investment, production, prices, exports, and integration with national suppliers. In return they would receive specified incentives and protection. The plan stated that "incentives must be granted in line with commitments and once agreed upon, they can be mandatory." Any firms found in noncompliance were subject to suspension of all incentives and "to the application of predetermined sanctions."[36]

After the plan was announced, leaders of the CCE, Coparmex, and Concamin campaigned against the government's applying mandatory goals to private sector firms. In a variety of public forums, bankers' alliance business leaders argued that the state should not impose its own objectives on private capital. In October 1980 López Portillo conceded that the plan would be binding only for public sector firms.

The evolution of the Global Development Plan (PGD) and its contrast with the Industrial Plan also reflects conflict between the two policy currents over industrial planning. The PGD, published in 1980, was a transformed version of a report Tello oversaw during his one year as minister of budget and planning. Tello's report, "Program for Public Action 1978–1982," outlined a strategy "based fundamentally on production of goods and services that are nationally and socially necessary." It stressed achieving food self-sufficiency and increasing production of wage goods—clothes, shoes, food, medicine, and consumer durables. It suggested the state increase participation in commercialization and distribution to facilitate price control for wage goods.[37]

---

[36]Story, *Industry, the State and Public Policy in Mexico*, p. 187.
[37]Carlos Marin, "En 1977 Programación y Presupuesto advirtió: El sistema a punto de estallar," *Proceso* 71 (1978), pp. 16–17.

When García Sainz took over at Budget and Planning, he decided to expand the report, including more emphasis on private sector participation. When de la Madrid replaced Sainz in 1979, he set about rewriting the plan yet again. The final version, published in April 1980, was more a rhetorical document than a technical program. In its final version the PGD placed greater reliance on the private sector and called for a more limited public sector role than the Industrial Plan had.[38]

The history of the PGD provides a typical example of the way the pressure of competing policy currents stymied public policy during the López Portillo administration. Despite the plan's nod in the direction of monetarist ideology through its reduction of the proposed public sector investment role, its ultimate author, de la Madrid, still publicly supported the national populist view of inflation and public spending. He believed it was necessary to combat inflation from the supply side as well as the demand side: "It is possible to achieve growth and diminish inflation." "Without sufficient public spending," he argued, "it will not be possible to attack bottlenecks and promote production and employment. . . . Lower public spending will retard production and social welfare programs in the coming years, we will lose time indispensable for preparing the economy to absorb oil wealth."[39]

Financiers and large-scale businessmen in the bankers' alliance saw the PGD as the result of a bureaucratic compromise between the two policy currents. They believed that de la Madrid, whom they otherwise tended to support, had compromised with the national populists in the administration. As a result, their support of de la Madrid's presidential candidacy in 1982 was moderate and cautious.[40]

Ironically, while private sector members of the bankers' alliance criticized the Plan from the "right," a group of national populists within the National Congress of Economists criticized it from the

[38]For example, the Industrial Plan called for 17.5 percent growth in public sector investment between 1980 and 1982 whereas the Global Development Plan called for only 14 percent.
[39]José Luis Ceceña Cervantes et al., *Planes sin planificación* (Mexico, D.F.: Proceso, 1980), p. 52.
[40]Saúl Escobar, "Rifts in the Mexican Power Elite, 1976–1986," in Sylvia Maxfield and Ricardo Anzaldúa, eds., *Government and Private Sector in Contemporary Mexico* (La Jolla: Center for U.S.-Mexican Studies, University of California–San Diego, 1987), pp. 776–777.

"left." The Congress, an association of professional economists that functioned partly as a government lobby group, was bitterly divided over whether or not to support the Global Development Plan. Critics drafted their own alternative report. They accused the PGD of favoring the private sector while ignoring the problems of workers. Their report set forth a series of hard-line nationalist recommendations, including the creation of a bigger role for the state and for labor, breaking the concentration of economic power and wealth among Mexican entrepreneurs and foreign investors, extending price controls, pushing land reform forward, and nationalizing the pharmaceuticals industry.[41]

In four policy debates—over public spending in the second half of the Echeverría administration, oil development strategy and public spending during the López Portillo administration, devaluation in 1981–1982, and industrial policy between 1976 and 1982—the story is one of confict and often stalemate between the national populists and the bankers' alliance. Just as the international financial situation strengthened the bankers' alliance in the 1950s, it weakened it in the 1970s. Foreign exchange was abundant and easy to get; the power the bankers' alliance gained in the 1950s from its role as international-loan-negotiating intermediary declined. Although the bankers' alliance was less likely to be able to impose its policy preferences, its decline in power did not guarantee that the national populists would be able to do so either. The result was often stalemate.

Policy Paralysis Evident in Public Sector Finances

The overall pattern of government income and expenditure in the 1970s, shown in Table 11, highlights how foreign borrowing substituted for the politically difficult alternative of increasing private sector taxes, reducing state subsidies, or more dramatically reorienting capital accumulation through lowered protection, as the bankers' alliance often suggested, or massive redistribution of wealth and income, which the national populists called for.

Three important trends stand out on the income side of the public sector balance sheet. First is a dramatic decline in the value of

[41]"Mexico's Report Card on Global Plan Gains Shows Positive Trends," *Business Latin America*, June 24, 1981, p. 195.

Table 11. Public income and expenditure, 1977–1981 (percentage of total income or expenditure)

	1977	1978	1979	1980	1981
Public Income					
Internal	72	70	64	66	55
Taxes	38*	38	59	48	41
State-owned enterprise (SOE) sales	23	23	19	18	13
External	28	30	36	34	45
Exports	5	8	11	19	18
Borrowing	21	21	23	13	26
Public Expenditure					
Internal	77	74	71	77	80
Interest	3	3	3	4	5
Personnel	24	22	20	19	17
Investment	21	24	35	50	30
External	23	26	28	23	20
Interest and amortization	14	16	20	11	10
Imports	8	8	8	10	8

*Subcategories do not add up to main totals because lesser subcategories are not listed.

Source: Data provided by the office of the Director General de Información e Evaluación Hacendaria, Secretaría de Hacienda y Crédito Público.

state-owned enterprise (SOE) sales as a portion of government income. Table 11 shows that they fell from 23 percent to 13 percent of internal income between 1977 and 1981. This decline reflects a subsidized price structure for SOE goods and services, with tremendous costs in forgone government revenue.

As oil exports became increasingly central to the Mexican economy, the cost in forgone income of keeping domestic oil prices below international prices rose. This subsidy was an explicit part of the Industrial Plan, under which private sector investment in priority sectors would be encouraged through low-cost state supply of inputs such as energy and transport. The foreign exchange bonanza kept the issue of SOE pricing policy off the agenda. Had foreign loans been scarce, the government would have been forced to consider revising SOE pricing policy. Since the sales of goods and services by SOEs represented a major source of public sector revenue, their pricing policy and cost structure directly influenced government solvency.[42]

[42]As mentioned in chapter 3, the 1972 tax reform effort began as an effort to raise SOE prices. In the end neither SOE pricing nor the tax structure was reformed. See Looney, *Economic Policymaking in Mexico*, p. 59.

In 1978, for instance, the difference between the domestic and international prices for state-produced oil, gas, and electricity equaled $5 billion, one-third of total internal government income in that year.[43] A study by Socrates Rizzo details how Pemex transferred resources to other SOEs and to the gas-consuming public through subsidized prices. In 1980 total domestic sales revenues for Pemex amounted to 95 billion pesos valued at domestic prices and $446 billion valued at international prices, which means that domestic consumers received a 79 percent subsidy. Using the difference between domestic and international prices to determine the total subsidy and analyzing Pemex's sales structure, Rizzo calculated the distribution of Pemex's implicit subsidy throughout the economy by sectors; 24 percent went to transport and 38 percent to industry, with only 11 percent going to households. Both transport and industry are capital intensive, leading Rizzo to conclude that Pemex's pricing policy further biased the Mexican economy toward capital-intensive activities.[44]

The SOE drain on government finances reflected an official policy, outlined in the 1979 Industrial Plan, of stimulating priority industrial sectors through public purchasing, direct subsidies, and indirect subsidies by way of SOE provision of inexpensive inputs.[45] Subsidies and transfer payments totaled 7 percent of GDP in 1977; by 1981 they had risen to 15 percent. Government pricing and subsidy policy transferred resources to the private sector in a way that especially favored a small group of large conglomerates. Between 1977 and 1979 ten economic groups received almost 20 percent of all government subsidies, fiscal exemptions, and development funds.[46] One Mexican economist estimates that the percentage of public spending going to support private sector investment hovered around 33 percent during the oil boom.[47] In 1979

---

[43]*Comercio Exterior* 31 (1981), p. 507.

[44]Socrates Rizzo, "Generation and Allocation of Oil Economic Surpluses," in Pedro Aspe and Paul Sigmund, eds., *The Political Economy of Distribution in Mexico* (New York: Holmes and Meier, 1985), p. 122. Data from the Finance Ministry comparing domestic and international energy prices for 1984 show that the domesic price subsidy ranged from 60 percent per liter of gasoline to 69 percent per kilowatt of electricity to 22 percent per cubic meter of natural gas.

[45]Eduardo Jacobs and Wilson Perez Nuñez, "Las grandes empresas y el crecimiento acelerado," *Economía Mexicana* 4 (1982), pp. 99–113.

[46]José Manuel Quijano, *La banca: Pasado y presente* (Mexico, D.F.: CIDE, 1983), p. 273.

[47]Interview with Carlos Rozo, Mexico City, May 1984.

Secretary of Industry de Oteyza complained that a figure equal to half the nation's expected oil income in 1980–1982 would be spent on subsidies to the private sector.[48] "The growing transfer of public resources to the private sector," write two other Mexican economists, "through low prices for public goods and services . . . signified a vertical transfer of oil funds from the public to private sector."[49]

The Global Development Plan included a general reference to restructuring energy prices but gave no details. At the same time the plan indicated that the state would use energy, transport, and communications subsidies to the private sector as one of the tools of industrial policy.[50] This ambiguity in government policy is highlighted in a statement by industry minister de Oteyza. "The idea," he said, "is to adjust prices to close the gap with international prices. But we are going to do it slowly, so that it doesn't create more problems than it solves."[51]

The second important trend in government financing is that although tax income grew, it rose erratically from a very low base, while public spending rose considerably faster. A key change in the Mexican·tax structure is that Pemex tax income rose as a percentage of overall tax income while general consumption and income tax fell. The average annual growth for Pemex taxes was 99 percent between 1977 and 1981; growth for both consumption and income taxes was only 35 percent, although the latter did grow absolutely.

Finally, as Table 11 shows, between 1977 and 1981 internal government income fell from 72 percent of total public income to 55 percent, with external income sources rising from 28 percent to 45 percent. Internal government income grew at an annual average of 28 percent while the growth of external income almost doubled that amount. Exports, mostly oil, account for 44 percent of the total five-year increase in external government income, and foreign borrowing, two-thirds of it by Pemex, accounts for the other 66 percent of the increase.

As government income came increasingly from external sources, the relationship between internal and external expenditure re-

[48]Judith Gentleman, *Mexican Oil Development* (New York: Peter Lang, 1984), p. 134.
[49]Jacobs and Perez Nuñez, "Las grandes empresas y el crecimiento acelerado," p. 17.
[50]Ceceña Cervantes et al., *Planes sin planificación*, p. 183.
[51]Reveles, "Podrán bailer sin codazos ni pistones, predice de Oteyza," p. 6.

mained relatively constant. As a result, the international payments account deteriorated rapidly. The public deficit went from 5 percent of GDP in 1977 to 14 percent in 1981 as the external balance of payments deficit declined. This deficit reflected government policy of turning external liabilities into peso liabilities, partly through the creation of so-called Mexdollars, dollar-denominated peso deposits in Mexican banks. Using foreign exchange revenue to support the peso was simply one of many ways in which the Mexican economy grew increasingly dependent on oil exports.

Both the policy debates outlined earlier in this chapter and the trends in state finances just surveyed highlight aspects of the interaction between changes in international financial markets and the domestic politics of economic policy making. Instead of reorienting domestic policy to cope with changes in the world economy and financial system, the Mexican government borrowed to buy time. Foreign loans allowed the government to continue selling the private sector artificially low-cost state-produced inputs. Together with the revenues from oil exports, loans hid the need for tax reform or any other measures that would increase the state's domestic income base.

Conclusion

Mexico's historical economic policy patterns left the government relatively ill equipped to control the negative side effects of international financial integration on industrial growth. The internationalization of finance, in turn, worked against economic policy adjustments that would have been necessary to optimize the return from liberal financial policies and internationalization. Access to foreign loans reduced the urgency for policy change. It weakened the bankers' alliance in the short run by temporarily undermining the rationale for monetary restraint. Although the bankers' alliance lost battles over public spending and exchange rates, its institutional base remained largely intact. The power over economic policy that this base gives the bankers' alliance is evident in the policy issues kept off the agenda in this period: financial regulation and exchange controls. Even when the banks were nationalized and exchange controls imposed, the bankers' alliance was able to limit and in some cases reverse the policy impact. But that is the story of the next chapter.

6

The Bankers' Alliance and the Mexican Bank Nationalization

The Mexican bank nationalization was a defensive, last-resort measure declared when Mexico's president felt *accoralado por los hechos* (cornered by events). Although it highlights the power of the Mexican presidency, it reveals how the division between national populist and bankers' coalitions hinders policy implementation. The nationalization decision reflected the temporary revenge of the national populists. As this chapter describes, the decision was made in frustration over declining state capacity to induce and guide industrial investment. Economic advisers sympathetic to national populist ideals linked this declining state control over allocation of economic resources to the internationally facilitated accumulation of wealth and power by financial-industrial conglomerates. The nationalization was a belated effort to implement policies that would help the government manage international financial integration, including exchange controls, state guidance of bank credit allocation, and the breakup of financial-industrial conglomerates.

Architects of the nationalization intended to break the power of financial-industrial conglomerates, increase state control over investment patterns, and improve the state's financial position. But the influence of the bankers' alliance hindered effective implementation of the nationalization decree. The weight of private bankers and their business and government allies is evident in disputes about the terms of indemnization for the former bank owners, the extent of reprivatization, and the duration of exchange controls

142

imposed along with the bank nationalization. This chapter details these aspects of the nationalization policy implementation, suggesting that, without fundamental changes in domestic structures, the nationalization decree could not achieve the lofty goals its architects set for it. The nationalization decree did not break the power of the financial-industrial conglomerates, increase state control over investment patterns through credit allocation, or improve the state's financial position.

The Nationalization Decision

As chapter 4 suggests, the combination of Mexico's historic economic policy patterns and international financial integration heightened the differentiation between small and medium-sized industry and large-scale commercial-industrial-financial groups. This differentiation provided a material basis for a growing dispute between policy currents. Furthermore, easy access to foreign loans eroded the institutional hegemony of the Finance Ministry–Central Bank alliance, leading to increased competition between stability- and industrialization-oriented wings of the state. As we saw in chapter 5, easy access to foreign exchange in the 1980s also weakened the bankers' alliance and contributed to a series of policy conflicts and stalemates between the bankers alliance and the national populist coalition. Architects of the 1982 nationalization saw it as a way to resolve the "fight for the nation" in favor of the populist vision.

In March 1982 López Portillo asked several advisers, including his longtime associate, Carlos Tello, and then head of the Ministry of Commerce and Industry, de Oteyza, to prepare a study of policy options for confronting the nation's financial crisis. Although Tello had been out of the cabinet since his resignation as planning minister in 1977, he had maintained a close relationship with the president. Simultaneously, a study group was set up in France under Mexican ambassador Flores de la Peña to evaluate Mitterrand's nationalization of the French banks. Flores de la Peña was labor minister for President Echeverría and is a "left-wing" economist and self-described socialist who taught at the Universidad Nacional Autónoma (UNAM) in the 1960s. Tello and de Oteyza were among his students there. Tello also studied economics in East Germany

143

and with Joan Robinson at Cambridge University. This academic background gave his economic views an unorthodox tint.

The authors of the nationalization decree defined their task in reaction to the internationally facilitated accumulation of wealth and power by private sector financial groups. Their argument for nationalization rested on the claim that the bankers' power challenged state command of the economic heights. The international integration of Mexican financial markets had created new short-term investment opportunities for capitalists and had fueled financial speculation. Incentives for short-term financial investment undermined state capacity to induce and guide new capital formation. Nationalizing the banks would break the political and economic power of Mexican bankers and of the large-scale industrialists with whom they were associated.

Architects of the nationalization and some sectors of civil society, including the more independent labor unions and intellectuals, believed that the internationalization of finance had spurred the bankers to excessively antisocial behavior. It had heightened *la disputa por la nación*. The nationalization was meant to help resolve the struggle over national economic strategy in favor of a "nationalist workers' project" instead of business's "neoliberal project."[1]

Expropriating the banks would allow the government to regain its lost control over the national financial system and would attach the financial sector to the goal of economic restructuring. A prominent left-wing economist summarizes this argument neatly: "If, in the past, the president and the government were increasingly helpless in the face of bankers and businessmen in general, with the internationalization of banking . . . the possibilities for sovereign action . . . were further limited. . . . In the absence of bank internationalization, the conflict would not have been the political conflict . . . that led to the nationalization."[2]

In June 1982, two months before the nationalization, the director of the National Banking and Exchange Commission exhorted Mexican bankers to act with "social" responsibility. He anony-

---

[1] See Carlos Tello, *La nacionalización de la banca* (Mexico, D.F.: Siglo XXI, 1984), and Rolando Cordera and Carlos Tello, *La disputa por la nación* (Mexico, D.F.: Siglo XXI, 1981). "Neoliberal" in the Latin American context refers to orthodox monetary policies such as those applied with textbook rigor in Argentina and Chile during the late 1970s.

[2] José Blanco, "La banca que quedó," *Nexos* 82 (1983), pp. 49–52.

mously criticized one "elitist bank in the service of a few privileged individuals which does not deserve to exist."[3] A little more than one week before the nationalization, the president of the Mexican Bankers Association implicitly admitted to the banks' "antisocial" behavior by suggesting they might consider creating a subsidized financing fund with the profits generated by exchange speculation and dollarization.[4] A former banker, citing the case of one of Mexico's two largest banks, admitted when interviewed shortly after the expropriation that the banks "had become greedy. . . . When Agustin's [Legoretta] father was alive, the bank [Banamex] tried to create at least one major business concern a year. But for the last five years it did not create one job. It bought up shares in existing companies. It created nothing but wealth for the bankers. The profit margins were as wide as the street out there."[5]

During August 1982 capital flight from Mexico reached previously unimaginable proportions. On August 5, 1982, López Portillo was presented with evidence that a single bank had taken $300 million out of the country in a single day. On that same day, a banker with $5 million in his suitcase was detained only momentarily at the airport as he left the country. Close friends of the president report that these incidents infuriated him. He was told that one industrialist had sent $1 billion to the United States; that Bancomer, one of the country's two largest banks, had transferred $5 billion to U.S. banks; and that Mexican ownership of real estate and other investments in the United States amounted $25 billion.

Discussions with his closest advisers—Tello, de Oteyza, Flores de la Peña, and José Ramon López Portillo, the president's son—convinced López Portillo that the bank nationalization would put a halt to this massive hemorrhaging of the nation's wealth. He also believed it would revitalize the image of the Mexican presidency, if not heal the nation's other political wounds.[6]

Exchange controls and government expropriation of the banks were imposed by executive decree. The Mexican constitution was later amended in accord with the decree. President López Portillo

---

[3]"Debe desaparecer la banca elitista: Creel," *Uno Más Uno*, June 4, 1982, p. 1.

[4]Carlos Ramírez, "La nacionalización de la banca, respuesta a la demanda popular," *Proceso* 305 (1982), p. 9.

[5]Alan Robinson, "Portillo Pockets the Banks," *Euromoney*, October 1982, pp. 47–53.

[6]Interview, Mexico City, February 1985.

announced his decision to the cabinet twelve hours before his address to the nation and asked for the resignation of anyone objecting. Miguel Mancera, head of the Central Bank, and Adrian Lajous, head of the state-owned Foreign Trade Bank, resigned. Finance minister Silva Herzog, then deeply involved in debt renegotiations with the international banking community, also tendered his resignation. The president refused to accept it. Mexico's economic future depended on successful renegotiation of the debt. Silva Herzog's key role in the negotiations left López Portillo no choice but to keep him in the cabinet. This role in the debt renegotiations later gave Silva Herzog considerable power in intra-government debates over implementation of the bank nationalization.

After the September 1 decree, Tello was appointed head of the Central Bank to replace Mancera. On September 4 Tello announced a series of specific measures designed to increase savings deposits, make more credit available to small and medium-sized industries, and reduce inflation. But as Tello himself points out in hindsight, simply changing bank ownership did not guarantee that bank operations, practices, and uses would change.[7] There were only three months left to López Portillo's *sexenio*, a very short time to engineer a complete change in the financial system. Tello faced pressures on many fronts.

Implementing the Decision:
Rearguard Action by the Bankers' Alliance

There was no consensus behind the nationalization decision within the Mexican government, either in the cabinet or in the ruling PRI. Opposition to the move within the cabinet and the PRI reflected pressures from the private sector and international creditors. Although the business community as a whole was divided in its response to the bank nationalization, the former bankers and several large-scale industrialists worked with sympathizers in the government and party to pressure, directly and indirectly, for limits on the impact of the bank nationalization. In the years immediately preceding the bank nationalization, as chapter 2 suggests was the case in most of post-1917 Mexican history, private bankers had

[7]Tello, *La nacionalización de la banca.*

considerable direct access to government through several staunch allies in the state. Miguel Mancera, for instance, campaigned strongly and effectively within the cabinet to prevent imposition of exchange controls when they were being considered in early 1982.[8] The owner/director of Bancomer (one of Mexico's two largest private banks), Manuel Espinosa Yglesias, was described as an "unofficial finance minister" to the López Portillo government. Agustin Legoretta, head of the other leading private bank, Banamex, was described as acting as "director of public debt for the state." Carlos Abedrop, director of another large bank, Banco del Atlántico, was also in close communication with López Portillo and president-elect de la Madrid. These three bankers sat on the board of directors of the Central Bank. The interests of the former bankers were also represented indirectly by the bankers' implicit allies in the government and the PRI, most notably Silva Herzog and incoming president de la Madrid. Finally, in combating the nationalization, the former bankers also reinforced behind-the-scenes bargaining with mild public protest statements.

On September 3, 1982, two days after the expropriation decree, the bankers began a series of secret meetings to discuss their possible response. Several days later they were joined by a small number of large-scale industrialists.[9] On September 5, Carlos Abedrop, president of the Mexican Bankers Association, issued a protest of the president's charges against the bankers to the daily Mexico City newspapers. Several present at the secret meetings wanted to pursue a strategy of open confrontation with the government.[10] But the

[8]In April 1982 Mancera published a treatise against exchange controls, "The Inconveniences of Exchange Controls." He listed geographic proximity to the United States, lack of skilled bank and border personnel, and the complex border economy among the reasons for his opposition to exchange controls. Excerpts are included in Clemente Ruíz Durán, *90 dias de política monetaria y crediticia independiente* (Puebla: Universidad Autonoma de Puebla, 1984), pp. 54–55.

[9]Interview Mexico City, March 1985.

[10]The business organization Coparmex along with a handful of business leaders from other associations took a radical position on the bank nationalization, arguing that the sudden, unilateral decision to expropriate the private banks was clear evidence of the "totalitarian nature of the presidentially dominated political system." The bank nationalization ushered in a period in which a radical faction of business began to campaign publicly for "a democratic Mexico." In the view of the "radical" segment of the business community and its allies from the PAN (National Action Party) and PDM (Mexican Democratic Party), the bank nationalization showed that Mexico needed a competitive two-party political system. Although a majority of businessmen agreed that the nationalization had broken the rules of government-business relations, they disagreed

majority, following their tradition of trying to avoid public confrontation, hoped that private pressure and negotiation would bring quick indemnization for expropriated property and return of the nonbank stocks that had been expropriated along with the banks.[11] The bankers had supported de la Madrid in the political juggling preceding the PRI's choice of presidential candidate and hoped their influence with him would help them negotiate successfully.

While Central Bank director Tello announced the first implementation measures on September 4, 1982, finance minister Silva Herzog, in Toronto for the annual World Bank and IMF meetings, called a press conference and stated his belief that the bank nationalization would not imply any change in bank operations. The tone and behavior of these two cabinet members during the days following the expropriation reflected deep political differences stemming from the different constituencies they each believed they served. Tello felt responsible to Mexico's "popular sectors": workers, peasants, lower-middle-class entrepreneurs. Silva Herzog checked his actions against the opinions of international and domestic bankers and their business associates.

Following the nationalization, Tello generally tried to avoid the press but indicated, contrary to what Silva Herzog said in Toronto, that the nationalization would mean a change in bank operating

---

regarding the appropriate business response. Immediately following the nationalization, the radical segment of the bankers' alliance pushed for a unified public protest, including the demand for a national plebiscite and a nationwide business strike. Divisions within the business community prevented this protest. Small and medium-sized entrepreneurs within Canacintra and Concamin supported the bank nationalization. The rest of the business community opposed the move but remained divided over the best response. On the one hand, Clouthier, then president of the CCE, Basagoiti, then president of Coparmex, and Emilio Goicochea, then president of Concanaco, wanted to respond forcefully through participation in opposition party activity and social mobilization. The former bankers and leaders of Concamin and Canacintra preferred a more cautious response, stressing behind-the-scenes negotiation and bargaining. These more moderate business leaders pressured the CCE to cancel a "business strike" called for September 7, 1982, and to suspend what had been announced as the "First National Businessman's Meeting." However, Coparmex and the CCE did launch a media campaign. The centerpiece was a series of meetings, "Mexico in Liberty," sponsored by the CCE and Coparmex and held during October and November in several cities in northern Mexico. These were public meetings with the purpose of "creating consciousness among individuals and citizens about the national reality."

[11]A partial list of bank holdings can be found in Sylvia Maxfield, "International Finance, the State and Capital Accumulation: Mexico in Comparative Perspective" (Ph.D. diss., Harvard University, 1988), appendix A.

principles. Interest rates would be lowered and credit would be allocated in accord with socially defined needs. Silva Herzog meanwhile assured the world press gathered at the IMF/World Bank meetings in Canada that the banks would continue to operate as before, paying attractive interest rates and following market signals. Many prominent Mexican journalists were in Toronto to cover Silva Herzog's negotiations with the international banking community. Through the reports they sent back to Mexico, Silva Herzog was able to undercut Tello's Mexico City announcements.

Before he left for Toronto, Silva Herzog, with another political manuever, had also managed to undermine Tello's capacity to use the nationalized banks to implement significant economic change. Herzog mistrusted several of the newly designated bank directors for sharing too much of Tello's "populism." The finance minister refused to leave for the meeting in Toronto until several names were stricken from the list of new bank directors. "There was a tremendous battle," recalls one government official. "But for Silva Herzog, Tello's old mentor, Flores de la Peña, would have taken over one of the big four banks." Silva Herzog also opposed appointment of Muñoz Ledo, a former minister of labor under Echeverría and a leader of the opposition Democratic Front in the 1988 presidential elections. In the end, the list included two former finance ministers, a host of former Central Bank officials, and a variety of government technocrats. As one bank analyst noted, "Some were inexperienced, but there was no one the former owners could object to."[12] A banker waiting with several colleagues at the home of banker Carlos Abedrop for word of the outcome of Silva Herzog's negotiation recalls a late phone call the night before the finance minister left for Canada. "The good guys won" was the message.[13] This incident reveals the extent to which Silva Herzog's leverage in the domestic debate stemmed from his links to international creditors and his key role in solving Mexico's extreme foreign exchange crisis.

While there was disunity within the Mexican cabinet over the nationalization, there was also disunity within the governing party. Incoming president de la Madrid was not enthusiastic about the nationalization. This disunity limited how far López Portillo could

[12]A list of the fifty-three new bank directors and their backgrounds is in Maxfield, "International Finance," appendix B.
[13]Robinson, "Portillo Pockets the Banks," pp. 47–53.

go before jeopardizing a smooth presidential transition. According to Tello, López Portillo's strategy vis-à-vis the bankers was *dar el golpe y no machacar* (hit but not smash).[14] If López Portillo and Tello had bound the incoming administration to pursue the extensive state control possible through bank nationalization by pushing detailed and binding legal and institutional changes or popular mobilization, they could have provoked a serious rupture within the PRI. "The whole system was already affected. . . . President-elect de la Madrid had not received the measure warmly," says a government official closely involved with the nationalization. "If on top of this, one had developed a legal system that bound the incoming government . . . this could have created a more conflictive situation for the Mexican political system than that which already existed."[15] López Portillo made this fear clear in a speech at the end of October 1982. "I would commit an unpardonable political imprudence," the lame-duck president proclaimed, "if I tried to definitively reorganize bank functions because this is the job of my successor. . . . My administration would be irresponsible if it moved further with reorganization, this reorganization will be in better hands than mine with the next administration."[16]

The weight of the bankers' alliance was also evident in subsequent debates over reprivatization of a portion of bank holdings, the terms of indemnization, and the duration of exchange controls. Negotiations over the amount and form of indemnization and resale to the private sector of nonbank stocks expropriated along with the banks began almost immediately after Tello took over as Central Bank director. Tello indicated shortly after assuming the Central Bank directorship that some portion of the expropriated stocks would be sold back to the private sector. He agreed to sell 34 percent of stocks in the banks themselves and all stocks in the nonstrategic industries the banks had owned. But the bankers were most interested in regaining control over the nonbank financial institutions their banks had owned. In the short term, these enterprises were more profitable than many industrial concerns—espe-

---

[14]Interview with Carlos Tello, San Diego, California, October 1984.
[15]Interview with Carlos Tello, San Diego, California, October 1984.
[16]"Reclama la crisis decisiones que ya no puedo tomar," *Excelsior*, October 29, 1982, p. 1.

cially when many industrial companies were heavily in debt.[17] Regaining the nonbank financial institutions that had been part of their economic empires would allow them to develop a parallel private sector financial market beyond government control. In 1984, after behind-the-scenes negotiations with the former bankers, the de la Madrid administration announced provisions for the sale of expropriated stocks of insurance agencies, stock brokerages, and other nonbank financial operations.

Regarding indemnization there were three areas of contention between the former bank owners and Tello: the actual extent of bank stock holdings, the valuation of those holdings once defined, and the form and time period of repayment. Defining the extent of bank holdings was difficult because bank books showed only an aggregate value for stock holdings, with no detailed breakdown of assets. Bankers or representatives from their stock brokerages would often go to company board meetings representing a percentage of stock holdings exceeding the bank's actual holdings. As is the case in other countries, such as West Germany, these bankers would represent their bank's holdings, the holdings of their bank's nonbank financial subsidiaries, the personal holdings of the bank owners, and the stock holdings of many of their clients. This package of stocks would give them significant influence over board decisions, but it did not correspond to their bank's book assets. It was particularly difficult to separate corporate bank holdings from the personal holdings of bank owners and directors. A final difficulty arose because most Mexican commercial paper is anonymous, marked "pay to bearer."[18]

There were also negotiations over the valuation procedure for bank assets. They could be valued according to their book value, according to their nominal capitalized yield at a specified interest rate, or by their market value. The maturity and interest rate on the government bonds issued as payment was another point of discus-

---

[17]Jorge Alcocer, "El displome financiero mexicano," *Cuadernos Políticos* 40 (1984), pp. 68–79. Maxfield, "International Finance," appendix A, presents a partial list of nonbank financial institutions owned by the banks.

[18]Sidney Wise and Hugo Ortiz Dietz, "La nacionalización de la banca," *El Inversionista Mexicano*, 1982, pp. 43–53; Salvador Corro and Juan Antonio Zuniga, "La banca usurera que esquilma a quien le presta y al que le pide," *Proceso* 267 (1982), pp. 12–13.

sion. Tello's proposal was to use an adjusted accounting value and issue ten-year bonds at a lower than market interest rate, placing total compensation at 69 billion pesos, roughly $1 billion. The owners of the three largest banks, Banamex, Bancomer, and Serfín, would have received a total of 47 billion pesos under this scheme. This proposal was not acceptable to the former bankers, and the negotiations extended into the de la Madrid presidency. They were concluded in 1983, with the three banks mentioned receiving compensation worth more than double that proposed by Tello, 118 billion pesos.[19]

The bankers' alliance also lobbied against the exchange controls imposed simultaneously with the bank nationalization to prevent capital flight and help the state regain the capacity to induce investment. The controls were soon lifted. Tello had originally hoped to use exchange controls to prevent capital flight and to institute government budgeting of foreign exchange. In his first public address as director of the Central Bank, Tello announced a two-tiered exchange rate: a preferential rate of 50:1 and a rate of 70:1 for nonessential transactions such as tourism.[20] But the bankers' alliance was vehemently opposed to foreign exchange controls, as it had been ever since Cárdenas considered exchange controls in 1938. López Portillo's own commitment was lukewarm, and his deputy, Carlos Tello, had little idea of how to implement exchange controls. Also, the long history of free exchange convertibility had made a wide cross section of Mexican society believe in a fundamental right to free access to dollars at a stable price. Knowledge that de la Madrid opposed the policy and intended to remove exchange controls as soon as he entered office also weakened the López Portillo administration's commitment to exchange controls. Another factor militating against a commitment to exchange con-

---

[19]Tello, *La nacionalización de la banca*, pp. 162–168.

[20]Priorities for allocation of dollars at the preferred rate were ranked as follows: obligations of the federal government, obligations of the rest of the public sector as determined by the Finance Ministry, obligations (including salaries) connected with Mexican representation abroad and membership in international organizations, obligations of credit institutions, authorized imports of basic foodstuffs and intermediate and capital goods for basic needs, imports of intermediate and capital goods for existing industrial plants or expansion according to government priorities, obligations of the private sector to foreign creditors contracted before September 1, 1982, necessary obligations contracted in the border free zone, and royalties and other obligations of foreign subsidiaries as approved by the Foreign Investment Commission.

trol was the IMF. The IMF expected Mexico to end exchange controls as part of the standby loan negotiation that was key to successful renegotiations with private international creditors. Mexico's 1982 Letter of Intent to the IMF stated: "The actual exchange system was established under crisis conditions. The Mexican authorities will adjust it to conform with . . . a policy of flexible exchange."[21] Exchange controls were relinquished, and private exchange brokerages, many owned by former bankers, continued to operate. Their power in the exchange market, in the absence of controls, was manifestly evident in the first half of 1985. On rumors of a stepped-up devaluation of the peso, border exchange houses bought dollars in such quantities that they squeezed the banks out of the market. To capture dollars, given stiff competition from private exchange brokers, the banks were forced to open their own exchange houses. One commentator suggests that in these events "paradoxically, the ex-bankers again robbed us [the nation]."[22]

Needless to say, Tello's goal of stemming capital flight was not met. The cumulative flow of capital flight from Mexico between 1983 and 1985, using a measure including unrecorded trade transactions, reached $16.2 billion. Although this figure represents an average annual reduction of $1 billion in capital flight over the previous three years, it was a severe drain on a heavily indebted, exchange-short economy. Furthermore, stemming capital flight was not the only goal never to be reached by the architects of bank nationalization.

Impact of the Bank Nationalization

The nationalization was designed to give the state a powerful new instrument for regulating the economy (*rectoría económica*). Architects of the bank nationalization intended that exchange controls and authority over credit allocation by the nationalized banks would give the state the capacity to discourage speculation and promote productive investment in agriculture, social services, and

[21]The letter to the IMF is reprinted in Tello, *La nacionalización de la banca*, p. 219.
[22]Rogelio Hernández Rodríguez, "La política de los empresarios después de la nacionalización bancaria," *Foro Internacional* 27 (1986), p. 253.

strategic (wage goods and basic infrastructure) industries. The Decree of Motives for the bank expropriation, the new bank regulations issued in December 1982, the Plan Nacional de Desarollo of 1983–1988, and the Programa Nacional de Financiamiento del Desarollo indicated that the newly nationalized banks should channel credit to a large number of small and medium-sized borrowers and should support production, distribution, and consumption of wage goods.[23] The goals of financial policy were to increase internal savings and decrease the cost of credit and its concentration among a small number of large corporate borrowers.[24] Architects of the nationalization also hoped the reorientation of financial flows would improve the state's financial position.

Despite these goals, neither the sectoral allocation of credit nor its concentration among a few privileged borrowers changed significantly following the nationalization. In the aftermath of the nationalization, Mexican government officials took the recommendations of the chief executives of companies formerly linked to the banks regarding nominees to the nationalized banks' boards of directors. A former director of the Bank of Mexico notes: "It is clear that the nationalized banks did not flee from possible influence of private corporations on the orientation of their financing and that the authorities do not consider it [business influence] contrary to the national interest as some enthusiasts of the nationalization seemed to think. . . . In fact it would be extremely disturbing if the part of the financial system most oriented to financing the private sector of the economy was not closely linked to it."[25]

Concentration in credit allocation grew rather than shrinking as architects of the nationalization had hoped. In 1981 there were 252 private sector borrowers obtaining loans greater than 500 million pesos. They accounted for 13 percent of all borrowers. In 1985 there were 924 borrowers in this category, representing 51 percent of all borrowers.[26] Borrowers able to obtain or needing only relatively small loans represented a much smaller portion of the borrowing population after the nationalization. The continued concentration of bank lending among a few privileged borrowers is

[23]Javier Márquez, *La banca mexicana* (Mexico, D.F.: CEMLA, 1986), pp. 182–183.
[24]Secretaría de Programación y Presupuesto, *Plan nacional de desarollo, 1983–1988* (Mexico, D.F.: SPP, 1983), pp. 183–190.
[25]Márquez, *La banca mexicana*, pp. 93–94.
[26]Ibid., p. 274.

Bankers' Alliance and Bank Nationalization

Table 12. Commercial bank credits by borrowing sector, 1981 and 1984 (percentage of total credits)

	1981	1984
Agriculture, livestock, mining, forestry, and fishing	10.8	8.4
Energy industry (oil and electricity)	2.7	6.7
Transformation industry (manufacturing, nonmetallic mineral products, steel and metal products, mechanical and electrical machinery)	24.1	23.0
Low-income housing	3.2	5.3
Transport	2.0	0.9
Consumer credit	5.9	4.4
Government	3.4	15.3

Source: Calculated from Banco de Mexico, *Indicadores económicos y de moneda y banca* (Mexico, D.F.: Banco de Mexico, various years).

not surprising given that there was little change in the composition of the banks' boards of directors.

The sectoral allocation of credit also hardly conformed to the expectations of the bank nationalizers. Although the proportion of financing going to public housing did rise, the architects of the bank nationalization were disappointed in other areas of social service financing. The proportion of total financing going to transportation and consumer credit fell. Financing for agriculture also fell. The sectoral allocation of credit and the continued short term of financial liabilities also indicated that the financial system was not contributing to investment in long-maturing industrial development efforts. If anything, it was facilitating increased oil dependence. The percentage breakdown of borrowing by sector presented in Table 12 indicates that between 1981 and 1984 the proportion of industrial financing going to oil rose while financing for manufacturing and construction fell. In mid-1984, 98 percent of all bank deposits were at maturities of less than one year.[27] A 1987 World Bank mission concluded that "the market for longer-term financial instruments has shrunk significantly in recent years."[28]

Patterns in allocation of commercial bank credit became increasingly irrelevant for guiding investment as the so-called parallel, nonbank financial markets began to attract savings at the expense

[27]Jack Sweeney, Telegram, Amembassy Mexico to SecState Washington, D.C., January 21, 1985.
[28]World Bank, *Mexico after the Oil Boom: Refashioning a Development Strategy* (Washington, D.C.: World Bank, 1987), p. xviii.

of the commercial banking system. By extending Tello's decision to relinquish expropriated nonbank stocks to include nonbank financial institutions, the de la Madrid administration allowed for development of a parallel financial system, which diverted resources from Tello's strategic development priorities, such as nonoligopolistic industry, agriculture, and housing.

Former bankers such as Banamex's Legoretta family and Bancomer's Espinosa Yglesias regained 100 percent control of the insurance companies, stock brokerages, leasing firms, and warehousing concerns that had been part of their financial empires. Agustin Legoretta, for example, bought back Casa de Bolsa Banamex, changed its name to INVERLET, and opened for business in 1984. His brother, Eduardo Legoretta, owned the Operadora de Bolsa brokerage house. Baillares of the Cremi Group, which had included Banca Cremi, bought back the securities brokerage Bolsa Cremi; Espinosa Yglesias bought back the insurance firm Seguros Bancomer (later called Seguros de Mexico). The Garza-Sada family, captains of the Monterrey Group enterprises, which had included the banks Banpaís and Serfín, bought back the group's nonbank financial enterprises, including Casa de Bolsa Banpaís, Arrendadora Banpaís, and Aseguradora Banpaís. Carlos Abedrop, former owner of Banco del Atlantico, formed Grupo Olmeca, which comprised a brokerage house and roughly ten formerly bank-owned companies in the electronic, chemical, petrochemical, and consumer goods sectors. Olmeca also formed an "international financial engineering" company.[29] These newly reprivatized nonbank financial institutions quickly began to compete for savings and create a parallel financial market beyond state control.

By 1985 the Mexican stock market, an important part of the parallel financial market, was booming. Placement of commercial paper grew 59 percent in real terms in 1985. Stock brokerages became major competitors with the banks for financial resources.[30] The twenty-nine private financial brokerage houses operating in

[29]"Nueva institución financiera en México," *Uno Más Uno*, May 23, 1985, p. 9; "Anuncian la institución de Ingeniera Financiera," *Uno Más Uno*, May 29, 1985, p. 12; Carlos Acosta Cordova, "Aun con IFI registrada al margen de la ley, la banca se desnacionaliza," *Proceso* 448 (1985), pp. 20–23.

[30]Tomas Peñalosa Webb, "El proceso de intermediación financiera y la banca comercial mexicana: 1970–1985," paper prepared for the workshop "Government and Private Sector in Contemporary Mexico," Center for U.S.-Mexican Studies, University of California–San Diego, La Jolla, 1986, p. 8.

1984 had a collective purse equal to approximately 40 percent of the assets of the nation's two largest newly nationalized banks: Bancomer and Banamex.[31] The development of nonbank financial institutions aggravated competition for bank credit while savings rates remained depressed. This credit shortage drove nominal interest rates up, leading representatives of small and medium-sized industry—by and large excluded from the stock market—to complain that financing was no easier to obtain and no less expensive than prior to the nationalization.[32] Financing obtained through the parallel financial system, by the selling of stock or commercial paper, was as much as 20 percent less expensive than that available through the banking system. However, access to this source of financing was limited to the two hundred Mexican corporations registered on the stock exchange.[33]

The boom in capital markets caused severe disintermediation in the banking system.[34] As data from the Central Bank reveal, total banking system deposits fell from 30 percent of GNP in 1982 to 27.1 percent in 1984. Deposits in formerly private banks (as opposed to national development banks) fell from 26.7 percent of GNP to 23.9 percent. Corrected for the irregular practices that these banks continued to use to inflate their deposit record, the real rate of bank deposit growth in 1984 was negative.[35] In real terms it fell 13 percent in 1985. The number of depositors did not rise ei-

[31]Hernández Rodríguez, "La política de los empresarios después de la nacionalización bancaria," p. 253.

[32]"Canacintra: poco importa la captación bancária, si el crédito sigue siendo caro e inaccesibile," El Financiero, March 30, 1984, pp. 4, 7, 12.

[33]Stock brokerages have earned high returns for their operations in the parallel non-government-controlled portion of the financial system. In addition to helping secure corporate financing, stock brokerages found a lucrative business in the mid-1980s Mexican merger boom reminiscent of that in the United States. In 1984 large-scale businessmen, most associated with former bankers, repurchased nonbank financial institutions and began to compete to purchase undervalued stocks of companies beginning to recover from the 1982 crisis. The process reached fever pitch in mid-1984, when several stock brokerages were shut down for using confidential information to buy and sell stock at spectacular profit. In 1986 the Mexican stock market index rose 600 percent, making it among the best performing in the world. Many observers took this increase as a sign of the strength of the Mexican economy, failing to note that there had been only one new stock issue between 1981 and 1986.

[34]The lack of public confidence in the nationalized banks is evident in the startling rise in accounts opened with Citibank in Mexico City in the year following the expropriation. A former bank employee estimates there was a 7000 percent increase.

[35]Among these irregular practices is making loans larger than needed by the borrower, who, by prearrangement, immediately redeposits part of the loan. This is a form of the "back-to-back" loan.

ther.[36] Dividing deposit levels by the money supply reveals that financial intermediation by banks was as low in 1984 as in 1981 and 1971, both of which were record low years.

The entry of the former bankers into nonbank financial activities was one reason for the boom in stock market activity and the growing irrelevance of commercial bank credit in industrial financing. A second reason for growth of the stock market was the Mexican government's own urgent financing need. Tello, chief author of the bank nationalization, expected it to improve public sector finances by lowering the cost of internal borrowing from domestic banks. Indeed the external debt crisis forced the Mexican government to turn to internal debt for its financing needs. During 1983 and 1984 the government financed expenditures through a system of bank reserve requirements—at negative real interest rates. But, on the premise that government financing should not be inflationary, the new banking legislation announced in January 1985 limited reserve requirements to 10 percent (they had been roughly 50 percent) and also placed a maximum nominal ceiling on Central Bank credits to the federal government and its state-owned enterprises.[37] Under the new government financing regime the public sector would try to raise funds through emission of government treasury bills known as Certificados de Tesorería (CETES). The government's increasing recourse to the domestic financial market to cover deficit spending pushed up nominal domestic interest rates. As the nominal domestic public sector debt rose, inflation conveniently lowered the real cost of the mounting debt. But inflation made the public wary of investing in CETES, particularly when there were other lucrative, very short-term financial opportunities. In 1985 the government had to offer an unprecedented real return of 9.2 percent on CETES to raise funds needed to cover government spending. The sale of CETES accounts for a large majority of Mexican stock market activity.

The growth in circulation of CETES had negative distributional consequences because of segmentation of the financial market between bank and nonbank credit circuits. The growth of the

[36]"Se estancó en 84 la cifra de depositantes de la banca," *Uno Más Uno*, April 7, 1985, p. 8. See also *Uno Más Uno*, April 6, 1985, p. 6, and April 8, 1985, p. 7.

[37]For more on the 1985 bank legislation see the trade journal *Ejecutivo de Finanzas*, June 1985, which is a special issue dedicated entirely to analyzing the legislation.

CETES market privileged large-scale industry while penalizing small and medium-sized entrepreneurs. Large-scale entrepreneurs, and the nonbank financial institutions with which they became associated through development of the parallel financial market, were the main economic actors with sufficient liquidity to invest in government bonds. In 1985 interest paid on these bonds to private enterprises amounted to 1.3 percent of GNP.[38]

Small and medium-sized entrepreneurs were squeezed much as they had been by prenationalization segmentation of financial markets between dollar-based and peso-based credit circuits. They had to rely on productive activity for profits, while large-scale enterprises maximized profitability through financial manipulations. Also, the rise in interest rates for companies without access to the stock market squeezed profit margins on productive activity. This squeeze led to repeated calls by the business organizations most representative of small and medium-sized entrepreneurs, Concamin and Canacintra, for a financial policy to increase the availability and lower the cost of working credit. The World Bank reported in 1987, "Borrowers ineligible for preferred credit are obliged to either self-finance (difficult in a recession), draw from foreign assets . . . or borrow from the costly free credit market, where effective, *ex post*, annual interest rates on short term loans were running 25 percent above inflation in 1986."[39] The government's high costs for bond market financing benefited both the holders of government bonds and the bond markets in general. The groups of financiers who had returned to the financial markets after the bank nationalization reaped the greatest benefits from the government's new financing mechanisms.

Although architects of the bank nationalization thought it would help improve the state's financial situation and lead to more equitable distribution of financial resources among small, medium and large-scale entrepreneurs, the rising dependence of the government on sale of CETES did just the opposite. So did other aspects of the postnationalization financial reorganization. The link between in-

---

[38]Celso Garrido and Enrique Quintana, "Financial Relations and Economic Power in Mexico," in Sylvia Maxfield and Ricardo Anzaldúa, eds., *Government and Private Sector in Contemporary Mexico* (La Jolla: Center for U.S.-Mexican Studies, University of California–San Diego, 1986), p. 119.

[39]World Bank, *Mexico after the Oil Boom*, p. xviii.

dustrial and financial capital in Mexico meant that the state took over not only banks but industrial enterprises as well. These takeovers saddled the government with the economic burdens of debt-ridden industrial companies.

As the economy heated up between 1979 and 1982, Mexico's largest banks extended more and more credit to their industrial associates. As described in chapter 4, the financial boom fueled group expansion. When the boom began to go bust in early 1982, many industrial enterprises found themselves overleveraged. Devaluation made their foreign credits and expenses costlier. Their financial difficulties threatened the stability of the banks with which they were linked. To some extent the nationalization served to bail out financially threatened banks and their industrial partners. Although the government immediately made plans to resell the industrial holdings of the nationalized banks, they could find no buyers for the shares in heavily indebted enterprises. To place industrial enterprises on a sounder footing and prevent widespread private sector bankruptcy, the government established a fund to absorb some of the cost and risk involved in private sector debt rescheduling. Under its Fideicomiso Para la Cobertura del Riesgo Cambiário (Fund for Exchange Risk, or FICORCA) program the government agreed to cover the difference between a subsidized exchange rate at which companies borrowed dollars and the later exchange rate at which they would have to make debt payments. FICORCA covered about 50 percent of private sector debts, including those of some of Mexico's largest, previously most dynamic corporations. The program essentially set up a government trusteeship over $11 billion of private sector debt. Added to the $10 billion worth of foreign debts inherited with the bank nationalization, this saddled the Mexican government with $21 billion worth of private sector debt.[40]

The benefits enjoyed by those corporations enrolled in the FICORCA program created significant differences between companies that joined it and those that did not. The program gave a substantial boost to private sector companies that participated because their debt repayment costs remained constant while inflation

[40]Garrido and Quintana, "Financial Relations and Economic Power," p. 15. For more on FICORCA see Robin King, "FICORCA: Mechanics and Effects," mimeo, Economics Department, University of Texas–Austin, 1988.

and revaluation pushed up the book value of their physical assets.[41] Between 1983 and 1985 companies covered by FICORCA received 38 billion pesos worth of financial support, according to estimates by the Ministry of Finance. The companies that joined FICORCA managed to accumulate liquid assets that they could profitably invest in the booming stock market. Although the most powerful banking groups lost their financial leadership through expropriation of private banks, they survived and profited through government support from FICORCA and the purchase of nonbanking financial intermediaries.

As in other areas, the nationalization fell short of its goal to help improve public sector finances. Although the public sector deficit relative to GNP fell from its astronomically high 1982 level, the public sector's financial situation remained weak after the bank nationalization. In 1983, according to data from the World Bank and the Inter-American Development Bank, the ratio of public deficit to GNP fell from the 1982 record high of 17.6 percent to 7.4 percent. But by 1985 the ratio was up to 9.5 percent again and in 1986 reached 16.8 percent. This increase is due partly to the rise in internal interest costs. Interest payments as a portion of total public sector expenditure rose from 9.5 percent in 1980 to 36.7 percent in 1985 as growth in internal debt replaced growth in external debt—at the cost of spiraling inflation. Interest on internal debt rose dramatically, from 3.2 percent of GDP in 1982 to 12.7 percent in 1986, while interest on external debt shrank from 5.4 percent of GDP in 1982 to 4.2 percent in 1986. Domestic borrowing relative to GDP rose from 2.4 percent in 1980 to 7.8 percent in 1985, while foreign borrowing went from .6 percent of GDP in 1980 to .2 percent in 1985. Relative to total public sector expenditure (current and capital), interest expenditure grew from 10.7 percent to 34.3 percent between 1981 and 1985, while public works expenditure fell from 9.8 percent to 2.8 percent and salaries from 17 percent to 11.6 percent.

Architects of the nationalization hoped it would give the state the capacity to discourage speculation and promote investment in wage goods industry, agriculture, and social welfare through control over credit allocation. Over all they expected a reduction in the

[41]Emilio Illanes Díaz Rivera, "La inversion privada en Mexico," *Ejecutivo de Finanzas*, November 1986, p. 122.

cost and concentration of credit allocation and an improvement in state finances. Instead credit allocation became more concentrated, sectoral allocation of credit changed little, and credit allocation became less important in guiding investment as its role in industrial financing was eclipsed by financial products available through the non-state-controlled parallel financial market dominated by the stock market. Growth in the circulation of government securities benefited financiers operating nonbank financial institutions while raising the cost of domestic government finance well over what it had been prior to the 1980s, when the commercial banking system was a primary source. To the extent the nationalization served to bail out financially overextended conglomerates it also added to the public sector's financial burdens and to inequalities within the entrepreneurial community.

Conclusion

The decision to nationalize the banks reflected a temporary comeback for the national populists, or Cárdenas coalition. They were spurred to action in part by the perception that changes in the international economy had strengthened the bankers' alliance. Nevertheless, the bankers' alliance managed to limit implementation of the nationalization decree, as is evident in debates over the extent of reprivatization, terms of indemnization, and duration of exchange controls. The goals of the nationalization—to change the cost, overall concentration, and sectoral allocation of bank credit and to improve public sector finances—were also frustrated. As Mexico's international financial position changed again, to one of desperation, the relative power of the bankers' alliance in domestic policy debates rose, as it had when Mexico was in need of international financial support in the 1920s and 1950s. In the aftermath of the nationalization and throughout the 1980s the weight of the bankers' alliance was evident as Mexico followed one of the most orthodox liberal economic trajectories in all of Latin America.

CONCLUSION

7

Mexico in
Comparative Perspective

This book has described the origins of a relatively strong bankers' alliance in Mexico, its influence on economic policy, and how these domestic factors interacted with changes in Mexico's international financial situation. The latter explain changes in the ability of the bankers' alliance to shape economic policy over time. The more vulnerable Mexico was to international capital outflows and, conversely, the greater the country's need for foreign inflows, the more leverage the bankers' alliance had in domestic policy debates.

The comparative emphasis shifts in this chapter to cross-national variation in the Latin American experience with international financial integration in the 1970s. Similarities among Mexico, Argentina, Chile, and Brazil suggest that international financial integration tends to divert national financial resources away from long-term investment in national industry. In all these cases we see a rise in short-term financial activity that profits financiers and their industrial associates at the expense of small and medium-sized entrepreneurs and the nation's industrial base.

Nevertheless, there are important differences in the magnitude of this effect. Among Latin American countries Brazil stands out. Geddes points out: "Nearly all Latin American countries borrowed too much in the late 1970s and very early 1980s. In Brazil, the borrowed money was not used optimally, but it was used to sustain growth and for projects which, though grandiose and somewhat inefficient, would eventually contribute to increased productivity.

165

Conclusion

The record in Argentina, Chile, and Mexico is far worse, with much of the debt spent on capital flight, luxury consumption, military imports and travel abroad."[1] In a survey of Latin American economic performance in the 1970s and 1980s Hirschman concludes that "while Argentina and Chile deindustrialized and Mexico 'de-substituted,' Brazil . . . vigorously consolidated its leadership."[2]

The explanation of Brazil's "exceptionalism" lies in the country's history of capital-controlling, or heterodox, economic policies, such as flexible exchange rates with controlled convertibility, heavy state intervention in domestic financial markets, and loose monetary policy. Historically these policies allowed the Brazilian government to influence the allocative decisions of national capitalists in favor of long-term industrial investment. This ability was crucial for managing capital accumulation in the context of increasingly internationalized capital markets in the 1970s and 1980s. In other words, Brazil's economic policy established a pattern of partially governing capital mobility. The relative weakness of the Brazilian bankers' alliance made this policy pattern possible. The historical development of state economic policy-making agencies and the organization of capital in Brazil provided only a relatively weak base for a bankers' alliance. As we have seen, the opposite was true in Mexico. Where the bankers' alliance was weaker, policy patterns that helped govern capital mobility evolved; where it was stronger, they did not.

There are, as noted eariler in this book, two theoretically controversial suggestions here. One is that economic policy reflects the economic interests of financiers, mediated by institutional and organizational circumstances. Chapter 1 explored the theoretical context of this claim. This chapter briefly compares it with alternative explanations of policy variation. The second claim, that in a world of increasingly international financial integration, policies that restrict capital mobility can have important benefits for the national industrial capacity of newly industrializing countries, is perhaps

[1]Barbara Geddes, "Building State Autonomy in Brazil, 1930–1964," paper prepared for the Latin American Studies Association meeting, Boston, October 1986, footnote 19.
[2]Albert Hirschman, "The Political Economy of Latin American Development: Seven Exercises in Retrospection," paper prepared for the Latin American Studies Association meeting, Boston, October 1986, p. 22.

even more controversial. This chapter ends with a discussion of the basis of this claim and opposing ones.

International Financial Integration and Economic Concentration: Regional Similarities

In the Mexican economic policy context, growing international integration of the financial system led (as chapter 4 outlines) to an increase in short-term financial activity and a decline in long-term industrial financing. Because of high concentration in credit allocation and financial market segmentation, the reduction in long-term industrial financing squeezed small and medium-sized borrowers. Large conglomerates, on the other hand, had access to plentiful and relatively low-interest foreign loans, which smaller borrowers could not obtain. Not only did this access allow conglomerate borrowers to obtain working capital at lower rates than those charged on scarce domestic credit, but it also brought them profits from arbitrage between the dollar- and peso-based portions of the financial market. They used these profits to buy up other enterprises, which were often vulnerable because of the financial squeeze on small and medium-sized business. It is also important to note that there was new industrial investment despite the boom in short-term financial activity that tied up resources that might have otherwise gone into long-term industrial investment. However, new capital formation in Mexico was driven by public sector investment in oil, not private sector activity. Private sector investment slowed and shifted away from manufacturing into services.

These trends are mirrored to varying degrees in the Chilean, Argentine, and Brazilian cases. The Argentine and Chilean cases provide extreme examples of the negative impact of international financial integration and liberal financial policy on national industrial development. In these two cases, in contrast to Mexico's, industrial employment and output stagnated or fell during the 1970s.

The military regime that overthrew the government of Chilean president Salvador Allende in 1973 instituted a financial reform based on ending government controls and internationally integrat-

Conclusion

ing the domestic financial system.[3] The rationale for these reforms was that they would increase savings, end financial market segmentation, and more efficiently channel financial resources into investment. Deregulating international capital flows would lead to domestic and international interest rate equalization.[4] Liberal financial policy and international financial integration did spur rapid growth of private financial institutions and markets. The share of total financial system assets held by private financial institutions rose, while those of the Central Bank and semiofficial public sector banks fell. The public sector share fell from 49 percent in 1970 to 25 percent in 1980, while the private sector share rose equally.[5] The share of short-term versus long-term assets also rose.[6] Although the financial sector's share in GNP grew rapidly, national savings and new capital formation fell. National savings fell from approximately 15 percent between 1960 and 1970 to 11.5 percent between 1974 and 1982.[7] The share of industrial output in GNP fell from 25 percent in 1970 to 20 percent in 1982, measured in constant prices.[8]

Financial sector growth reflected an increase in foreign liabilities and interest earned on the inflated value of short-term financial

[3]Following the blueprint of monetarist financial reform, the military government freed interest rates, eliminated credit controls, reduced barriers to entry for new financial institutions, and reduced reserve requirements (Diego Portales, "El capital financiero transnacional en la 'restructuración capitalista' de la economía chilena," in Jaime Estévez and Samuel Lichtensztejn, eds., *Nueva fase del capital financiero* [Mexico, D.F.: Editorial Nueva Imagen, 1981]). Financial institutions that had come under state control or ownership during the Allende administration were sold to their former private sector owners or to newly formed economic conglomerates; this sale contributed to a merger boom. (Alejandra Mizala, "The State, the Role of Finance and Industrialization in Chile, 1940–1982," paper prepared for the Latin American Studies Association Meeting, Boston, October 1986.) The government also gradually lifted restrictions on international capital flows. The main mechanism for foreign borrowing was Article 14 of the International Exchange Law. Until 1977 bank borrowing was restricted, so most Article 14 borrowing was done by industrial and commercial firms. The International Exchange Law was modified in 1978, removing limits on bank borrowing and allowing banks, under Agreement 1196, to relend borrowed dollars domestically. (Vittorio Corbo, "Economic Policy and International Economic Relations since 1970," in Gary M. Walton, ed., *The National Economic Policies of Chile* [Greenwich, Conn.: JAI Press, 1985].)
[4]Luz Carmen Latorre, "The Chilean Crisis: A Note on the Consequences of Liberal Policies towards the Private Sector," *Developing Economies* 22 (1984), pp. 289–308.
[5]Ibid., p. 294.
[6]José Pablo Arellano, "El financiamiento del desarrollo," in Alejandro Foxley, ed., *Reconstrución económica para la democracia* (Santiago, Chile: Editoriales Aconcagua, 1985), pp. 132, 203.
[7]Latorre, "The Chilean Crisis," p. 292.
[8]Mizala, "The State, the Role of Finance and Industrialization in Chile," p. 35.

assets. Industrial investment declined as the financial boom channeled resources into short-term financial speculation, consumption,
and purchases of existing companies. A survey of the balance
sheets and income statements of 233 publicly held Chilean manufacturing concerns reveals that those doing well in the 1973–1983
period minimized their physical assets and maximized their financial assets.[9]

International financial integration did not succeed in equalizing
domestic and international interest rates. Between 1975 and 1982
the differential between peso interest rates and devaluation-
adjusted international rates averaged between 35 percent and 65
percent.[10] Segmentation of the market for corporate finance, aggravated by government restrictions on foreign indebtedness, guaranteed larger corporations greater access to foreign loans; such
privilege meant access to profits from short-term financial maneuvering. Small and medium-sized firms had almost no direct access
to foreign loans and were forced to borrow from domestic financial
institutions, which charged prohibitively high interest rates.[11] Of
Article 14 foreign borrowing, 60 percent was by the country's two
largest conglomerates: BHC and Cruzat-Larrain. The six largest
conglomerates accounted for 82 percent of foreign funds.[12] Conglomerates used these funds to buy out smaller, weaker enterprises
and to engage in short-term financial market operations. One of
the most profitable activities for economic groups was obtaining
cheap foreign credit and deposits from the general public and lending them at high rates in the domestic market. Several enterprises
even reported to the 1978 World Bank mission to Chile that they
were willing to import goods for resale at little or no (even negative) profit in order to acquire the accompanying trade credits that
could be turned over in the domestic money market.[13]

A study of 190 publicly held Chilean manufacturing firms gives a
clear picture of financial market segmentation and its impact on
industrial enterprises. The financial costs of enterprises linked to

[9]Ibid.

[10]Ibid.; World Bank, *Chile: An Economy in Transition* (Washington, D.C.: World
Bank, 1979), p. 136.

[11]Stephany Griffith-Jones and Enzo Rodríguez, "Private International Finance and In-
dustrialisation of LDCs," *Journal of Development Studies* 21 (1984), pp. 47–74.

[12]Mizala, "The State, the Role of Finance and Industrialization in Chile," p. 54.

[13]World Bank, *Chile: An Economy in Transition.*

economic conglomerates were substantially lower throughout the 1975–1982 period than those of small and medium-sized firms not linked to conglomerates. The financial costs facing manufacturing firms integrated into conglomerates averaged 30 percent less than for nonconglomerate firms. Firms linked to conglomerates were able to keep financial costs low by increasing their foreign borrowing. For large enterprises, the share of direct Article 14 foreign loans grew from 3.5 percent in 1977 to 9.2 percent in 1981. For small enterprises, it was 1.8 percent in 1977 and 2.6 percent in 1981. "Enterprises with a direct link to the financial sector clearly have an advantage over rival firms not so connected," stated the 1978–79 World Bank Mission Report.[14]

The Argentine military regime that overthrew the government of Juan Perón's widow, Evita, in 1976 pursued a liberal financial policy similar to Chile's and, even more rapidly than in the Chilean case, removed restrictions on international capital movements. As in Chile, unrestricted international capital mobility was intended to correct financial market segmentation and bring about interest rate equalization.[15] As in the Chilean case, Argentina's liberal financial policy and international integration engendered financial sector growth but no increase in national savings or net new capital accumulation. Finance was the only sector with steadily growing income between 1977 and 1986.[16] The boom reflected the rise of a large, rapid-turnover, short-term financial market. Between 1976 and 1981 the share of time deposits, most short term, in total commercial bank deposits grew from 40 percent to 79 percent. In 1981, 70 percent of all time deposits were for maturities of thirty days or less.[17]

Opening the capital account of the balance of payments to large inflows did not suffice to bring domestic lending rates in line with international rates, as was the case in Chile also. The foreign (dollar) interest rate, adjusted by the programmed peso devaluation,

[14]Ibid., p. 272.

[15]Ibid.; Luis Beccaria and Ricardo Carciofi, "Recent Experiences of Stabilisation: Argentina's Economic Policy, 1976–1981," *IDS Bullletin* 13 (1981), pp. 54–55; Julio J. Nogues, "The Nature of Argentina's Policy Reforms during 1976–1981," *World Bank Staff Working Papers* 765 (1986).

[16]Adolfo Canitrot, "Teoría y práctica del liberalismo: Política anti-inflacionaria y apertura económica en la Argentina, 1976–1981," *Estudios Cedes* 3 (1980), p. 923.

[17]World Bank, *Argentina: Economic Memorandum*, vol. 1 (Washington, D.C.: IBRD/World Bank, 1979), p. 210.

remained below the domestic rate. Firms that did not have access to foreign credit had to borrow at higher domestic rates. Only banks and a few large corporations had direct access to foreign loans. Small banks had to borrow from banks that converted their dollar loans into high-cost peso credits.[18] Therefore, access to foreign finance was a considerable competitive advantage.[19] Kosacoff finds a partial correlation between access to foreign loans and ranking among the top Argentine industrial corporations.[20]

Smaller enterprises went bankrupt as a consequence of intensified competition resulting from tariff reductions and differential access to relatively cheap foreign credit. Large industrial companies with access to foreign credits participated actively in recycling foreign resources in the domestic financial system, using profits from this intermediation to cover operating losses.[21] Banks used the profits gained from intermediating between the international and domestic markets to buy up bankrupt enterprises and group them into financial-industrial-commercial conglomerates.[22]

Data collected by Carvallo and Petrei from the balance sheets and income statements of a sample of small and large Argentine industrial corporations indicate that between 1976 and 1980 the debt leverage of smaller firms increased less than that of larger firms, partly because smaller firms had reduced access to long-term credit and foreign financing. Less reliance on debt financing did not help the smaller firms obtain higher profit rates, however, because of the losses associated with small firms' inability to collect the subsidies implicit in foreign financing. Financial costs for small firms, restricted to local borrowing, were almost three times higher than those for large firms.[23]

In the Brazilian context, increasing international financial integration also encouraged corporate financial managers to manipu-

[18]David Felix, "El monetarismo latinoamericano en crisis," *Investigación Económica* 170 (1984), pp. 11–27.
[19]Aldo Ferrer, "El monetarismo en Argentina y Chile," *Comercio Exterior* 31 (1981), pp. 3–13.
[20]Bernardo P. Kosacoff, "Industrialización y monetarismo en Argentina," *Economía de America Latina* 12 (1984).
[21]Aldo Ferrer, *Puede Argentina pagar su dueda?* (Buenos Aires: El Cid Editorial, 1982), p. 73.
[22]Felix, "El monetarismo latinoamericano en crisis," p. 21.
[23]D. T. Carvallo and A. H. Petrei, "Financing Private Business in an Inflationary Context," in Pedro Aspe, Rudiger Dornbusch, and Maurice Obstfeld, eds., *Financial Policies and the World Capital Market* (Chicago: University of Chicago Press, 1983).

late financial assets for short-term gain rather than putting them to work in long-run industrial investment projects. The incentive to move into finance and away from productive assets was reinforced by the country's subsidized credit system. Interest rates on agricultural credits provided by the Banco do Brasil were negative. State industrial credits also carried low or negative interest rates. Borrowers with access to subsidized credits invested them in the open market for indexed and nominal government bonds, making large profits. As this form of intermarket financial arbitrage caught on, the average holding for these government bonds fell from 11.4 days in 1973 to 1.8 days in 1979.[24] Brazilians called this arbitrage between financial market segments the *ciranda financiera*, or financial "ring around the rosy." "The role of internal debt was totally perverted," writes Brazilian economist Jaime Serra. "Instead of providing development financing or permitting monetary control, it came to represent a base for . . . speculation."[25] As a result of short-term financial maneuvering the "nonoperating" profits of Brazil's five hundred largest firms in 1978 were larger than profits on operations.[26]

The high rates on government bonds attracted liquidity within the Brazilian financial system to the primary and secondary market for government bonds. Yet credit available in the commercial bank market (as opposed to the indexed bond market) became increasingly limited. Although data are scarce, it appears that the financing available in the commercial bank market and through foreign borrowing was biased toward a limited number of dynamic industrial sectors dominated by the larger domestically owned groups, as it was in Mexico, Chile, and Argentina. Debt to equity ratios rose for most major Brazilian firms—rising fastest in the capital goods sector. Summarizing the available data, Frieden concludes that "the more dynamic sectors and the larger firms were more heavily indebted; they could borrow because of their size and dynamism, and their access to finance increased both."[27]

Policies to stimulate the private financial sector, and the resulting

[24]José Serra, "Notas sobre el sistema financiero brasileño," *Economía de America Latina* 7 (1979), p. 65.
[25]Ibid., p. 161.
[26]Ibid., p. 165.
[27]Jeff Frieden, "The Brazilian Borrowing Experience: From Miracle to Debacle and Back," *Latin American Research Review* 22 (1987), p. 114.

concentration in credit allocation, accentuated market imperfections in the productive sector. Larger, more creditworthy firms turned to foreign credit and used it to speculate in the Brazilian money market and in the more loosely organized market to which most smaller, less creditworthy Brazilian firms had to resort to obtain credit (at well above average cost). Smaller firms without access to subsidized credit or foreign loans were forced into the exorbitantly priced free market for working capital credit. Some credit and other incentives were provided for smaller enterprises, but the overall effect was too little, too late.[28] Oligopolistic firms could use their market power to pass on high domestic credit costs to the consumer—whether they were forced to rely on high-cost markets or not. Monetary and financial policies combined with the effect of increased foreign borrowing to "reinforce the oligopolistic tendency of production, regardless of production efficiency criteria," while the financial backing and the market power of the large firms put inflationary pressures on the economy.[29]

To varying degrees all over Latin America, international financial integration in the 1970s increased the liquidity and segmentation of financial markets, spurring speculation and economic concentration. Industrial and financial conglomerates profited heavily from short-term financial activity. The incentive structure created by international financial integration and government policy drew resources away from industrial finance. Small and medium-sized industrialists without preferential access to credit markets were financially squeezed. Wealth and financial resources became increasingly centralized and concentrated in the hands of a relatively small number of conglomerates.

Explaining Variation: Bankers' Alliances and Economic Policy in Mexico and Brazil

Despite these broad similarities, significant differences also exist among these countries. Perhaps the most puzzling differences are

[28]William Tyler, *The Brazilian Industrial Economy* (Lexington, Mass.: Lexington Books, 1981).
[29]Christian Anglade, "The State and Capital Accumulation in Contemporary Brazil," in Christian Anglade and Carlos Fortín, eds., *The State and Capital Accumulation in Latin America* (London: Macmillan, 1985), p. 80.

between Brazil and Mexico. Of the four countries examined, Mexico and Brazil are the most similar in terms of size and level of economic development. Yet in the late 1970s the Brazilian government successfully redirected subsidized federal credit to orient private investment toward new government priorities: energy substitution and agricultural and manufactures export. Capital flight between 1976 and 1985 amounted to $10 billion, compared with $53 billion from Mexico in the same period. Brazilian nonbank deposits held abroad as a percentage of domestic deposits grew from 8 percent in 1981 to 22 percent in 1985. In Mexico they stood at 13 percent in 1981 and rose to 43 percent by 1985. Between 1982 and 1985 private sector investment in Mexico contracted 19.4 percent, while in Brazil it expanded 20 percent. Why did Mexico, the Latin American country most similar to Brazil, fail to harness the benefits of international financial integration, as Brazil did? The answer lies in the relative strength of the bankers' alliances in the two countries and in their impact on economic policy.

The organizational and institutional environment was less conducive to formation of a bankers' alliance in Brazil than in Mexico for three reasons. First, in contrast to Mexico's Central Bank, the Brazilian Central Bank was founded late and enjoyed relatively little authority until 1987. It was founded through the legislative efforts of government technocrats opposed by the agricultural export elite. Together with the government, this elite held a large share of stock in the nation's largest commercial bank—a bank that also enjoyed central banking privileges. Second, compared with Mexico, Brazil has a more developed state planning apparatus, which enjoys considerable support from the nation's several monetary authorities. This planning apparatus developed in response to demands for protection from market forces by Brazil's coffee growers. Given this state structure, policy tended to focus more on credit creation, planning, and credit allocation than on monetary stability. Finally, thanks to both state structure and the organization of capital, Brazilian state planning and industrialization authorities have had much more control over the flow of investment finance than have authorities in Mexico.

Institutional Foundations of the Brazilian Bankers' Alliance

In contrast to Mexico, where the Central Bank was founded in 1925 with the close collaboration of private sector bankers, the

Brazilian Central Bank was not founded until 1964 and did not enjoy complete authority as a central bank until 1987. It was founded strictly through the efforts of state actors. Until 1945 the role of central bank was played by the Banco do Brasil, which was 55 percent state owned and 45 percent privately held. Its private owners represented the agrarian and commercial elite tied to coffee and sugar exporting. Even after the 1930 "revolution" against the old elite, the Banco do Brasil continued to serve the interests of agricultural exporters and to resist government efforts to strip away the central bank privileges it enjoyed. The struggle between urban reformers and agrarian elites linked to the Banco do Brasil was such that the latter referred to any efforts to change the Banco do Brasil's status as coup attempts.[30]

Beginning in the 1940s, government officials and advisers pushed heavily for formation of a genuine central bank. The Banco do Brasil, and the agricultural and commercial elite represented among its owners, resisted. This resistance was successful thanks to the heavy representation of agrarian interests in Congress. Congress normally approved institutional changes in the financial system. In 1945 government economist Octávio de Gouvêa Bulhões convinced President Getúlio Vargas to take advantage of a long congressional recess and decree the creation of a Superintendência da Moeda e Crédito (Superintendency of Money and Credit, or SUMOC), intended as a precursor to a central bank.[31]

From 1945 to 1964 central banking functions in Brazil were shared by three institutions: the Banco do Brasil, the National Treasury, and SUMOC. SUMOC was supposed to be the overarching institution in charge of formulating and implementing monetary and exchange rate policy, but it did not enjoy executive power over the other two monetary authorities. Furthermore, five of its eight original voting directors were Banco do Brasil executives. The Banco do Brasil continued to act as the primary monetary authority. The treasury issued currency, but the Banco do Brasil acted as

[30]Leslie Armijo and Sylvia Maxfield, "The Political Economy of Development Finance in Brazil and Mexico," paper prepared for the Latin American Studies Association meeting, Boston, October 1986; Maria Lucia Teixeira Werneck Vianna, *A administração do Milagre: O conselho monetário nacional, 1964–1974* (Petrópolis, Brazil: Editora Vozes, 1987); José Carlos de Assis, *A chave do tesouro: Anatomía dos escandolos financieros* (Rio de Janeiro: Pax e Terra, 1983).

[31]Leslie Armijo, "The Political Economy of Brazilian Central Banking," paper prepared for the American Political Science Association annual meeting, Washington, D.C., September 1988, p. 29.

its bank while also operating as lender of last resort for the financial system, as a private commercial bank, and as a private investment bank.

The 1964 financial reforms created two new monetary authorities: the Brazilian Central Bank and the National Monetary Council. The latter replaced SUMOC. Ironically, however, the reforms legally reinforced the role of the Banco do Brasil as a monetary authority.[32] The legislation also gave the Banco do Brasil an account ("movement account") at the Central Bank with automatic and unlimited overdraft facilities. The Banco do Brasil continued to enjoy autonomous money-creating privileges. These Banco do Brasil privileges limited the extent to which the new Central Bank of Brazil could be a genuine central monetary authority. Furthermore, although the Central Bank was formally independent from the president and the executive branch, its president and directors were often political appointees.[33]

Over the twenty years following establishment of the Central Bank, central banking functions were "wrested away . . . one by one if necessary" from the Banco do Brasil.[34] The Banco do Brasil's overdraft account with the Central Bank was not closed until 1987. In exchange for giving up its "movement account" the Banco do Brasil demanded and received authorization to operate as a financial conglomerate. This authorization angered other private banks, which had always viewed themselves as being at an unfair advantage vis-à-vis the Banco do Brasil.[35] When the Banco do Brasil was finally stripped of its overdraft privileges with the Central Bank, the latter became a nominally autonomous central monetary authority. This autonomy was gained fully half a century after the Mexican Central Bank had gained sole monetary authority.

The relationship between state monetary and financial authorities and other state economic policy-making agencies in Brazil was

---

[32]John Welch, *Capital Markets in the Development Process: The Case of Brazil* (Pittsburgh: University of Pittsburgh Press, 1989), p. 199. Mario Henrique Simonsen, "A imaginação reformista," in R. Campos and M. Simonsen, eds., *A nova economía brasiliera* (Rio de Janeiro: Livraria José Silva Editora, 1974), p. 125.

[33]The most notorious instance of a politically motivated staff change involves then–finance minister Delfim Netto, who forced out the first military government's appointees in 1967 and appointed his own men (Armijo, "The Political Economy of Brazilian Central Banking," p. 31).

[34]Ibid.

[35]Ibid.

also quite different from that conducive to the formation and sur-
vival of a strong bankers' alliance. In Mexico, until the mid-1970s,
the Finance Ministry, allied with the Central Bank, sat at the top of
the hierarchy of state economic policy-making institutions. But in
Brazil there was no genuine central bank. Furthermore, although
the Mexican state did not have a specific planning aparatus until
1976, the Brazilian state had long had a variety of agencies concerned with planning; and these agencies exercised considerable
power within the state. The national development bank, founded
in 1952, the Development Council, and later the Council for Industrial Development performed national planning functions until the
Secretariat of Planning was formed in 1974. The Foreign Trade
and Foreign Exchange departments of the Banco do Brasil, together
with the so-called Executive Groups, were central to plan implementation. The Foreign Exchange department reviewed industrial
projects for complementarity with existing industry, the Foreign
Exchange section of the bank allocated the necessary foreign exchange, and the Executive Groups, with representatives from all
relevant state ministries and the private sector, helped streamline
implementation.[36]

The primary instrument of plan implementation was allocation
of subsidized credit. This allocation necessarily involved the chief
monetary authorities—the Ministry of Finance, the Banco do
Brasil, SUMOC, and later the National Monetary Council
(CMN)—in the planning process. For example, after 1964 the
CMN exercised ultimate authority over the so-called monetary
budget, which became "the main instrument of strategic economic
development policy through the use of selective credit policy."[37]
The existence of a relatively elaborate planning aparatus and the
absence of a strong independent-minded central bank created an
ideological and institutional environment conducive to close cooperation between the monetary and planning authorities—an environment that is strikingly absent from the Mexican scene.

In Mexico, where income and outlays were tightly controlled by
the Finance Ministry and the Central Bank, the monetary authorities' primary emphasis was on monetary stability, not credit cre-

---

[36]Barbara Geddes, "Building 'State' Autonomy in Brazil, 1930–1964," paper presented at the Latin American Studies Association meeting, Boston, October 1986, p. 29.
[37]Welch, *Capital Markets in the Development Process*, p. 206.

ation. In contrast, in part because there were several monetary authorities with autonomous money-creating power, Brazilian monetary authorities as a group were oriented more toward credit creation than toward monetary stability. Unlike the situation in Mexico, the Central Bank was virtually nonexistent and the Finance Ministry was relatively unable to impose monetary stability even when it so desired. A former Brazilian finance minister laments that "the system is too flexible."[38]

The degree of fusion between industrial and financial capital is a final important difference between Mexico and Brazil—and one that helped create the different institutional possibilities for a strong bankers' alliance and orthodox economic policy. Until the 1982 bank nationalization, Mexican capital was organized into several large financial-industrial-commercial conglomerates. In contrast, there was a relative lack of integration between industrial and financial capital in Brazil.[39] This lack of integration may partly explain why Brazilian businessmen, representing both large and small industry not closely tied to finance or commerce, are committed to the idea that growth can be reconciled with inflation. In Mexico small and medium-sized industrialists have generally been supported only by labor in their calls for looser credit. But in Brazil, with conglomerates segregated into separate industrial and financial groups, large industrialists have often joined small and medium-sized industry in calling for lower interest rates and reflationary economic policy.[40]

The extent of integration between industrialists and bankers, both shapes the strength of the stabilization coalition versus the growth-oriented coalitions and increases the possibilities for "internal" investment financing. Greater internal financing tends to reduce the effectiveness of investment incentives administered through

[38]Mario H. Simonsen, "Inflation and Anti-Inflationary Policies in Brazil," *Brazilian Economic Studies* 8 (1984), pp. 1–37.

[39]Wendy J. Barker, "Banks, Industry and the State in Brazil," paper prepared for the Latin American Studies Association meeting, New Orleans, March 1988; Harry M. Makler, "Financial Conglomerates in Brazil and Mexico," paper prepared for the Latin American Studies Association meeting, Albuquerque, April 1985; José Serra, "Notas sobre el sistema financiero," *Economía de America Latina* 7 (1981), pp. 155–167; Maria da Concepção Tavares, "El sistema financiero brasileño y el ciclo de expansión reciente," *Economía de America Latina* 5 (1980), pp. 95–116.

[40]Thomas E. Skidmore, *Politics in Brazil* (London: Oxford University Press, 1967); Robert Kaufman, *The Politics of Debt in Argentina, Brazil, and Mexico* (Berkeley: Institute of International Studies, University of California–Berkeley, 1988).

government regulation of the cost and availability of external financing. Relative lack of integration with private sector financial intermediaries is one reason that private Brazilian industrialists, with one or two notable exceptions, such as the Votorantim group, have been relatively dependent on external financing. The best estimates put internal financing of investment by Mexican private manufacturers in the 1950s and 1960s at between 65 percent and 90 percent.[41] Brazilian firms, in contrast, used only 43 percent internal financing.[42] The lower the level of internal financing, the greater the likelihood that government credit allocation policies will effectively induce industrial investment in targeted sectors.

The history of central bank founding, its place in the hierarchy of state economic agencies, and aspects of the organization of capital created the basis for a strong bankers' alliance in Mexico. As chapter 3 describes, Mexico's economic policy reflects the strength of the bankers' alliance. There is an emphasis on preserving monetary stability and protecting unregulated capital mobility—both domestically and internationally. The institutional and organizational environment in Brazil was not so conducive to development of a bankers' alliance. Brazilian economic policy reflects the relative weakness of the bankers' alliance. The emphasis is on credit creation rather than monetary stability, and there is considerably more state regulation of capital mobility than in Mexico.

Policy Patterns

Mexican and Brazilian policies regarding domestic financial capital mobility differ according to their emphasis on regulation versus ownership and on direct versus indirect control of credit allocation. The Mexicans have used regulation and indirect control. The Brazilians' greater ownership stake in the financial system has allowed Brazil to guide private investment credit allocation directly to a greater extent than does Mexico. The difference between the two countries is even more pronounced in the case of regulating international capital mobility. The Mexicans have long been committed

[41]Joseph La Cascia, *Capital Formation and Economic Development in Mexico* (New York: Praeger, 1969), p. 53; Dwight Brothers and Leopoldo Solís, *Mexican Financial Development* (Austin: University of Texas Press, 1966), p. 101.

[42]Economic Commission for Latin America, *The Process of Industrial Development in Latin America* (New York: United Nations, 1966), p. 188.

Conclusion

to free exchange convertibility and fixed exchange rates, whereas the Brazilians were among the first in Latin America to adopt exchange controls. The Brazilians have also focused more on credit creation than monetary stability.

Partly because of its ownership stake in the commercial banking sector, the Brazilian government's direct allocation of credit to the private sector was much greater than in Mexico, where the government had to rely more on indirect control of allocation. Of total monetary system financing to private enterprises and individuals in Mexico in the early 1960s, roughly 15 percent was by public institutions.[43] The comparable figure for Brazil is approximately 70 percent to 75 percent.[44]

The Brazilian state's ownership position in the financial system comes largely from its stake in the Banco do Brasil. The Banco do Brasil is by far Brazil's largest commercial bank. Government ownership of Banco do Brasil stock dates to 1905. In that year the weakness of the nation's leading national private bank, the Banco do Republica, forced the state to intervene. The state reorganized the bank, restored it to solvency, changed its name to the Banco do Brasil, and took a dominant ownership position. Brazil's coffee and sugar planters were the bank's minority private owners and favored clients. This agrarian elite supported the partial nationalization on the grounds that it would stabilize the financial system and restore credit flows.

Until the Mexican bank nationalization in 1982, the Brazilian government's ownership stake in the Banco do Brasil, and the latter's overwhelming dominance in the commerical credit system, provided a marked contrast to Mexico. In the mid-1970s the Banco do Brasil accounted for close to half the loans made by the nation's fifty largest commercial banks.[45] In Mexico the commercial credit market was slightly less concentrated and was largely privately owned. It took the nation's two largest commercial banks to account for 50 percent of commercial bank financing. These banks were both 100 percent privately owned. The Mexican government

[43]Economic Commission for Latin America, *The Process of Industrial Development in Latin America*, p. 188.
[44]Brothers and Solís, *Mexican Financial Development*, p. 105.
[45]Werner Baer, Isaac Kerstenetzky, and Annibal V. Villela, "The Changing Role of the State in the Brazilian Economy," *World Development* 11 (1973), p. 75.

did take over two failing banks in the 1970s: Banco Internacional and Banco Somex. But together these banks accounted for only 13 percent of all commercial lending in the mid-1970s. This was a relatively small percentage of commercial lending potentially subject to direct government allocation criteria, compared with the Banco do Brasil's 50 percent.

The Brazilian government's ownership stake in the Banco do Brasil had three important implications. First, it allowed the government to collect working-class and middle-class savings through the bank and redistribute them to the agrarian elite and, to a lesser extent, industrial entrepreneurs, without resorting to taxation and raising interest rates. Second, the privilege accorded the Banco do Brasil through its partial government ownership put other commercial banks at a competitive disadvantage and stifled their growth. Finally, as mentioned earlier, direct ownership of a large commercial bank increased the ease and success of using selective government credit controls to induce and guide industrial investment. In the mid-1970s, for example, 35 percent of the Banco do Brasil's assets were targeted and subsidized agricultural and industrial credits.[46]

The Brazilians also provided more direct investment credit to private entrepreneurs through public development banks than did the Mexicans. The most important of the Brazilian public banks was the Banco Nacional do Desenvolvimento Econômico (National Bank for Economic Development, or BNDE), which provided investment loans and administered a dozen special funds that did the same. Its funds came from two "forced savings" programs. During the 1970s the BNDE shifted from funding primarily state-owned enterprises to funding private business. In contrast, the Mexican national development bank, Nafinsa, continued to fund primarily public sector ventures.

Even the Brazilian Central Bank functioned partly as a development bank. In the mid-1970s roughly 8 percent of its assets were for agricultural price support programs and targeted credits passed on to public and private financial institutions.[47] The Mexican Central Bank also underwrote development bank issues but did not

---

[46]Calculated from Brazilian Central Bank data presented in Armijo, "The Political Economy of Brazilian Central Banking," p. 14.
[47]Ibid.

directly provide funds for targeted lending, as the Brazilian Central Bank did.

As private nonmonetary investment funding grew in the late 1960s in both Brazil and Mexico, the ability to regulate stock and bond transactions became increasingly important. The Brazilians had an advantage over the Mexicans in this regard because there was relatively less anonymity in the Brazilian financial system. For example, the Brazilian Finance Ministry requires owner name registration of many financial assets and liabilities.[48] In contrast, anonymous ownership of financial assets and transactions has been a cornerstone of Mexican financial development. Efforts to require registration of bond ownership, for instance, have been defeated by private sector lobbying.

Differences between the two countries' regulation of international capital movements is even greater than their differences in domestic regulation. Where Mexico has been committed to free exchange convertibility, Brazil has a long history of exchange controls. Brazilian authorities have also not shied away from devaluation the way Mexican authorities have. The exchange rate has occasionally been kept undervalued, and since 1968 Brazil has followed a policy of "minidevaluations" similar to the crawling peg.

The first Brazilian government institution for regulating foreign exchange was created in 1906. The Caixa de Conversão bought and sold foreign exchange in an effort to keep the exchange rate undervalued in order to favor agricultural exports and subsidize the purchase of machinery, instruments, and even raw materials for industrial development.[49] Strict exchange controls were imposed during World War I. These controls became a permanent mechanism of peacetime economic policy through legislation passed in 1921. After World War II foreign exchange controls became a key instrument for promoting industrialization.[50] Exchange controls were briefly lifted after the Estado Novo in 1946 but were reimposed after a balance of payments crisis in 1947. From 1947 to

---

[48]Walter L. Ness, "Financial Markets Innovation as a Development Strategy: Initial Results from the Brazilian Experience," *Economic Development and Cultural Change* 22 (1974), p. 458.

[49]Steven Topik, *The Political Economy of the Brazilian State, 1889–1930* (Austin: University of Texas Press, 1987), pp. 40–43.

[50]Werner Baer, *Industrialization and Economic Development in Brazil* (Homewood, Ill.: Richard D. Irwin, 1965), p. 16.

1953 government-controlled multiple exchange rates covered most international economic transactions. The system of multiple exchange rates became more complex and slightly less comprehensive from 1953 to 1963, with only a very brief period of free exchange in 1961. From 1946 to 1953 the exchange rate was fixed and increasingly overvalued. From 1953 to 1968 there were periodic devaluations that prevented severe overvaluation. In 1968 the Brazilians adopted a policy of frequent minidevaluations, which helped control speculation against the cruzeiro.

Brazil's policy of exchange controls and frequent devaluation limited the extent to which the threat of capital flight could be used to oppose economic reform. In the Mexican case, Central Bank and Finance Ministry officials often ruled out policy changes expected to displease bankers and large-scale industrialists, on the grounds that they would cause capital flight. The strength of agricultural exporters partly explains the difference in these two countries' foreign exchange regimes. Exchange controls and devaluation were both policies initially adopted in Brazil to favor and protect coffee exporters. The latter also dominated the nation's largest commercial banks. In Mexico the revolution left the agricultural elite, never as closely tied to private financiers as in Brazil, politically weak. The financial elite moved in to fill the postrevolutionary vacuum in economic policy leadership and set the tone for a half-century of foreign exchange policies less favorable to agricultural exporters than to bankers and urban industrialists.

Monetary policy is a third area of striking policy difference between Brazil and Mexico—and one that reflects the relative strength of bankers' alliances in the two countries. Mexico's monetary policy has been consistently tighter than Brazil's. Where Brazil had only two sustained stabilization efforts between 1906 and 1980, the Mexicans attempted and succeeded at monetary stabilization in the 1920s, from 1954 to 1970, and again after 1982. The pattern of loose credit and a relatively undervalued exchange rate in Brazil goes back to close to the turn of the century. From 1906 to 1914 Brazil had a series of presidents who broke with the previous orthodox monetary policy. In accord with the wishes of coffee and sugar planters their administrations freely distributed credit and intervened to keep the mil-réis (renamed the cruzeiro in 1942) cheap. After World War I, Brazilians elected a champion of orthodox economic policy, but he died before taking office. João Pessoa,

183

elected instead, continued the loose credit policy of the 1906–1914 period. He had the Banco do Brasil open a rediscount window, which was heralded as a "permanent defense of national production."[51]

A 1923 British financial mission to Brazil demanded a return to monetary conservatism, which engendered serious domestic conflict. President Arthur Bernardes tried to comply because he wanted to increase the value of the mil-réis and control inflation in order to calm urban unrest. The president of the Banco do Brasil, however, refused to comply with Bernardes's order to restrict credit. The finance minister joined in the opposition to tight credit. Bernardes fired the Banco do Brasil head and the minister of finance and presided over the first period of restrictive monetary policy since before 1906.

President Washington Luis oversaw a financial reform in 1926 that loosened credit once again. In 1929 he reversed this policy, inducing a severe recession that contributed in part to his ouster in a 1930 military coup. President Vargas's populist Estado Novo progressively devalued the mil-réis but pumped money into the economy through government spending.

After the Estado Novo period there were brief attempts at monetary stabilization under the Eurico Dutra administration in 1946, under Vargas in 1953, João Café Filho in 1954, Jânio Quadros in 1961, and João Goulart in 1963. None of these efforts lasted more than a year. Echoing the dispute that erupted after the British financial mission in 1923, a pattern developed in these stabilization efforts where the Banco do Brasil refused to cooperate, highlighting the impotence of the finance minister and often leading to his resignation. For example, finance minister Horácio Lafer left office in 1953, claiming the president of the Banco do Brasil never even consulted with him about the Banco's credit policy.[52]

The 1946 stabilization effort was led by finance minister Eugênio Gudin (who was also a member of the IMF board of directors). In this case, tight credit policy led to several bank failures and to negotiations between President Dutra and Quadros, the governor of São Paulo, to expand credit again. Gudin and his team resigned. The situation in 1958 was very similar to that in 1953. A finance

[51]Topik, *The Political Economy of the Brazilian State*, p. 40.
[52]Skidmore, *Politics in Brazil*, p. 116.

minister committed to stabilization resigned, frustrated by the Banco do Brasil's refusal to cut credit in the face of protest from São Paulo businessmen. Shortly thereafter Brazil became the first Latin American country ever to break off negotiations with the IMF. Protests by industrialists and workers, and in the 1963 case also military officers, quickly brought both the Quadros and the Goulart stabilization efforts to an end. In sum, all these stabilization efforts faced strong opposition not only from organized labor and the popular sector but also from São Paulo industrial elites and coffee planters and their allies in government, often including the Banco do Brasil.[53]

The military government that took over in 1964 carried out the first sustained stabilization program since 1923. Even here, however, government economists rejected the IMF's shock treatment in favor of a more gradual approach involving the distinctly unorthodox procedure of financial indexation. The second and third military governments again relegated the fight against inflation to second place, behind growth. Antônio Delfim Netto, minister of finance in both the General Arthur da Costa e Silva and General Emilio Garrastazu Medici administrations, believed inflation was cost determined. He followed a heterodox policy of price controls combined with active credit expansion.[54] General Ernesto Geisel's economic policy and response to the first oil price hike was also heterodox. A short-lived stabilization effort in 1974 rapidly gave way when a major bank group failed. In mid-1976 finance minister Mario Henrique Simonsen attempted a heterodox stabilization program combining government investment spending, monetary stringency, and heavy foreign borrowing.[55] "Stop-go" cycles in monetary policy persisted for the rest of the decade. Even as international pressure for monetary stabilization grew in the 1980s, Brazil responded with a "heterodox shock." At the same time, Mexico chose to pursue orthodox stabilization policies, at least until electoral pressures mounted in 1987.

[53]Kaufman, The Politics of Debt, p. 19.

[54]Donald E. Syvrud, Foundations of Brazilian Economic Growth (Washington, D.C.: American Enterprise Institute, 1974), pp. 81–89.

[55]Albert Fishlow, "A Tale of Two Presidents: The Political Economy of Brazilian Adjustment to the Oil Shocks," Working Paper No. 202, Department of Economics, University of California–Berkeley, February 1986.

Conclusion

Alternative Explanations and the Case for Heterodoxy

This book suggests that the strength of bankers' alliances, shaped by organizational aspects of the state and capital, helps explain economic policy patterns. It also suggests that differences in policy patterns, particularly in the extent to which they have historically restricted capital mobility, explain differences in the impact of international financial integration. Comparison between Mexico and Brazil appears to confirm these hypotheses. Nevertheless, there are plausible alternative explanations. Fully evaluating the relative weight of different causal variables in explaining cross-national variation in economic policy and investment patterns would require exploring more comparative cases. We would need to conduct paired comparisons, matching similarities and differences, in order to try to isolate the impact of different variables on policies and their outcomes. Although such investigation is beyond the scope of this book, superficial comparison with other cases does lend plausibility to the argument outlined here.

A world systems, or *dependencia*, approach might suggest that differences in policy and investment patterns are due to the different international positions of the two countries. Mexico, the argument goes, is more vulnerable to pressures for orthodoxy and to financial speculation and capital flight because it shares a two thousand-mile border with the United States. Although I have suggested that a country's international situation is important in explaining longitudinal variation in the ability of a bankers' alliance in any given country to influence economic policy, there are several reasons to doubt the plausibility of an international position argument for cross-national variation in policy. First is the confounding case of Canada; like Mexico, Canada shares a long border with the United States, but it has generally followed more heterodox economic policies than Mexico. Capital flight and financial speculation in the 1970s also were not the problems that they were in Mexico. An in-depth comparison of Mexican and Canadian policy patterns and the factors explaining them would probably suggest that, to a large extent, degrees of dependency are themselves a function of the interplay between domestic policy and the international situation.

Another variant of this argument might suggest that the explanation lies in differences in the degree of international financial integration in Brazil and Mexico. The greater the integration, the more negative its impact on industrial investment. I find that, by the measures suggested in chapter 1, international financial integration is higher in Brazil than in Mexico. In the 1970s there were more foreign banks with subsidiaries or representative offices in Brazil than in Mexico. Brazilian banks also operated more international offices than Mexican banks. Foreign borrowing was roughly similar. With Brazil having more international banking links than Mexico, we would expect the pressures for orthodoxy and the negative impact of international financial integration on industrial investment to be greater in Brazil than in Mexico. Yet Brazil responded to the mid-1980s debt-induced economic crisis with a new version of heterodoxy, whereas Mexico pursued orthodoxy to the hilt. As I have noted, Brazil also experienced less capital flight and financial speculation relative to industrial investment than Mexico.

A second possible explanation rests on differences in the two countries' political regimes. Brazil was more authoritarian than Mexico and could therefore impose more "statist" policies on society. We would expect capital-regulating policies to be more effective. Although certain aspects of the comparison outlined earlier are related to the relatively more authoritarian nature of the Brazilian regime, other comparative cases raise doubts that would have to be explored through more in-depth structured comparison.[56] For example, Brazil and Argentina have both had similar histories of intermittent authoritarianism. Yet, although Argentina's political regime bears much more resemblence to Brazil's than to Mexico's,

[56]One of these aspects is evident in the political underpinnings of Mexico's tight monetary policy in the 1950s and 1960s. Private bankers agreed to the high reserve requirements that made the policy possible as part of an implicit bargain; the government would leave the private banks, particularly the *financieras*, free from other regulations so they could earn profit enough to compensate for reserve requirements. The Mexican government's fiscal base in these reserve requirements, the success of its monetary policy, and its system of indirect credit controls all depended on private bank cooperation. This dependence, combined with the need to maintain popular legitimacy, left the Mexican government with little policy flexibility. The government could not finance spending through forced savings, as the Brazilians did, because of the political importance of the working class. It also had to move carefully in increasing pressure on private financiers for fear of losing their cooperation. The Brazilian regime, more authoritarian than the Mexican, could and did force the working class and middle class to make their savings directly available for state use without using private bankers as intermediaries. This ability gave the Brazilian government more flexibility in the area of monetary and fiscal policy than the Mexican government had.

187

Conclusion

the country's economic patterns are orthodox and its levels of financial speculation and capital flight relative to long-term industrial investment in the 1970s were far higher than in any other Latin American country. Despite its authoritarian regime, Argentina's economic policies and investment patterns in response to international financial integration are similar to Mexico's. Although this casts doubt on the political regime explanation, we cannot dismiss it without further research.

Another plausible explanation for the difference in economic performance in Mexico and Brazil in the 1970s is oil. Terry Karl suggests that heavy reliance on exports inhibits industrial diversification and leads to policy paralysis and other forms of political malaise.[57] Again the doubt about this argument rises from the experiences of other Latin American countries. In non-oil-exporting countries such as Chile and Argentina, liberalized financial policies and international financial integration appear to have had ill effects similar to those experienced by Mexico.

A fourth explanation rests on characteristics of the state bureaucracy other than those highlighted here. As noted in chapter 1, both Sikkink and Geddes focus on merit-based hiring and efficiency criteria inculcated in the Brazilian bureaucracy under President Juscelino Kubitschek to explain Brazil's relative industrial success.[58] Although this explanation appears to fit the Brazil-Argentina comparison Sikkink makes, evidence suggests it works less well in explaining variations between Brazil and Mexico. Schneider's analysis of the relationship between bureaucracy and economic policy in Mexico and Brazil suggests that the similarities outweigh the differences. His depiction of Brazilian bureaucracy contradicts Sikkink's and Geddes's picture of a relatively merit-driven organization. In both Brazil and Mexico, Schneider finds, bureaucrats advance on the basis of presidential decisions largely unrelated to merit. If Schneider is correct, this kind of bureaucracy-based argu-

---

[57]Terry Lynn Karl, "Oil Booms and Petro-States: Democracy over a Barrel in Venezuela," manuscript, nd.

[58]Kathryn Sikkink, "State Autonomy and Developmentalist Policy Making in Argentina and Brazil," paper prepared for Latin American Studies Association meeting, New Orleans, March 1988; Barbara Geddes, "Building State Autonomy in Brazil, 1930–1964," paper prepared for Latin American Studies Association meeting, Boston, October 1986.

188

ment also does not appear to explain differences between Mexico and Brazil.[59]

One way neoclassical economists, or those sharing their economic ideology, would react to the argument presented here is to suggest that whether or not the correlation between bankers' alliance strength, economic policy patterns, and the impact of international financial integration on financial versus industrial activity is correct, it ignores the efficiency and social welfare costs of heterodox policy. In other words, the benefits that may be gained from governing capital mobility are outweighed by the costs associated with these policies.

Tremendous debate surrounds economic evaluations of financial, exchange rate, and monetary policy. Beginning with financial regulation, "structural monetarists" such as McKinnon argue that insofar as government intervention in financial markets distorts interest rates, it leads to inefficient allocation of financial resources and too little savings.[60] Shaw and Cameron argue that unrestricted growth of financial markets is a primary factor driving investment and growth in developing economies.[61] Insofar as the argument presented here suggests that governments closely regulate financial market growth, these authors would say it condemns developing countries to slow growth. Other arguments against financial regulation are that government intervention makes the business environment less predictable and raises the risk and cost of doing business. It also leads to corruption.

Defense of financial regulation rests on three arguments: the neoclassical theory of second-bests, mercantalism, and post-Keynesian or Marx-inspired theories of financial instability. Neoclassical theory suggests that government intervention in financial markets is a second-best policy in cases where noneconomic factors or long-

---

[59]Ben Ross Schneider, "Partly for Sale: Privatization and State Strength in Brazil and Mexico," *Journal of Interamerican Studies and World Affairs* 30 (1988–1989), pp. 89–116.

[60]Ronald T. McKinnon, *Money and Capital in Economic Development* (Washington, D.C.: Brookings Institution, 1973); Ronald T. McKinnon, "Financial Policies," in John Cody, Helen Hughes, and David Wall, eds., *Policies in Industrial Progress in Developing Countries* (Oxford: Oxford University Press, 1980).

[61]Edward S. Shaw, *Financial Deepening and Economic Development* (New York: Oxford University Press, 1973); Rondo Cameron, *Banking and Economic Development* (New York: Oxford University Press, 1972).

term economic structures distort financial markets. Díaz-Alejandro's work provides considerable empirical evidence that in the context of segmented financial markets such as those in Latin America, liberalized financial policies have high costs in terms of equity and industrial investment.[62] A second argument for financial regulation rests on the essentially mercantilist idea that the international environment is hostile for late-developing countries and that state intervention in financial markets is necessary so that these economies can catch up.[63] A third defense rests on financial instability theory, which suggests that business cycles make unregulated financial markets inherently unstable.[64]

Exchange controls are a form of financial regulation, and the arguments against them are similar to those against financial regulation. They lead to corruption and inefficient allocation of resources. They increase capital flight by undermining business confidence. Defense of exchange controls rests on both Keynesian and mercantilist ideas and empirical evidence. Andrew Dexter White, one of the chief architects of the Bretton Woods monetary system, recognized the potential need for exchange controls to protect nations against capital flight. Even better than national-level controls, he believed, would be an international mechanism. At Bretton Woods he argued vigorously for an agreement whereby Bretton Woods member governments would lose International Fund facilities if they accepted deposits or investments from any other member country without permission of that country's government. The same penalty would apply if a member government refused any other member government's request that it make available for "repossession" all property (deposits, investments, securities) purchased by members of that country.[65] Needless to say, such a proposal involved ceding so much national autonomy that there was

[62]Carlos Díaz-Alejandro, "Some Unintended Consequences of Financial Laissez-Faire," in Alejandro Foxley, Michael S. McPherson, and Guillermo O'Donnell, eds., *Debt, Democracy, and the Art of Trespassing* (Notre Dame, Ind.: University of Notre Dame Press, 1986).

[63]Alexander Gerschenkron, *Economic Backwardness in Historical Perspective* (Cambridge: Harvard University Press, 1962).

[64]Hyman P. Minsky, "The Financial Instability Hypothesis," in C. P. Kindleberger and J. Laffrage, eds., *Financial Crises* (Cambridge: Cambridge University Press, 1982); David Harvey, *The Limits to Capital* (Chicago: University of Chicago Press, 1982), pp. 239–329.

[65]Fred L. Block, *The Origins of International Economic Disorder* (Berkeley: University of California Press, 1977), p. 45.

considerable opposition from within the U.S. camp and from other countries also. The parties to Bretton Woods did recognize a temporary need for exchange controls on essentially mercantilist grounds. They exempted Europe from the requirement of complete foreign exchange convertibility until 1961 to facilitate economic reconstruction and development.

Historically, developing countries with capital controls have had relatively low levels of capital flight. A study of Latin American countries in the 1970s and 1980s shows that the four with the lowest percentage of capital flight—Brazil, Chile, Colombia, and Peru—all had exchange controls during the period examined. Meanwhile, the study's author notes with irony that countries "free of the 'impediments to social welfare' imposed by capital controls, literally hemorrhaged resources."[66] Some orthodox economists have come to believe that the benefits of capital controls in developing countries with serious capital market imperfections may outweigh the social welfare costs.[67]

The argument against easy credit is that it leads to inflation, which in turn causes investment and growth to fall. In this view inflation is caused by excess demand. The Keynes-inspired argument for loose credit suggests that inflation is caused by exogenous shocks or structural rigidities. Loose monetary and fiscal policy are seen as the only way to overcome these rigidities and guarantee growth.[68]

The approach taken here looks for the political determinants of economic policy. The assumption is that policy makers do not merely respond passively to market signals. As the Mexican bank nationalization shows, international market pressures can lead to mercantilistic market-blocking behavior as well as to market-conforming behavior. Approaching economic policy from a political viewpoint sensitizes the investigator to evidence of market imper-

[66]Manuel Pastor, Jr., "Capital Flight and the Latin American Debt Crisis," paper prepared for the Latin American Studies Association meeting, New Orleans, March 1988, p. 24.
[67]See John T. Cuddington, "Macroeconomic Determinants of Capital Flight: An Econometric Investigation," in Donald R. Lessard and John Williamson, eds., *Capital Flight and Third World Debt* (Washington, D.C.: Institute for International Economics, 1986).
[68]For a sophisticated statement of the structuralist view see Lance Taylor, *Structuralist Macroeconomics* (New York: Basic Books, 1983). For more on the debate see Susan M. Wachter, *Latin American Inflation* (Lexington, Mass.: Lexington Books, 1976).

Conclusion

fections and casts doubt on policy prescriptions based on assumptions of perfect competition. Although it involves trespassing in another discipline, the comparative case study with which this book closes is meant to add to the debates over economic policy just described. The suggestion is that unorthodox, capital-controlling policies can have benefits that may, for newly industrializing countries in an increasingly internationalized world, outweigh their social welfare costs.

Index

193

Index

Index

Index

197

Index

Library of Congress Cataloging-in-Publication Data

Maxfield, Sylvia.
    Governing capital : international finance and Mexican politics / Sylvia Maxfield.
        p. cm.
    Includes bibliographical references.
    ISBN 0-8014-2458-5 (alk. paper)
    1. Capital movements—Government policy—Mexico. 2. Banks and banking—Government ownership—Mexico. 3. Investments, Foreign—Mexico. 4. Investments, Mexican. 5. Mexico—Economic policy—1970–   I. Title.
HG3891.M39   1990
332.4'5'0972—dc20
                                                              90-55137